Child Care and Preschool
Development in Europe

Child Care and Preschool Development in Europe

Institutional Perspectives

Edited by

Kirsten Scheiwe
University of Hildesheim, Germany

and

Harry Willekens
University of Antwerp, Belgium and
University of Hildesheim, Germany

palgrave
macmillan

First published 2009 by
PALGRAVE MACMILLAN

Palgrave Macmillan in the UK is an imprint of Macmillan Publishers Limited,
registered in England, company number 785998, of Houndmills, Basingstoke,
Hampshire RG21 6XS.

Palgrave Macmillan in the US is a division of St Martin's Press LLC,
175 Fifth Avenue, New York, NY 10010.

Palgrave Macmillan is the global academic imprint of the above companies
and has companies and representatives throughout the world.

Palgrave® and Macmillan® are registered trademarks in the United States,
the United Kingdom, Europe and other countries.

ISBN-13: 978–0–230–53744–6 hardback
ISBN-10: 0–230–53744–8 hardback

This book is printed on paper suitable for recycling and made from fully
managed and sustained forest sources. Logging, pulping and manufacturing
processes are expected to conform to the environmental regulations of the
country of origin.

A catalogue record for this book is available from the British Library.

A catalog record for this book is available from the Library of Congress.

10 9 8 7 6 5 4 3 2 1
18 17 16 15 14 13 12 11 10 09

Printed and bound in Great Britain by
CPI Antony Rowe, Chippenham and Eastbourne

Contents

List of Illustrations   vii

Notes on Contributors   ix

Introduction: Path-dependencies and Change in Child-care
and Preschool Institutions in Europe – Historical
and Institutional Perspectives   1
Kirsten Scheiwe and Harry Willekens

1   Public Child Care in Europe: Historical Trajectories
    and New Directions   23
    Thomas Bahle

2   How and Why Belgium Became a Pioneer
    of Preschool Development   43
    Harry Willekens

3   Public Child Care and Preschools in France:
    New Policy Paradigm and Path-dependency   57
    Claude Martin and Blanche Le Bihan

4   Child Care in Spain after 1975: the Educational Rationale,
    the Catholic Church, and Women in Civil Society   72
    Celia Valiente

5   The Paradox of Public Preschools in a Familist
    Welfare Regime: the Italian Case   88
    Eva Maria Hohnerlein

6   Public and Private: the History of Early Education
    and Care Institutions in the United Kingdom   105
    Helen Penn

7   Danish Child-Care Policies within Path – Timing,
    Sequence, Actors and Opportunity Structures   126
    Anette Borchorst

8   Child Care as an Issue of Equality and Equity:
    The Example of the Nordic Countries   142
    Pirkko-Liisa Rauhala

9   The Politics of (De)centralisation: Early Care
    and Education in France and Sweden   157
    Michelle J. Neuman

10 Slow Motion – Institutional Factors as Obstacles to
    the Expansion of Early Childhood Education in the FRG   180
    Kirsten Scheiwe

11 Private Family and Institutionalised Public Care for
    Young Children in Germany and the United States,
    1857–1933: An Analysis of Pedagogical Discourses   196
    Meike Sophia Baader

12 Maternalism and Truncated Professionalism – Historical
    Perspectives on Kindergarten Teachers   210
    Ursula Rabe-Kleberg

13 Money Matters – Experiments in Financing
    Public Child Care   222
    Margarete Schuler-Harms

14 Basic Legal Principles of Public
    Responsibility for Children   234
    Ingo Richter

Index   247

Illustrations

Figures

1.1   Childcare services in Europe, around 2000   25

1.2   Childcare services: Coverage rates, Europe 1990–2004   35

9.1   France and Sweden: Summary of decentralisation trends   158

9.2   Sweden: Proportion of children aged 1–5
      in preschool, 1975–2005   168

9.3   Sweden: Number of children in preschool and
      family day care, 1975–2003   170

9.4   France: Increasing numbers of assistantes
      maternelles, 1990–2001   170

9.5   Sweden: Deregulation in the 1990s is associated
      with larger groups   172

Tables

1.1   Childcare coverage rates, Europe *ca.* 2000   26

1.2   Family policy profiles   32

1.3   Childcare patterns, selected countries 2004   38

7.1   Number of children in publicly supported childcare
      services in percentage of all children. 1980–2006   128

7.2   Number of children in different types of
      services. 1980–2006   129

9.1   France and Sweden: Early care and education
      policy functions decentralised   158

9.2   France and Sweden: Consequences of
      decentralisation changes   166

9.3   Sweden: Proportion of 1–5-year-olds enrolled
in preschool by municipality type, 1997–2005   169

9.4   France: Decreasing average group size in École
maternelle, 1960–2001   171

9.5   Sweden: Increasing average number of children per
group and child-to-staff ratio in preschool, 1980–2003   172

Annex

5.1   Table on preschools, classes, pupils and teachers   102

Graph

10.1   Legal entitlement to public child care   191

Contributors

Meike Sophia Baader is Professor at the Pedagogical Institute of the University of Hildesheim, Germany, and a member of the Board of the Early Childhood Excellence Centre at this university. Her major research interests are in: the history of childhood, youth and education; education and religion; education and democracy; gender and education; education and the 1968 movement.

Thomas Bahle teaches sociology at the University of Mannheim. At the time of writing his contribution for this book he was Marshall Fellow at the London School of Economics. His main research interest is in the comparative sociology of welfare states.

Anette Borchorst is Associate Professor at the Department of History, International and Social Studies, Aalborg University, Denmark. Her research focuses on Scandinavian child-care policies.

Eva Maria Hohnerlein is a senior researcher at the Max-Planck-Institute for Foreign and Comparative International Law in Munich. She is the author of *Internationale Adoption und Kindeswohl* (Baden-Baden: Nomos, 1991) and of many publications on comparative social law.

Blanche Le Bihan is a researcher at the Laboratory for the Analysis of Social and Health Policies at the School of Studies in Public Health at Rennes, France. Her main research interests are in child-care policies and policies regarding the frail elderly in Europe.

Claude Martin is a senior researcher at the *Centre national de Recherche Scientifique* at the University of Rennes, France, and Director of the Laboratory for the Analysis of Social and Health Policies of the School of Studies in Public Health. His main research interests are in the sociology of the family and in social policy issues regarding the family, children and the elderly in Europe.

Michelle J. Neuman is Senior Program Officer with the Open Society Institute's Early Childhood Program. Prior to joining OSI, Dr Neuman designed and carried out international studies of early childhood care and education for UNESCO and the OECD. Her research interests include education governance, child and family policy, and comparative politics.

Helen Penn is Professor of Early Childhood at the University of East London and co-director of its International Centre for the Study of the Mixed Economy of Childcare. Her current interest is the marketisation, corporatisation and globalisation of child care. She has also worked for the OECD and the EU on policy issues in early childhood.

Ursula Rabe-Kleberg is Professor of Pedagogy and the Sociology of Education and Director of the Institute for Early Childhood Education and Care at the University of Halle-Wittenberg, Germany. Her research focuses on the professionalisation of teachers in early education, cooperation between professionals and parents, and general issues of family and childhood.

Pirkko-Liisa Rauhala is Reader in Social Work and Social Policy at the University of Helsinki. From 2001 to 2006 she was Visiting Professor at the University of Tartu, Estonia, and a member of the Welfare Research Committee of the Nordic Council of Ministers.

Ingo K. Richter is Emeritus Professor of Constitutional and Administrative Law and Honorary Professor at the University of Tübingen, Germany. He serves as President of the Irmgard-Coninx-Foundation at the Social Science Research Center, Berlin. His main interest is in educational law and policy. Recent publications are on human rights and transnational civil society.

Kirsten Scheiwe is Professor of Law at the University of Hildesheim, Germany. Her research is interdisciplinary and oriented towards gender studies questions, mainly in the fields of family law, social law and comparative law.

Margarete Schuler-Harms is Professor of Public Law, especially Public Economic Law and Environmental Law, at the Helmut-Schmidt-University in Hamburg. She has a special research interest in family policies, especially questions of family benefits and the taxation of families.

Celia Valiente is Associate Professor in the Department of Political Science and Sociology at Universidad Carlos III de Madrid, Spain. Her main research interests are gender equality policies and the women's movement in Spain from a comparative perspective. Her latest book in English is *Gendering Spanish Democracy* (with M. Threlfall and C. Cousins, Routledge, 2005).

Harry Willekens teaches legal sociology at the University of Antwerp and law at the University of Hildesheim. His main research interest is in the sociology and history of the legal institutions constructing and influencing the family.

Introduction:
Path-dependencies and Change in Child-care and Preschool Institutions in Europe – Historical and Institutional Perspectives

Kirsten Scheiwe and Harry Willekens

1 The approach – historical, institutional, comparative

Public child care and collective forms of education in early childhood have already been well researched, not only from a national but also from a comparative perspective.[1] It might not be very productive to add to this literature, were it not that the available research is strongly dominated by a relatively short-range social policy perspective. Where comparison is practised, it focuses on developments of the last decades, which are virtually all connected with the rise in mothers' labour market participation and the ensuing increase in the need for public child-care arrangements.[2] Broadening the temporal horizon of our view to include long-range developments since the nineteenth century allows us to see questions bound to be rendered invisible by the shorter-range perspective.

As will become clear throughout this book, present-day tendencies in the development of public child care and of preschool organisations have their roots in different national traditions, themselves having their origins in different eras of social and economic development. These traditions have been crystallised in different institutions, in socially and legally structured ways of doing things which tend to facilitate the introduction of some innovations and to stand in the way of others. To understand the development of public child care and preschool organisations and the range of accessible solutions for contemporary social policy issues, it is imperative to see how these institutions create openings at the same time as being obstacles for certain kinds of solutions. For that reason, an institutional perspective and a focus on the issue of path-dependency are central to this book.

It cannot, of course, be the purpose of this book to further develop the theory of path-dependency[3]. Path-dependency for our purposes is just a means to better understand the development of preschool systems in the different European countries. We start with the notion of path-dependency as 'processes in which choices made in the past systematically constrain the choices open in the future' (Myles and Pierson, 2001, p. 306), which may lead to 'institutional stickiness'. In our research into and interpretation of changes and historical turning points we come close to the ideas of Hall (1993), who distinguishes changes of different orders. There are the overarching goals of policy-making, the policy instruments and the precise settings of these instruments. From this distinction three orders of change follow. First-order change is a process whereby *instrument settings* are changed while the overall goals and instruments of policy remain the same. Second-order change involves altering the *instruments of policy* as well as their settings, but still leaves the overall policy goals untouched, while third-order change is marked by the radical changes in the overarching terms of policy discourse associated with a paradigm shift.

The question whether and to what extent a given path, once entered upon, pushes social policy in a given direction and keeps it from developing in other directions is dealt with by most of the authors of this book, but keeping an open mind. We investigate *as a matter of fact* whether the ways of organising public child care chosen – or more probably stumbled upon – in the past have shaped the later development of child-care policies, closed off certain venues, prevented debates from getting underway and/or stimulated innovative policy steps. Important questions in this respect have proven to be: how competences regarding child care are divided between state and church[4]; whether decision-making on child-care issues is centralised on the state level, decentralised towards lower levels of the polity or entirely left to private initiative[5]; whether public care for children under school age is defined as a matter of education, of protection or of the emancipation of women (and, as a corollary, which political actors are supposed to produce discourses and policies with regard to public child care).[6]

Our approach in this book is comparative and interdisciplinary. The comparative study of the institutional structures underlying the provision of public child care obviously requires an input from sociology, political science and history, but also from the law. Most of the relevant institutional factors take a legal form, and, though the analysis of this form is far from sufficient to understand in how far institutions steer policies onto predestined paths, it is nevertheless indispensable: the fixedness which the law gives to institutions and the rigidity of the procedures which have to be followed to change the law form additional barriers to straying from the path entered upon. Although the leading research questions of this book are not of a pedagogical nature, the pedagogical perspective also has an important role to play here. The pedagogical goals pursued by preschool public child care and the historical shifts in these goals are of obvious importance in the formation of social policies, as appears from the contributions of Penn, Baader, Borchorst and Rabe-Kleberg in this volume.

The need for a comparative approach does not only follow from scholarly concerns. The policy issues under study here have in the meantime acquired a European dimension.[7] The European Council set targets for child-care development in the EU at the summit of Barcelona in 2002: in 2010, 33 percent of children under three years old and 90 percent of children aged from three to obligatory school age must have access to a form of child care in order to diminish disincentives for women's employment. If one wants to be able to foresee the difficulties which countries may have in meeting such international targets and to understand why some can meet them effortlessly, it is necessary to take a look at the differences between the countries and to try to understand the causes of these differences. We have tried to accomplish the comparative goals pursued with this book by the inclusion of three kinds of contributions. Bahle's general overview of developments in a wide range of European countries is followed on the one hand by a series of country studies (Willekens on Belgium, Martin and Le Bihan on France, Valiente on Spain, Hohnerlein on Italy, Scheiwe on Germany, Penn on the United Kingdom, Borchorst on Denmark and Rauhala on the other Nordic countries), and on the other hand by several essays exploring specific issues by way of restricted and focused comparisons (Neuman on centralisation/decentralisation in France and Sweden, Richter on the basic legal principles of public responsibility for children, Schuler-Harms on models of financing public child care, particularly focusing on Germany and France, Baader on the relevance of pedagogical paradigms in the United States and Germany, Rabe-Kleberg on guiding ideologies such as maternalism and their impact on differences in professionalism in early childhood education).

2   Different policy motives: ideal types of the institutionalisation of child care

Looking at European developments from a long-range historical perspective, two *policy motives* for institutionalising public child care and early childhood education can be discovered. One is the idea that even children below the age of obligatory schooling are in *need of public education* (an idea which presupposes children to be already of an age at which they can be publicly educated). The other is to promote the *reconciliation of care work and paid work* – a goal which may justify public child care for children of any age. These motives of course do not in themselves constitute social policies. They are ideal types from which particular sets of organisational and institutional principles can be derived and from which different kinds of questions and problems follow. No actually existing system conforms in its entirety to the logic of one of the ideal types; looking at the degree to which reality corresponds to an ideal type and at the ways in which the two ideal types are combined within a public child care system which really exists enables us, however, to see how the different systems are positioned in relation to each other. The ideal types tie in with dominant notions of gender and class relations and thus make it also easier to see how such notions are incorporated within different social policies.

Policies inscribed within one of the ideal types may nevertheless have different roots and be embedded in different ideologies of the family and of its relation to the state and to society at large. The first 'foundational idea', the notion that young children are in need of public education, comes in many variations, which, however, may be grouped into two basic types, one child-centred, the other state- or society-centred.

There are different strains of the child-centred variety. One is the idea that normal child development is only possible if from a certain age onwards children are together with other children and adults from outside the family. Another rests on the presumption that even young children benefit from systematic, school-like learning (see especially Valiente on Spain and Willekens on Belgium, and also the contributions on Italy and France in this volume); the reason why they do not simply attend school is then no more than that young children have special needs which make it advisable from a practical point of view to separate them from the older schoolchildren. Kindergartens are in this case explicitly conceived as parts of the public educational system and as preparatory to school. The supply of public child care may also be rooted in ideas of equal opportunities for children from different social, cultural and linguistic backgrounds: the inevitable inequalities resulting from differences in children's family backgrounds have to be compensated by the availability of public educational services equally accessible to all. Ironically, this last notion has been the most influential in the Nordic countries (see Rauhala in this volume), where over the last centuries social, cultural and linguistic cleavages have been *less* pronounced than in other parts of Europe (Battail, Boyer and Fournier, 1992).

There is, of course, also a collective interest dimension to all of these reasons why public child care is good for children. It is in the obvious interest not only of the children themselves, but also of society and the state, for children to be integrated and educated and for the talents of the socially deprived to be saved by equal opportunities policies. But young children's need for public education may also be justified more directly by the interests of the state or society. To integrate all within the state, it may be deemed necessary to inculcate the values of the political system in the citizens from the youngest possible age: such was the main reason given for the early development of the preschool system in France (see Martin/Le Bihan and Willekens in this volume) and one of the reasons for generalised preschoolisation in the former Communist countries of Eastern Europe. A similar argument may even be decisive in a society *without* a strong state, as is shown in Baader's contribution to this volume: in the late nineteenth and early twentieth centuries, kindergartens were strongly argued for in the United States on the ground that a culturally mixed migration society can make its new members into citizens only by virtue of imbuing them with the same set of basic values.

It is from the first foundational idea, that is young children's need for public education, that the first preschool systems developed which were universalist in both their ideology and practice. In Belgium and France, the idea that it is normal or even necessary for children between three and six to attend kindergarten was already well-established by the early twentieth century.[8] At least in urban areas, kindergarten attendance became generalised in these countries at a time at which it was still a minority phenomenon in all other countries. In one sense, these developments were no more than straightforward consequences of the pedagogical goals pursued by kindergartens: if children should attend kindergarten to be taught republican values (France) or to be well prepared for life in a modern society (Belgium), then it follows from this that *all* children should be targeted. What calls for an explanation, however, is that this ideo-logic was translated into the generous allocation of public money to the preschool sector at a time when the welfare state was only just budding in both countries, and that this breakthrough took place in overwhelmingly Catholic countries where a strong ideal of the mother as caretaker/homemaker was dominant (Lenoir, 2003). As can be gathered from Willekens' and Bahle's contributions to this book, the explanation for the willingness of the State to pay for kindergartens is to be found in the fierce competition between the State and the Church in these countries – which explains why the pioneers of the universal supply of kindergartens were Catholic countries: in Protestant countries there simply was no religious organisation with sufficient power to challenge the hegemony of the state and thus to drive it to invest in kindergartens. The kindergarten system as it developed in France and Belgium also proved to be reconcilable with the prevailing ideology of motherhood. Kindergarten attendance was not – as in public child-care systems targeting working mothers' children – conceived as an alternative to motherly care, but as a supplement to it, as a means of smoothing the transition from the unique mother–child relation to participation in the school community; and the kindergarten teachers were supposed to emulate maternal attitudes and behaviour.

Pedagogical goals, whether child-centred, state-centred or both, were present in early developments in public child care in nearly all the countries under review in this book, and such developments were therefore nearly all carrying the seeds of universalism. For several reasons, though, outside France and Belgium those seeds were unable to grow into something substantial. For one thing, in most cases there were no forces pushing the state to make the preschool sector into a budgetary priority. Left to their own financing, preschools, whatever their underlying ideology, could not blossom into universalism. For another thing, the child-centred pedagogical goals were in some countries either pursued by the bourgeoisie alone or defined diversely by different social classes, with the result that no pedagogical platform for a universal provision existed (see for example Penn on the United Kingdom and Rabe-Kleberg on Germany in this volume).

The second basic motive for having public child care (the *reconciliation of care with paid work*) also comes in different varieties. The main purpose of policies of this kind may be *to protect children* whose both parents or single parent are so unfortunate as to have to work to earn a family income – this was, historically, the first wave of policy in the nineteenth century, addressed towards the children of parents working in agriculture or industry who left their children unattended and on their own. The consequence of such a goal formulation is, of course, that public child care should only be provided to those in dire need of it, so that it remains residual and targeted; a public child-care system covering the whole population can never be built on this foundation. The main policy goal may also be *to liberate women* from their economic dependence on men by enabling them to enter the labour market (or to diminish children's poverty risks through maternal employment), *or to liberate women's labour power* so as to make it available for the market and enhance economic efficiency (as in the actual debates on the 'social investment strategy'; see the contribution of Martin and Le Bihan).

On the face of it, the two main policy motives ought to have very different implications for the organisation of public child care for pre-school children: a system pursuing educational goals tends, as already mentioned, to be universalist – all children must be educated – whereas a system aiming for the reconciliation of paid work and care might be expected to target those children whose working parents are unavailable for care. This correlation holds very well for the period before 1970. From the 1970s onwards, the correlation starts to break down, as is witnessed by the development of a universal supply of preschool places in the Nordic countries, which had started out with a residual and targeted child-care system[9]. The obvious explanation is that universalism may also be derived from our second policy motive, but only on condition that the *whole* adult population is supposed to be in paid work – which has been the tendency in the Nordic countries over the last decades and which is also the implied goal of European policies, illustrated by, for example the Lisbon and Barcelona targets.

The two ideal–typical policy motives have quite distinct implications for class relations. In the *educational model* access is not class-related, while the *reconciliation model* in its narrowest interpretation focuses on children in need and on poor parents who have to work; child-care institutions are then seen as a makeshift for the lower classes, as was the case in the nineteenth century. Even in a broader understanding, the reconciliation model has to work with priorities: if places in public child care are scarce, children with both parents or a single parent in employment or children 'at risk' with disadvantaged family backgrounds will get preferential access. If a parent loses her employment, the child may lose its place in a child-care institution (as used to be the case in Sweden until 2002, but not in Denmark[10]), or the child of a mother who is a housewife or temporarily at home to care for another child may be excluded. A system which gives preference to working parents' children – and, among them, to the children of the disadvantaged – gives those parents not fulfilling the conditions of access and especially the better-off an incentive to look for alternative modes of child care, with the result that two tiers of child care can emerge: one for the working class and one for the bourgeoisie (see, for example, Penn's article in this volume). Such a split also occurs in systems in which the two basic motives for public child care exist side by side; it emerged for instance in nineteenth-century Germany, where daycare for lower-class children coexisted with the Fröbel kindergartens frequented by the middle classes (see Scheiwe). It is much less likely in those unambiguously education-oriented systems in which all children are assumed to attend preschools, as has been the case for many decades in France and Belgium and has recently become the rule in Spain and Italy; in such systems, not having attended preschool is a handicap upon school entry, and the well-off therefore have a disincentive for developing alternative private solutions for child care. This is not to say, though, that the educational model cannot also produce its alternatives: as appears from the texts of Valiente and Martin/Le Bihan in this volume, some features of the educational model (long school holidays, fixed hours not necessarily concurring with parents' working hours) are not optimally adapted to the needs of working parents. As a result, alternative child-care arrangements (such as professional childminders working in their own home, or nannies) flourish as a *supplement* to the public supply.

3   Developmental paths, policy arenas, actors, institutional dimensions and constraints

Even if both of the foundational policy motives can end up with universalism, they can make a big difference in terms of development paths, of the institutional assignment of child care to different policy arenas (educational policy, employment policy, welfare policy, family policy, gender policies) and of the principles by which public child care is organised. The two models may make differences with regard to the assignment of legislative, administrative and financial competences to different actors within the state, to the degree of centralisation and decentralisation of competences, to the training requirements of the staff, to the question whether access to public child care is free or fee-bound, etc. Let us take a look at a simplified overview of the institutional dimensions affected by the different goal-setting of public child-care systems:

Institutional dimensions	'Educational model'	'Work–care reconciliation model'
Access	Universal	Targeted
Entitled person	Child	Parent/child with special needs
Pedagogical concept	Educational goals (learning)	Mainly care
Group size and organisation	Relatively big groups (similar to school classes)	Smaller groups
Professionalisation of staff, payment	Teacher training and pay	Lower level of professional education and payment than teachers
Fees	No fees for school (eventually for meals etc.)	Subsidised, but parental fees
Financing bodies	As for schools (national or regional financing)	Mixed financing with a share of communal authorities (less centralised)
Administrative competence	School authorities	Social welfare authorities
Time patterns	Opening hours and holidays like schools	Varying

Some European countries can, for the whole of the period under review here, unambiguously be categorised as belonging to the left or right side of this table. Belgium, France, Luxemburg, Italy, and Spain clearly follow an educational model for children above the age of three or two. Other countries clearly started out with a residual reconciliation model exclusively or predominantly targeting the working poor, but, with the extension of this model to more and more children, pedagogical considerations unavoidably had to enter the equation. The general trend is that these countries move in the direction of the educational model; the idea that learning and education are important also for very young children nowadays tends to become more and more accepted. However, moves in this direction happen among the countries of the 'work–care reconciliation model' at different speeds, to varying degrees and in varying combination with other policy goals and arenas, such as (un)employment policy, antipoverty policy or family policy. In some countries, even basic organisational and legal principles (such as the division of competences between the education and social welfare administrations, decentralisation or centralisation, financing modes) are subject to change, whereas in other countries their unchangeability proves to be a stumbling block for any reforms whatsoever. For example: in Sweden, in 1996 child-care institutions were renamed 'preschool' institutions and the relevant decision-making competences were hence shifted from the social welfare ministry to the education ministry (although the competence – and duty – to organise preschool services remained with the local authorities) (see Neuman); in Germany, on the contrary, modernisation is retarded as a result of the complex distribution of legislative, administrative and financing competences between the Federal state, the regional and the local authorities, which stands in the way of any swift change (see Scheiwe and Richter). The United Kingdom has to be considered as a case apart here, since the regulatory level of child care and early childhood education has been traditionally very low and much was left to the market, while many changes have been introduced since 1997.

4   Critical junctures and radical shifts or smooth adaptation and slow motion?

A central question of the different contributions collected in this book is whether and how change happened, whether there was a move – particularly in countries starting out with the 'work–care reconciliation' model – from a targeted towards a universal model, whether shifts towards the educational model happened even at some institutional levels, but not at others. One of the predictions of path-dependency theory is that path-dependency leads to institutional stickiness and that it is very difficult to change the shape institutions have been given by past political decisions. A distinction is made between, on the one hand, path-dependent reforms as 'incremental modifications of existing policies' (Hall, 1993, p. 278), which usually happen continuously, through marginal and unspectacular adaptations, and radical changes on the other hand. Fundamental change may happen, and 'critical junctures' (Collier and Collier, 1991) can be identified which bring about rapid change in a short time. But path-dependency implies that this will be the case only under particular external and internal pressures, especially in times of revolutions, war, catastrophes, occupation, high pressure by actors or the breakdown of parts of the system. Applying this conceptual distinction to our story, we investigate the course of reform processes (if any): did radical change occur, did the systems change by incremental, possibly smooth modifications or have they got stuck in stasis? Answering these questions is complicated by the fact that making the distinction between modifications and fundamental changes or between the three orders of change theorised by Hall (see above) is not so easy in practice. Applying these distinctions only makes sense if changes are measured starting from a clear point of reference in the past – ideally from the same point in time for all the national systems under review, but this makes little sense in practice, because for some countries (e.g., Belgium and France) path-defining events already took place during the nineteenth century, whereas for other countries (e.g., the Nordic countries or Britain) very little is to be reported for this era.

Let us now, always keeping in mind the two basic paradigms of public child care, take a look at what our authors have found.

The countries represented in our research which follow the 'educational' paradigm are the forerunners of preschool education, Belgium and France, and the latecomers Italy and Spain.

Willekens argues that Belgium, besides France the most important pioneer in preschool development, presents a strong case of path-dependency. The path was cut out as early as the 1880s, a period of struggles over education between the State and the Catholic Church which led to 'pillarisation' and competition in the educational sector. As a result of this unusually fierce competition, Belgium was the first country in the world to approach universal availability of kindergarten places.

Martin and Le Bihan investigate the French case. On the basis of an in-depth historical and institutional analysis of the development of different family policy instruments in France from the late nineteenth century onwards, they argue that French developments, focused as they have always been on the goal of educating children, show a good deal of continuity. They argue that preschool development has been a strongly path-dependent process since a first law of 1887 institutionalised preschools as a part of public education. However, the picture looks different if arrangements for younger children below preschool age and the whole of child-care policies are taken into consideration. Martin and Le Bihan argue that child-care policies reached a turning point during the 1990s, when tackling unemployment and employment policy gained priority over other considerations and the reform of child-care policies was used as a way to restructure the labour market. The 1990s brought a

move towards reconciling work and family responsibilities and the introduction of the 'free choice' option for parents. This argument is backed
up by Neuman in her comparison of changes in governance in France
and Sweden during the processes of decentralisation between 1980 and
2005. She points to the differences between preschool development and
trends in service provision for children from birth to three in the French
bifurcated system. France thus clearly belongs to the educational paradigm only with regard to children in the preschool age group (from two
till the age of obligatory schooling).

The latecomers within the educational paradigm are Italy and Spain.
Hohnerlein sees the turning point towards the development of preschools in Italy in 1968, when the Act on Establishing Maternal Schools
was adopted (Act 44/1968), which transformed the former residual
approach of targeted welfare intervention for children into a universal one, conceptualising child-care institutions as places of education
and instruction. Former struggles between the Catholic Church and
the State over schooling had not led to the rise of new concepts until
a State–Church compromise was reached in 1968. For Hohnerlein, the
driving forces of change in 1968 were the changing power relations in
the political system and a consensus on the need for modernisation of
society and the educational system.

The other latecomer is Spain. Valiente analyses 30 years of child-care
development after the breakdown of fascism in 1975, when postauthoritarian policy-makers converted a preschool programme of limited
coverage into a nearly universal educational scheme. Particular attention is paid to the role of the Catholic Church as a principal actor
in education, interested in the expansion of preschooling as long as
part of it is private and subsidised by the state, as well as to the position of women in civil society and the women's movement. Spain is
a strong example of a country developing early childhood facilities
on the foundation of an educational paradigm and within the institutional framework of public education. Even care for children under
three is administered by educational, not by welfare authorities. This
may have its shortcomings; Valiente argues that the features of the
preschool setting cause difficulties for working mothers, since the
characteristics of the preschool model – long holidays, big groups/
classes, rigid hours – are too inflexible and do not satisfy working
mothers' needs.

With regard to these countries of the educational paradigm, attention should be drawn to one conclusion of Bahle's research into the
variations in public child care in Europe from the late nineteenth

century onwards. Bahle finds that the initial stronger State–Church competition in Catholic countries from early on led to higher levels of provision than in religiously mixed countries. Welfare pluralism or welfare competition (especially between State and Church), the conflict over the decision-making competences regarding education and socialisation, and the issue of the legitimacy of state intervention into the family are seen to have played an important and path-setting role. Bahle explains the variations between the national systems with reference to different historical trajectories. The first trajectory was related to industrialisation and nation-building, and in this historical context the main issue was education. The second historical trajectory (starting in the early 1970s) was the transition to a service economy and the rise of female employment. In this second historical context the main issue is not education but family policy. This argument is helpful to understand why even the historical pioneers of early childhood education, the countries with the educational paradigm, at a later historical stage were confronted with the problem of integrating educational policies with other political goals stemming from different political arenas, such as gender equality, the compatibility of employment and family life, antipoverty issues or the reduction of unemployment. But in different policy arenas distinct internal logics and regulations prevail and different actors are at work. Different policy arenas are combined in varying modes, which makes international comparison a very complex undertaking. From a comparative perspective, however, the educational paradigm shows a higher degree of stability and path-dependency than the 'reconciliation approach'.

Looking now at the countries representing this second paradigm (in this book: Germany, the Nordic countries, the United Kingdom), one can observe that the 'work–care reconciliation model' has undergone a variety of policy changes at different stages in time and different institutional levels. Again, the question is what has happened at 'critical junctures' and how change should be characterised – as path-dependent smooth adaptation, even stickiness, or as a paradigm shift. It has already been mentioned that the model which started out as a residual approach targeting children and families with particular needs can develop towards a universal approach and move in the direction of the educational model. Such a transition, however, runs into special difficulties and has to do battle with institutional constraints inherent to the residual welfare approach.

Borchorst argues that in Denmark a transition from a residual to a universal approach has occurred. The Danish model is characterised by a high level of public commitment, the principle of universalism and social–pedagogical objectives. The critical path-breaking development occurred in 1964 as universalism replaced the former residual approach as the guiding principle of child-care policies. To explain continuity and change, Borchorst goes back to the historical development from 1919 onwards, when the social–pedagogical tradition was institutionalised and the path was set. For the next 45 years public child care was based on the principle of residualism. Public subsidies were only granted on condition that two-thirds of the children in a kindergarten came from low-income families. As in Britain and other countries, the starting point in Denmark was a two-tier, class-based child-care model, but in Denmark (as opposed to, for example, Germany or the United Kingdom) this was gradually replaced by people's kindergartens. A change in the financing principles was an important step towards universalism. The change to universalism was framed in relation to children's needs and educational arguments, while women's employment and gender considerations did not play a central role in framing policy at the beginning of the 1960s – the time analysed as a critical juncture by Borchorst. Obviously, the extensive child-care facilities foster and allow the high female employment participation in Denmark; but access of a child to a place in kindergarten has not been linked to the employment status of the mother – the child-centred discourse stands in the way of a child losing its place in kindergarten if the mother becomes unemployed (contrary to Sweden, where a child of an unemployed parent or of a mother at home, up to 2002, had no right to a place in kindergarten). All in all, Denmark takes a special position within the comparative spectrum. The first decades of the development of public child care in Denmark are clearly to be situated within the social welfare paradigm. There then occurred a switch to the pedagogical paradigm, which, however, did not require fundamental changes in the organisation of public child care, because social–pedagogical considerations – albeit originally restricted to the lower classes – had always been central to the structure of public child care.

This book does not contain a country report on Sweden as such, but the developments in Sweden are dealt with by Bahle in his comparative contribution, by Rauhala, who focuses on the common features of the organisation of public child care in the Nordic countries as they have developed mainly since the 1970s, and by Neuman in her comparative contribution on decentralisation trends and governance changes in Sweden and France since the mid-1970s. Bahle explains the development of child-care institutions towards universalism in the Protestant

Scandinavian countries by 'integration' as the institutional mode of Scandinavian child-care systems. By 'integration' is meant the absence of cultural divisions and conflicts and the weakness of class antagonism. Integration also means that children are seen primarily as individual members of society, not as members of a family. This explanation helps to understand how the Scandinavian countries, though starting from a residual welfare model, could nevertheless find the path towards universalism. At the institutional level, important steps in Sweden were the shift of decision-making competences from the ministry of social welfare to the ministry of education in 1996, the change of the name of the services from child care to preschool in 1998, and changes in the financing and organisational principles in the direction of decentralisation. The importance of pedagogical concepts was emphasised through the introduction of national curricula for children aged one to five in 1998. Subjective rights of children to kindergarten places were gradually extended, but were for a long time based on a targeted approach making the employment of the parent/s a precondition for the child's entitlement. This last restriction fell only in 2002, when children of non-employed parents became entitled to at least three hours' child care a day.

Germany is an example within this group where strong path-dependency has led to stickiness in the expansion of early childhood education. Scheiwe analyses the German case as a 'late-comer' in the expansion of early childhood education and explains this slow motion historically (going back to the nineteenth and early twentieth centuries). Institutional constraints, especially legal features of federalism, the resulting split of legislative and administrative competences between the federal state, the regional authorities and local municipalities, and the presence of rules inhibiting efficient political cooperation between the federal and the regional authorities (named the 'joint decision trap' by the political scientist Scharpf, 1988) have played an important role as impediments to the expansion of public child care. A rigid institutional separation between kindergarten and child care on the one hand and schools and formal education on the other hand is upheld by institutional rules and by a lack of political consensus among actors with competing interests in a federal system of multilevel governance. Since the beginning of the twentieth century, child-care institutions have been conceptualised as targeted welfare services for families in need and were integrated into the social welfare sector, administered and financed by the municipalities. As the social welfare sector is subject to the legal principle of subsidiarity (see Richter in this volume), which posits that the state only has to intervene when intermediary organisations fail to do so, the Churches and other nongovernmental organisations play a dominant role in the field; they are in fact the biggest employers of child-care staff in Germany. This whole approach was reinforced by a traditional family and gender model in (Western) Germany (see also Rabe-Kleberg). The first wave of expansion in the 1990s only became possible as a result of the German unification of 1989 and the incorporation of the formerly socialist GDR, in which public child care had been a universal provision. And the actual plans towards an upgrading of rights to early childhood education for under-threes are a result of EU targets and of political compromises within a great coalition of Christian Democrats and Social Democrats, which move towards retarded modernisation – but on a fragile basis, since some actors might be tempted to question the constitutional basis of the compromise package and bring the Federal Constitutional Court into play, an important actor in German politics with the power to reverse even the slow motion visible at present.

The United Kingdom is a country which, even up to the present, has been comparatively slow and hesitant in developing public child care. Helen Penn minutely analyses the relevant developments and the ideological debates surrounding them since the nineteenth century. She points to the importance which social class has always had and still has in the provision of different kinds of child care in the United Kingdom. Over the last years, there have been several initiatives to restructure public child care in the United Kingdom, but the author argues that they have not brought any spectacular breakthroughs and have tended to subject the organisation of child care to the logic of the market. Thus, the door to universalism in Britain was shut by the strong class barriers and the split system involving a public system for the poor and a private one for the better-off (see Bahle in this volume, who describes the British system as a pattern of 'separation' in terms of social class). It is difficult to classify the British system as it does not properly fit either of the two paradigms described here. The residual system of nursery schools for the poor was traditionally integrated into the school system, following an educational paradigm (however limited, and with strong emphasis on social control). Compared with the state nurseries, there were only a few local authority day nurseries, and even these were under the inspection and control of the Educational Board – arguments which might lead us to assign the British case to the first paradigm. However, the public sector of early childhood education was closely linked to class politics for the poor, while the better-off classes relied on nannies, private schools, boarding schools and private services, so that the guiding paradigm is separation, not universal education. One might characterise the British model as a 'targeted educational approach' instead of a universal one; a model apart and an exceptional case within the 'educational paradigm', which is normally associated with universalism.

With regard to recent developments under New Labour since 1997, opinions are split. Is this a significant, path-breaking change, or simply a gradual catching-up process? In England, ministries have been reorganised and all children's services are under the Department for Children, Schools and Families (the former Department for Education and Skills). Children aged three and four have guaranteed access to nursery education in schools (although on a part-time basis). Employed parents of children aged 0 to 5 have access to nurseries outside the school system, and fees are subsidised by child-care tax credits. Separate targeted programmes were developed (see Penn for a detailed account). Is this a path-breaking development and a radical shift? Penn says no; the public–private split has been upheld, and a turn towards an equitable system would require public funding and a separate and coherent system of education and care, not watered-down schooling or a commercial baby park. Bahle agrees in so far as he considers separation along class lines still to be characterising the child care system in the United Kingdom, but points out that the whole range of innovations which have taken place in the United Kingdom over the last decade appear to move the system away from its initial paradigm of child care as a private matter.

5   Cleavages, actors, power relations

In the field of early childhood education, we deal with relationships between different groups of actors: the State, the churches and parents, especially mothers, play a role in the provision of education, socialisation and care for children. Ideological notions of how children should be raised and of what they need come into play. Different paths may be set depending on whether children are perceived primarily as future citizens or as members of the private family, on whether they are perceived as being more in need of 'citizenship education' than of 'home-made education',[11] or on whether the provision of such services is seen as a state task or left mainly to the family, the state stepping in only as a last resort for children deprived of maternal care, as used to be the case in the United Kingdom (Penn in this volume).

The assignment of responsibilities to maternal or family care and/or to publicly provided or financed education for young children has important gender implications which go beyond the reconciliation issue. The status of educational work and the professionalisation of educational activities are affected at different levels, such as training and career opportunities, pay, recognition of skills and abilities etc. of professionals as teachers or as lower-paid and less trained educators (Oberhuemer and Ulich, 1997). The history of the professions and of different associations and unions in this area provide rich material for an understanding of the struggles about recognition and status and about exclusion and inclusion (see Rabe-Kleberg on maternalism and professionalism in this volume).

Other important actors in civil society are indeed *professional organisations and trade unions, NGOs and private initiatives,* as well as private and *commercial suppliers* of marketed or publicly funded child-care services and education. Their role in national processes of the development and change of early childhood education is highlighted in different contributions. Borchorst shows that the turn towards universalism in 1964 in Denmark was strongly influenced by educational professionals, who were able to gain strong support from the civil servants charged with drafting the reform bill. Penn presents many details of the numerous professional and voluntary organisations who tried to influence the reform process in the United Kingdom over a long period, though much less successfully than the reform pedagogues in Denmark. Rabe-Kleberg argues that the comparatively low status and low level of professionalisation of the staff in the German child-care system, who have had little organised influence and played a negligible role as promoters of change, have their roots in the ideology of *maternalism* and the initial exclusion of women from teaching as a profession and from teachers' organisations.

The French example shows an important influence of trade unions upon developmental paths, and Neuman claims that the strong role of trade unions in the highly centralised educational sectors, of which preschools are a part, prevented further decentralisation and spending cuts in this area. Her focus is on how governance shifts have affected the position of different political actors. The shift from 'governance by rules' to 'governance by objectives' in Sweden has increased professional responsibilities of teachers and school directors at the local level. Decentralisation has shifted the main venue for advocacy, political debate and decision-making from the national to the local level, with local elected officials as new players who hold greater discretion in setting early childhood policy. As a result national organisations representing local actors have also gained power. While this may be a new development in formerly more centralised systems, in systems with multilevel governance local and regional actors traditionally have had a stronger impact upon decision-making processes. This power constellation may lead to reform blockages, as Scheiwe shows for Germany with regard to the distribution of legislative, administrative and financial competences under the federal system. This 'joint decision-making trap' also characterises other political systems, such as the EU. Richter's contribution also addresses the distribution of authority within federal systems and its impact on the influence various actors can have upon the development of institutions. Within the same state, power relations are different within more centralised subsystems (characteristically the school sector) from what they are within more decentralised subsystems (for example, typically, the targeted public child-care systems) where local municipalities shoulder more responsibilities for implementing and creating services which meet demand, but also enjoy more discretion. It would be interesting to study in more depth how voters or organisations on the demand side (parents' initiatives, women's groups etc.) can affect local services' provisions and policies, a point that is mentioned by Borchorst – Danish politicians are aware that parents who expect high-quality child care make up a large and visible part of the electorate, she says. Since the early childhood education sector is under reform, sometimes highly contested, more comparative research is desirable on power relations and political conflict in this area.

The *financing* of preschools and public child care is a critical issue, especially in times of welfare cutbacks. Recently, financing principles have become a focus of reform, as Schuler-Harms shows in her contribution. A major shift in financing principles currently under discussion is the one from object-related subsidies (for the institution) towards subject-related financing (through vouchers for parents), which is aimed at increasing the power of the recipients (parents) by enabling them to make choices and which introduces more competition and market-related elements. Schuler-Harms investigates these alternative ways of financing public child care and analyses the legal framework of vouchers, underlying voucher experiments in England, the United States and Germany. She also compares the voucher experiments to another alternative mode of financing public child care: the French 'caisse familiale' (CAF), an institution with far-reaching powers in French family policy and in the child-care system, with a unique financing mechanism which has since the 1920s been based predominantly on employers' contributions (see also the contributions of Martin/Le Bihan and Neuman in this volume). Because of the specificities of the French institutional context (which grants a highly independent and influential position to the Caisse in a thoroughly centralised state system and integrates the employers into public financing structures) and of French family politics – geared as it is to explicit demographic goals – Schuler-Harms is, however, rather sceptical as to the possibility of exporting the Caisse Familiale financing model to other countries.

Finally, we would like to thank Dr Gretchen Wiesehan for her efficient help with English language editing of the contributions by non-native speakers, and acknowledge the helpful comments of an anonymous referee who draw our attention to inconsistencies in the original manuscript.

Notes

1. Comparative literature on child-care arrangements and policies in different countries started up in the 1980s and 1990s. The subject gained attention in the following years, fuelled by different policy initiatives and research funding through international organisations, such as the OECD, the ILO and the European Commission. In 1986, the EU-Childcare Network started its work and initiated various comparative investigations. The OECD Directorate for Education initiated country studies and comparative investigation of child-care issues in 1998; in the context of the 'Starting Strong (Early Childhood Education and Care) Network' 20 countries were investigated up to 2004 and several comparative issues were analysed. The scientific body of literature and the number of research networks and projects have spread widely in the meantime. Comparative work concentrates on issues such as quality aspects, professional training and education of staff, costs and finances, preschool programmes and curricula, interaction processes, parental involvement and child development.
2. The strong emphasis of child-care research upon the reconciliation aspect and the employment and work relationship is visible, for example, in the contributions to the EU conference held in 2004 in Groningen on 'Child care in a changing world', which concentrated on the socioeconomic aspects of child care (see http://www.childcareinachangingworld.nl/downloads/conference_report.pdf). From the scientific comparative literature, we especially want to mention the publication 'Child care policy at the crossroads – Gender and welfare state restructuring' (Michel and Mahon, 2002): while many other comparative publications remain very much at the surface of empirical analysis of the actual situation, the contributions assembled in the book edited by Michel and Mahon develop a conceptual framework that focuses on welfare state restructuring and the decline of the male-breadwinner family to analyse the development

of child care from a feminist perspective, thus widening the perspective to integrate historical and institutional analysis as well as actor- and policy-related questions with the purpose of understanding divergent development patterns in the politics of child care. This comes closest to our approach; however, even in this book the historical perspective for the most part only extends to the period from the 1960s onwards, and in the present volume we go much further back.

3. For the theoretical debate on path-dependency see North (1990), Pierson (2000; 2004) and Mahoney (2000).
4. Compare the contributions of Bahle, Willekens, Valiente, Hohnerlein and Martin/Le Bihan in this book.
5. Compare the contributions of Penn, Neuman, Scheiwe, Richter and Martin/Le Bihan in this book.
6. Compare the contributions of Willekens, Scheiwe, Martin/Le Bihan, Valiente, Baader, Borchorst and Neuman in this book.
7. The first initiative of the European Council dates back to 1992 when a legally non-binding recommendation on child care was enacted (recommendation 92/241/EC of 31 March 1992).
8. For more information on this whole paragraph, see the contributions of Willekens and Martin/Le Bihan. It becomes clear from *all* the other contributions to this book that the early developments in Belgium and France were unique.
9. See Rauhala and Borchorst in this volume.
10. See the contributions of Neuman and Borchorst in this volume.
11. Baader (in this volume) on pedagogical discourses and the reception of Fröbel in the United States and Germany from 1857 to 1933.

Bibliography

J. F. Battail, R. Boyer and V. Fournier, *Les sociétés scandinaves de la Réforme à nos jours* (Paris: Presses Universitaires de France, 1992).

R. Collier and D. Collier, *Shaping the Political Arena: Critical Junctures, the Labor Movement, and Regime Dynamics in Latin America* (Princeton: Princeton University Press, 1991).

P. A. Hall, 'Policy Paradigms, Social Learning, and the State. The Case of Economic Policymaking in Britain', *Comparative Politics*, 25 (1993) 275–296.

R. Lenoir, *Généalogie de la morale familiale* (Paris: Editions du Seuil, 2003).

J. Mahoney, 'Path Dependence in Historical Sociology', *Theory and Society*, 29 (2000) 507–548.

S. Michel and R. Mahon (eds), *Child Care Policy at the Crossroads – Gender and Welfare State Restructuring* (London/New York: Routledge, 2002).

J. Myles and P. Pierson, 'The comparative political economy of pension reform', in P. Pierson (ed.), *The New Politics of the Welfare State* (Oxford: Oxford University Press, 2001) 305–333.

D. North, *Institutions, Institutional Change and Economic Performance* (Cambridge: Cambridge University Press, 1990).

P. Oberhuemer and M. Ulich, *Working with Young Children in Europe. Provision and Staff Training* (London: Paul Chapman, 1997).

P. Pierson 'Increasing Returns, Path Dependence, and the Study of Politics', *American Political Science Review*, 94 (2000) 251–267.

P. Pierson, *Politics in Time – History, Institutions and Social Analysis* (Princeton: Princeton University Press, 2004).

F. Scharpf, 'The Joint Decision Trap: Lessons from German Federalism and European Integration', *Public Administration*, 66 (1988) 239–278.

1
Public Child Care in Europe: Historical Trajectories and New Directions

Thomas Bahle

1 Introduction

Today public child care is primarily regarded as a service for working parents rather than for the child. Its major purpose seems to be to assist parents in balancing work and family life. In this view, child care is part of family policy and a core issue related to gender equality. Anttonen and Sipilä (1996) take this perspective in their comparative analysis of social service systems in Europe. Consequently, they analyse the variations in public policies between countries with respect to different degrees of 'women-friendliness'. Thereby, almost unavoidably, the Scandinavian pattern becomes the reference and all other countries are analysed with respect to 'deficits' compared with this model.

This Scandinavian-centred perspective is greatly misleading, however. Not only are alternative historical routes of development neglected, policies are also evaluated with regard to attitudes pertaining in Scandinavia. Even more problematic from a scientific point of view is that this approach tends to overlook alternative explanations for variations in child-care systems. With respect to welfare regimes, Esping-Andersen's well-known typology (1992) has been widely criticised for such a Nordic bias, but in child care and family policies the Scandinavian model still seems to be uncontested. Yet the Scandinavian road to public child care was not the only model, but simply one of several, because it is based on specific cultural traditions and historical circumstances. Other European countries have followed different paths of development.

The significance of historical–cultural variations for the comparative analysis of social services is emphasised by Alber (1995). His conceptual framework, which is based on the comparative–historical approach by Rokkan and Flora (Rokkan, 2000), highlights an aspect that was also crucial for the historical development of public child care: the conflict between state and church over the competence for education and socialisation. The strength (or absence) of this conflict and the way it was 'institutionalised' in different societies influenced the early formation of public child care in Europe, long before family policy and gender equality became the dominating themes.

In such a historical perspective, this chapter aims at a comparative analysis of public child care in Europe. The analysis focuses on public (or publicly subsidised) care for children aged 0 to compulsory school age. Care for school children is excluded. In the first part, variations in public child-care provision in Europe are presented. This is followed in the second part by a historical explanation and interpretation which tries to reconstruct different paths of development in public child care. The third part concludes with a discussion of new developments in two selected countries: Britain and Germany. In both countries, a policy shift has taken place which seems to follow a renewed interest in children's socialisation and education.

2   Variations in public child care in Europe: an overview

Unfortunately very little comparative longitudinal data on child care is available. The EU collected data in the Child Care Network and the Observatory on National Family Policies; both have been discontinued, however, because the treaties of Maastricht and Amsterdam define family policy as a national domain for which the Union has no competences. The OECD has also collected data and undertaken some studies related to labour market issues and early childhood education programmes. With respect to the educational aspect of child care, the EU information system EURYDIKE also provides some comparative data, as does UNICEF for the former communist countries in Eastern Europe. Despite these efforts comparative data are incomplete and sometimes inconsistent.

A major problem is the borderline between public and private child care, of which the latter is usually badly documented. In some countries public agencies provide almost all child care; in others the majority of places are provided by not-for-profit organisations which are, however, often largely funded by the public purse. In still others, parents receive subsidies or tax concessions for the use of private, for-profit child-care institutions. Another major problem for comparability is the borderline between child-care institutions and care at home provided by persons who do not belong to the child's family. Some countries rely almost exclusively on child-care centres whereas others have institutionalised systems of childminding.

Despite these differences, comparative data are quite consistent with respect to the broad indicator on child-care provision as used in Figure 1.1 in cross-sectional perspective.

Here a distinction is made between children aged 0–2 and those aged 3 up to compulsory school age. In most countries this is age 6, in some 5 (the United Kingdom, the Netherlands, Ireland), in others 7 (Sweden, Denmark). The indicator shows the coverage rate of publicly provided (or subsidised) child care as a percentage of the child population by the year 2000. Countries are ranked by the coverage rate for children aged 3–5, which in all countries is higher than for the younger age group. For the older age group coverage rates vary from 100% in France to about 50% in Poland (no data for Ireland), for the younger age group from almost 70% in Denmark to less than 2% in the Czech Republic and Poland. Interestingly enough, it is not the Scandinavian countries but four continental European nations which provide the most places for children aged 3 to 5: France, Belgium, Italy and the Netherlands. In the Netherlands, however, most places are part-time. Moreover, there is no strong correlation between the two different coverage rates: countries which score high for one age group do not necessarily score high for

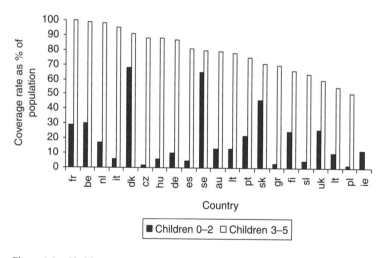

Figure 1.1   Childcare services in Europe, around 2000

Sources: OECD (2001, 2003, 2005); EURYDIKE (2005); UNICEF (1999) Bahle/Pfenning (2002); Neyer (2003).

the other. This clearly shows that the comparative patterns in the two different age groups need to be explained by different factors.

A first clue to explaining these variations institutionally and historically is provided in Table 1.1, in which countries are cross-classified by the two different coverage rates. Quite interestingly, most countries with high coverage rates for children aged 3 to 5 (above 80% coverage) are Catholic and have established preschools. Among them, France and Belgium have a long preschool tradition, dating back to the end of the nineteenth century. In Italy and Spain the development was more recent, starting after World War II. Only one Scandinavian country, Denmark, offers the same amount of child care in this age segment. Four continental European countries also have high coverage rates for this age group: the Netherlands, Germany, the Czech Republic and Hungary. Yet their institutional development was different from the preschool countries. In Germany kindergartens have a long tradition, but coverage has only recently increased to such an extent. Before the 1990s Germany was situated (in the table) near Austria in a middle position. The same is true for the Netherlands. Here too the growth in coverage was more recent. The Czech Republic and Hungary have partly retained their child-care systems from the communist period. In this regard, they are something of an exception. Overall, the preschool tradition, a specific institutional arrangement, is the best condition for a high coverage rate in this age group.

For the younger age group (0–2) public child care is more limited in all countries. The growth in this age segment came only after the

Table 1.1   Childcare coverage rates, Europe *ca.* 2000

Children 3–5 Children 0–2	> 80%	70%–80%	< 60%
> 20%	**France** **Belgium** Denmark	Sweden Finland Portugal Slovakia	United Kingdom
10%–20%	**Netherlands** Germany	Austria Latvia	Ireland
< 10%	**Italy** **Spain** Czech Republic Hungary	Greece Slowenia	Poland Lithuania

Note: **High preschool coverage rate**; Subsidized family day care.

1970s. Also for children aged 0–2 there is an institutional factor, which explains why some countries have higher coverage rates (above 20%). All these countries share an institutional characteristic: they have a system of family day care, that is, a publicly subsidised and regulated network of child care provided for small groups in family-like settings. The Scandinavian nations and Finland are among these countries, as are France and Belgium. Although in Belgium and France child care institutions like crèches play an important role, it is the public system of childminding (*assistentes maternelles*) which constitutes the biggest difference to countries with lower rates of coverage (DREES, 2003b; DREES, 2005). Portugal, Slovakia and the United Kingdom also have high coverage rates for this age group. Yet Portugal is a well-known exception among the Southern European countries because of its high female labour force participation. In Slovakia, one may speculate about a kind of 'exceptional' heritage from the communist past. Finally, for the United Kingdom the position among the leading countries for very young children is quite recent (as for Germany above). In Britain, as in Germany, there has been a significant change in child-care policy which will be discussed in part 4.

3 Historical trajectories: welfare competition and family policy

How can these variations be explained historically? In a long-term perspective, the comparative pattern of child-care services in Europe was shaped by two different historical contexts: the first was related to industrialisation and nation-building, the second to the transition into a service economy and the parallel rise of female employment. In the first phase the conflict between state and church and the differences between social classes were highly important for the formation of early public child care, in the second the women's movement and state family policies. The first historical context was crucial for the development of preschools (for children aged 3 to 5). The second context is located in time about 100 years later and was dominated by family policy and gender equality issues from the beginning.

The historical development of public child care can therefore be understood as a process of stepwise institutionalisation and continuing growth. The two different phases of institutionalisation laid the foundations for the subsequent quantitative expansion of the systems. The first period is characterised by the problems of industrialisation and the conflicts related to the expansion of the state into society. It was a period of male-dominated work in which the male-breadwinner family model ultimately reached its historical zenith in the 1960s. It was also a time in which strong ideological conflicts based on social class and religion pertained. The second period, starting in the early 1970s, was characterised by the growth of female employment as part of a general shift to a service-dominated economy. In this period the nuclear family started to disintegrate and differentiate as well. The two periods are analysed in the following.

The first period of institutionalisation needs to be understood in a perspective in which child care was not regarded as a 'service' for working parents. Early child-care institutions had rather different aims. Through them the state tried to impose a kind of social control on the poor and disadvantaged strata of the working class. At the same time both state and church aimed at socialising and integrating children into the value systems of the nation-state or the religious community. The first issue is thus related to class structures, the second to the conflicts related to nation-building and the penetration of the state into society. Hence, I will focus on two aspects of child-care systems here: their institutional fragmentation (or integration) across different population groups and the actors which have driven their expansion. In this respect I distinguish between four patterns which have followed different historical trajectories: the patterns of competition, pluralism, integration and separation.

The first, competition, is found in Catholic countries of Europe in which there was a conflict between the state and the church regarding the competence for education and socialisation of children. Since both actors competed for the same group, in principle the whole population in these territories, competition was strong. Although child care also originated within the context of early industrialisation, the cultural conflict between the liberal state and Catholicism soon overshadowed distinctions by social class. Since state and church competed with each other over the integration of large population groups, the competition was 'open'. This may explain why these systems tended to high coverage, indeed eventually to universality. Still, of course, there was a big difference between the industrially more advanced countries of France and Belgium on the one hand and the less modernised Southern European countries on the other. This explains why child care remained historically limited longer in the South. Yet a general striving towards universality, the institutionalisation of an educational focus of child care and a clear separation from the demands of working life have characterised all the 'competition' countries. This institutional pattern resulted in a relatively early development and current high coverage for preschool children.

The second pattern, pluralism, is found in the two religiously mixed countries, the Netherlands and Germany (Switzerland is a different case because of its strong decentralisation and predominance of liberalism). In both countries competition was weaker than in the Catholic world, because the different confessional population groups were separated. Therefore competition was somewhat 'closed'. Yet there was also direct competition between the state on the one hand and the different churches on the other, but this was also limited. The historical–cultural heterogeneity in these societies thus led to welfare pluralism in which the different actors served different population groups. Competition between these different groups was naturally limited. Pluralism has therefore favoured fragmentation rather than integration of the child-care system. Yet also for these countries the conditions for an expansion of public child care were not unfavourable, in particular in the Netherlands with its strong pillarisation. Here the early socialisation and integration of children in the respective 'pillar' was regarded as highly important. This may explain why in the Netherlands the pre-school tradition was stronger than in Germany. Yet there was no such strong motive to extend the system as in the more 'competitive' purely Catholic countries.

In Protestant Europe the historical conditions were completely different. First of all, there was no conflict between state and church over the competence in social and family matters, including the issues of education and child care. Following the Reformation, church and state were integrated. The Scandinavian countries were characterised by a kind of church monopoly. Thus there was neither 'open' nor 'closed' competition as in purely Catholic or religiously mixed Europe. No actor wanted to mobilise the population through education or socialisation against a competitor. Yet in Britain the situation was more complicated. There has always been a sizeable Catholic minority in Britain. In addition, the various Protestant sects which do not belong to the Anglican state church had a strong influence on state politics and policies. Despite this plurality of actors, however, it was not pluralism which developed in Britain, but a 'reluctant state' which has followed a general leitmotif of nonintervention in social affairs. The minorities were too weak for a balanced pluralism, but they contributed to a structure in which the state did not want to become too involved with social and family issues. In Protestant Europe class divisions could more easily become a major factor in structuring child-care institutions because of the absence of cultural divisions. Yet the class factor became dominant only in Britain, not in Scandinavia. There are two reasons for this British exception. The first was early and strong industrialisation, the second the formation of a real industrial working class almost completely detached from agrarian conditions. In Scandinavia, by contrast, industrialisation came later and there were sizeable agrarian population groups living well into the twentieth century. Moreover, the Scandinavian countries were characterised by a very low level of social inequality historically. For all these reasons the idea of universalism, bridging class distinctions, became predominant in Scandinavia, whereas in Britain class differences permeated all kinds of social institutions including child care. Hence, in Protestant Europe one can distinguish two different patterns: integration and separation.

Integration is the institutional mode of Scandinavian child-care systems. It means first of all absence of cultural divisions and conflicts. Second, it means that class differences were weak. Therefore child-care institutions could become potentially universal, aiming at integrating all members of society into the same system. Integration also refers to the idea that children as individuals are members of society, not only members of a particular family. The state was therefore widely regarded with sympathy when taking responsibility for society's children. Yet, due to the initial lack of competition between different actors, child-care institutions could not unfold their potential to universal expansion from early on. They did so only after the social conditions in the economy and within the family had changed. Indeed, the Scandinavian child-care systems increased rapidly and extensively only after the 1970s, when the labour market and the family had started to change.

In Britain, by contrast, the door to universalism was shut by the strong class barriers that characterise the early interventions of the welfare state focusing on the poor. Public child care long remained limited to the disadvantaged strata while the middle classes relied on private nannies. Thus the child-care system was split from the beginning by class differences into a public system for the poor and a private one for the better-off (see Penn in this volume). In addition, the influence of the religious minorities hindered development of a comprehensive system of public child care. The British system can therefore be described as a pattern of 'separation' in terms of social class rather than 'pluralism' in terms of religious heterogeneity.

Comparatively speaking, the competitive environment was the most fertile soil for early and high development of child care. In economic terms, it was characterised by a duopoly, which is a highly competitive environment. Pluralism was ready for a less extensive development. This situation may be described as an oligopoly, in which competition is controlled and therefore less forceful. The integrative model was shaped by a kind of state monopoly. This condition first hindered development, but unfolded its encompassing expansive potential when the welfare state was massively extended, starting in the 1970s. In this sense we may speak of a heavily subsidised monopoly that has a tendency to expand. The special British case of separation by social class was the least favourable for growth in public child care, which also remained severely limited due to the state's non-interventionist tradition in economic and family affairs. In economic terms this situation can be described as a state monopoly that decided for various reasons to limit supply. On the other hand, of course, the private market was 'open', but it could only serve the higher income groups.

The second major 'juncture' in the development of public child care came when the transition to a service-dominated economy was accompanied by a strong increase in female employment and the pluralisation of the nuclear family. This was the case around the 1970s. Since then child care has again become an important political and social issue, but the context is now completely different from the first historical period. Now the main issue is not education but family policy (see also Gornick et al., 1997).

The shift to a service-based economy was a general problem for all countries, but the extent and timing of this change and the reactions of the state varied greatly. The rise of child care for very young children was strongest in two groups of countries: the Scandinavian nations on the one hand and Belgium and France on the other. In the first group the issue of gender equality was predominant. The 'socialisation' of family functions was extensive, also because there was no idea of the family as an autonomous social institution. Scandinavia with its integrative social institutions was best prepared for a rapid expansion of child care, including for the younger age group. Child care was socialised to an extent then unknown in the Western world. Another important factor was that the model of the male-breadwinner family had never really been dominant in Scandinavia, because the period of industrialisation (in which this model was strongest) was short and still permeated by the agrarian past with its more egalitarian gender role model. The Scandinavian context thus was most open for a rapid and huge expansion of child care when the need for it arose and political demands were successfully expressed, in particular by the women's movement.

France and Belgium are the two outstanding examples of developed public child-care systems on the European continent. These nations were the pioneers of family policy in Europe and the world. Family policy was able to gain a very strong and highly legitimate position in politics and policies which paved the way for its extension and further development. In addition, particularly in France there was a tradition of working mothers, in contrast to both Germany and the United Kingdom where the male-breadwinner role model was predominant. France and Belgium thus displayed a unique combination of factors that was favourable for the development of child-care services. Their 'old' historical context of conflict between state and church resulted in the highest level of preschool coverage all over Europe and the 'new' context of transition to a service economy was embedded in a unique high legitimacy of family policy which opened the door to an expansion of child care to the younger age groups as well. In this respect it is also interesting that the established preschools (which originally served children aged 3–5) were partly opened for younger children as well, in France for example from age two and a half.

The rise of care for very young children is thus part of family policies which also vary widely within Europe (see Table 1.2).[1] One can broadly identify three country groups characterised by a typical dominant mode of intervention in the relationship between the family and the labour market: neutrality, subsidiarity and compatibility.

Table 1.2   Family policy profiles

| Income support | Family-work relationship | | |
	Compatibility	Subsidiarity	Neutrality
High	Denmark Finland Sweden Belgium France	Austria Germany Luxembourg Hungary	Malta
Medium	Estonia Latvia		Cyprus Ireland The Netherlands United Kingdom
Low	Slovakia	Czech Republic Lithuania Poland	Greece Italy Portugal Slovenia Spain

Source: own compilation.

The first mode, neutrality, is characterised by undeveloped policies both in public child care and in measures which support the care of children at home, for example paid parental leave. In these countries the state is simply nonactive in this field, supporting neither a parental work nor a parental care model. The family is regarded as being able to take care of itself and the state takes a neutral position towards the various role models within families. This group consists basically of Southern Europe, but also includes Ireland, the United Kingdom and the Netherlands. Unlike the Southern European countries, however, the Netherlands, the United Kingdom and Ireland have a more elaborated income policy in favour of families. The Southern European countries have generally weakly developed family policies.

The second group of countries demonstrates a subsidiarity approach to family policy. Here the state supports the family so that it can better fulfil its social tasks, including early child care at home. Therefore parenting policies are more developed than public child-care services (see also Bertelsmann Stiftung, 2002). The typical role model in this profile is the caring mother. The countries included in this category are typically located in central Western and Eastern Europe. Also here we have two subgroups: in the first (Austria, Germany, Luxembourg and Hungary) income policies for families are also generous and support the general leitmotif of subsidiarity; in the second, income support for the family is low (Czech Republic, Poland and Lithuania).

The third group of countries follows a compatibility approach in family policy and has the most developed public child-care systems. Their family policy profile can be described as work-oriented, because the working parent is the pivotal role model. In five of these countries family policy is generally highly developed, including income transfers. The Scandinavian countries (including Finland) form the core of this group, but France and Belgium also belong to it. In the other three countries with good child care, financial transfers play a smaller role. This is the case in the Baltic states and Slovakia.

This group is particularly interesting for the purpose of this chapter, because these countries have the highest child-care coverage rates for children below the age of 3. Denmark and Sweden were latecomers in family policy development, but, once they started, their systems expanded rapidly and to high levels. Yet child care for the older age group is still less developed than in the Catholic European countries with a tradition of preschools. Belgium and France, on the other hand, were the pioneers of family policy in Europe. As a consequence, family policy became firmly institutionalised both in politics and in social institutions. The high legitimacy of family policy was the crucial basis for its later modernisation and also for the extension of services when family and labour market structures started to change. In this respect path-dependency is rooted in the unique strong institutionalisation and high legitimacy of family policy, and less in specific policies. Since Belgium and France now belong to the countries with the most 'modernised' child-care policies, they have moved towards Scandinavia in terms of their family policy profile (Bahle, 2008a; Fux, 2002).

The former communist countries have followed a specific historical trajectory (see Dörfler, 2002; Pascall and Manning, 2000; Rostgaard, 2004; UNICEF, 1999). Communism was a significant break with previous institutional structures, in particular with respect to industrialisation, female work patterns and child-care arrangements. The strong female worker model under communism went together with high public child-care coverage rates, although individual countries differed from each other. The most 'socialised' pattern took shape in the German Democratic Republic, whereas in Hungary and Poland the family continued to play a more important role. With the end of communism this pattern changed dramatically. High unemployment, lower female labour force participation and the crisis in public finances resulted in the closure of many child-care institutions (Commander and Bornhorst, 2004). Yet since birth rates had also strongly declined, coverage rates remained relatively high. Very interesting is the fact that, after having abandoned their communist traditions, these countries went back to their even older historical paths of development inspired by the common Central European idea of subsidiarity. Indeed, today most former communist countries show a family policy similar to Western and Central European countries like Austria or Germany, although benefits are still lower. The historical aberration of communism was put aside and replaced by a return to the historically older path of subsidiarity. There are two major exceptions, however. The first are the two Protestant Baltic states Estonia and Latvia, which were part of the Soviet Union before the end of communism. Today both countries appear to have moved closer towards their geographic and cultural neighbours in Scandinavia with respect to family policy patterns. The other exception seems to be Slovakia, which is the only Central European country that did not move towards the common Central European pattern. On the one hand, it retained elements of the former communist system (high child-care coverage) while on the other it introduced elements of a radical liberal approach as in the

United States, exemplified by the low legal provisions regarding maternity or parental leave.

4 New directions: Britain and Germany in the European context

Recently some countries have changed their policies significantly. This raises the question whether one can interpret such changes as a break with the historical path of development. If so, the next question is what the reasons for this shift have been. Do these changes really show a significant break with traditional structures or are these countries simply catching up with their more advanced European neighbours?

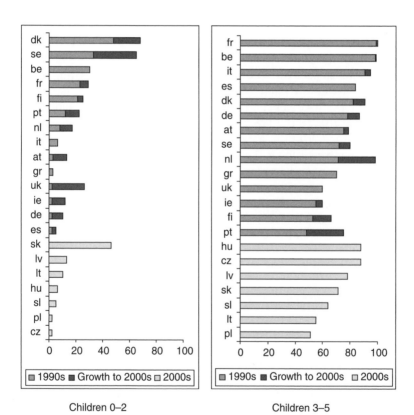

Children 0–2   Children 3–5

Figure 1.2   Childcare services: Coverage rates, Europe 1990–2004
Sources: OECD; Bahle 2008a.

Over the past 15 years the comparative pattern of child care in Europe has not changed dramatically, but some countries (which had been lagging behind) have caught up, in particular the United Kingdom and the Netherlands. Also in Germany one can already observe a small change. Yet in absolute terms, coverage for children 0–2 grew most in Sweden and Denmark, the two countries which already had the most developed systems.

Britain and Germany are two examples of a reorientation in public child care which needs to be analysed further. This shift has taken place recently and is therefore not yet fully reflected in the figures. The growth for the younger age group is already visible in the United Kingdom, though not in Germany. But Germany has far-reaching plans. The most recent plans to which federal and state governments agreed in 2007 will increase coverage for children aged 0–2 from about 10 percent to more than 30 percent in 2013.

In both Britain and Germany child-care services were very limited, for some of the same reasons (see above). In both countries, the strong and lasting impact of industrialisation resulted in a persisting male-breadwinner family model. In Britain this model was even more sustained by the state's liberal policy which limited state intervention to children at risk. In the 1980s child-care services developed on a larger scale, but the role of the state remained limited. The major policy shift came under New Labour. There was a new emphasis on the child and the problems of socialisation. The state became active in the development of child care. Guarantees for part-time places in educational facilities were given and the number of services increased rapidly. The core institution in this respect was the nursery school, which had developed as part of the school system. In Britain, young children go to primary school at the age of 5 (compulsory school age) and the system of nursery schools was recently extended to integrate children aged 4 and 3, although on a part-time and voluntary basis only (Lewis, 2003). The British policy shift can be explained by the combination of two factors: the rapid change to a service-based economy after the massive deindustrialisation since the 1980s and the renewed interest in socialisation and education.

In Germany the development was different, but the policy shift was also great. Also in Germany the male-breadwinner family model was deeply rooted and the transition to a service-based economy came later than in most other countries. But reunification changed the situation dramatically and permanently. Suddenly Germany was faced with massive deindustrialisation as well, not only in the new *Länder* (states) of the former German Democratic Republic, in which an even larger proportion of the workforce was employed in the industrial sector. Still, in Germany too, the policy shift in child care had to wait until the issues of socialisation and education were added to the agenda. At the same time, the pro-child care discourse which had developed within the family policy domain received strong support. Hence, also in Germany it was the combination of family policy change and the renewed interest in early childhood education which brought about the massive (planned) expansion of child care.

In Britain and Germany the recent shift in child-care policies can be explained by a change in the political and social constellation. In both countries a massive transformation from industrial to service-based employment took place (on the foundations of a historically strong industrial society). At the same time, there was a renewed interest in the child and the socialisation of children in society. This interest in education and socialisation was fuelled by a debate on child abuse and the failure of some parents living in poor conditions to socialise their children properly. In addition, there was also growing public concern about the problems of social integration for migrants and their children. Child care and early childhood education were seen as appropriate means to influence these processes positively. This agenda also has strong support from conservative politicians. In the German context of party politics, for example, it is very interesting to see the changing debate within the Christian Democratic Party in that respect. It was therefore no accident that only the grand coalition government, which came to power in 2005, was able to initiate this policy shift on child care where the previous Social Democrat – Green coalition had failed. Only when the interests of the child were given priority did the window open for change.

Is this shift in Britain and Germany already reflected in social practice, for example in daily patterns of child care in families? The answer is not yet clear. Still the situation in both the United Kingdom and Germany differs from that in Scandinavia or even France (see Table 1.3).

The United Kingdom and Germany have a similar daily pattern of child care in which parents and other family members, in particular grandparents, play a greater role than in other countries. Grandparents, for example, are the major caregivers in both countries in about one-quarter of families with children below the age of 12. With this data, the United Kingdom and Germany are close to Spain and only a little behind Poland, the two countries in the sample with

Table 1.3 Childcare patterns, selected countries 2004

	Germany	Germany-West	Germany-East	France	United Kingdom	Sweden	Denmark	Spain	Poland
Grandparents	25,5	27,7	15,6	12,7	24,0	2,1	12,2	25,6	31,6
Former partner	2,0	1,9	2,3	3,9	1,3	0,7	2,0	7,2	8,5
Other family members	9,6	9,9	8,6	5,5	13,5	1,2	3,7	5,1	7,1
Unpaid care in private household	0,6	0,5	1,1	1,0	0,9	0,7	1,7	0,7	0,7
Paid care in private household	2,5	2,5	2,8	16,1	6,7	6,7	3,4	4,4	1,8
Cost-free childcare centre	2,1	1,6	4,0	1,5	1,3	1,9	0,8	0,7	0,5
Paid childcare centre	15,6	12,1	31,6	13,0	8,4	49,6	43,9	5,5	5,2
Child stays alone	7,4	7,1	8,4	8,2	0,7	11,9	11,3	2,0	3,8
Parent at home: no childcare needed	32,9	34,5	25,6	35,5	42,1	24,5	13,0	46,5	38,5
Other	1,8	2,2	0,0	2,8	1,0	0,7	7,9	2,4	2,5
Total	100,0	100,0	100,0	100,0	100,0	100,0	100,0	100,0	100,0

Note: Families with children below the age of 12; one item to select only.

Source: European Social Survey 2004; own computations.

the most traditional, family-centred child-care patterns. In Britain, the parents themselves provide even more care than in Poland and much more than in Germany. In this respect, public child care in Britain is still much less developed than in most other European countries.

This contrasts sharply with the situation in Sweden and Denmark. In the two Scandinavian countries, paid child-care centres are by far the most important form of child care while the family takes second place. There is one interesting difference between Sweden and Denmark, however: in Sweden, the parents themselves are more and the grandparents less important than in Denmark. This may be due to the unique Swedish parental insurance system, which allows parents to stay at home and care for children for a long time while being paid and retaining the right to their jobs. In Denmark, parental leave is shorter, which means that grandparents take a more active role when parents are back to work and children do not go to public institutions. It is also interesting that in both Scandinavian countries children spend more time at home alone than in all other countries. Viewed positively, this may be an indicator for confidence in children's ability to cope by themselves (probably rooted in the individualised culture in Scandinavia generally), but it may also reflect the fact that the need to work outside the home creates problems even in the most developed public child-care systems.

France lies between the Scandinavian and the other continental European countries, which nicely confirms our historical–institutional analysis. On the one hand, in France the family, in particular parents, still plays an important role. Grandparents, however, are less important than in all other countries except Scandinavia. The alternative to parental care is not primarily grandparents but public child care, with 'paid care in private households' playing a unique role in France compared with other countries (see Martin and Le Bihan in this volume). This is very likely due to the institution of the *crèches familiales* or the day-care mothers (*assistantes maternelles*), which is highly developed (DREES, 2003a; OCDE, 2004). It is not quite clear, however, whether the preschools (for children 3–5) are included in these data at all, because the term 'child-care centre free of charge' is less frequently used than 'paid child-care centre', which seems strange in the French context. A reason for this may be that the table refers to children under age 12 (and not specifically to preschool children); another reason may be the fact that also in France parents have to pay for child care provided at preschools outside regular school opening hours.

The German pattern of daily child care clearly differs between the eastern and western parts of the country (Statistisches Bundesamt, 2004). In the west, parents and grandparents dominate; in the east, paid child-care centres. Grandparents play a limited role in the east. This difference is partly explained by the different working patterns in both parts of Germany. In the former GDR women tended and still tend to work universally and full-time, whereas in the west the male-breadwinner model is strong even compared with most other Western European countries. In this respect, the former GDR was more 'modernised' than all other communist countries and the (old) Federal Republic was more 'traditional' than most Western European countries.

Overall, the survey data confirm the findings of the comparative–institutional analysis. Although Britain and Germany recently invested in the extension of public child-care systems (Bahle, 2008b), there is still a long way to go. The growth in public child care is not yet reflected in comparative data on patterns of daily child care as used by families. One reason for this is that the policy shift has occurred only recently, another that most places are still provided on a part-time basis. This is especially the case in Britain, where most of the expansion was in part-time educational arrangements (Department for Education, 2003). This means that parents and other family members will continue to play a dominant role. Yet at the same time children are increasingly integrated into public programmes. This allows the state to have a minimum of public supervision and control with respect to socialisation. Quite clearly then, the main aim of these programmes is not balancing work and family life (for parents), but integrating children into society and improving the conditions for socialisation. In Germany, the policy change still needs to be implemented and is therefore not yet reflected in the data presented here. Here the change was also made possible by a renewed interest in socialisation, but compared with Britain family policy continues to play a more important role. Therefore what one can see is in both cases a change in child-care policy, but more continuity in family policy more generally. It depends much on the perspective taken whether this is interpreted as a path-breaking or a path-continuing form of development.

Note

1. For a more detailed discussion and explanation of family policy profiles see Pfenning and Bahle (2000); Bahle (2008a); Fux (2002).

Bibliography

J. Alber, 'A framework for the comparative study of social services', *Journal of European Social Policy*, 5 (1995) 131–149

A. Anttonen and J. Sipilä, 'European social care services: is it possible to identify models?', *Journal of European Social Policy*, 6 (1996) 87–100

T. Bahle, 'Family policy patterns in the enlarged EU', in J. Alber, T. Fahey and C. Saraceno (eds), *Handbook of quality of life in the enlarged European Union* (London: Routledge, 2008a), 100–125

T. Bahle, 'The state and social services in Britain, France, and Germany since the 1980s: reform and growth in a period of welfare state crisis', *European Societies*, 10 (2008b) 25–47

T. Bahle and A. Pfenning, 'Angebotsformen und Trägerstrukturen sozialer Dienste im europäischen Vergleich'. Mannheimer Zentrum für Europäische Sozialforschung, *Working paper No. 42* (Mannheim: MZES, 2003)

Bertelsmann Stiftung (ed.), *Vereinbarkeit von Familie und Beruf. Benchmarking Deutschland Aktuell* (by Werner Eichhorst and Eric Thode) (Gütersloh: Verlag Bertelsmann Stiftung, 2002)

S. Commander and F. Bornhorst, 'Integration and the well-being of children in the transition economies'. UNICEF Innocenti *Working Papers No. 98*, 2004 (Florence: UNICEF, 2004)

Department for Education, *Statistics of Education: Provision for Children under 5 Years in England, January 2002* (London: DfE, 2003)

J. Donzelot, *Die Ordnung der Familie* (Frankfurt: Suhrkamp, 1980)

S. Dörfler, 'Familienpolitische Leistungen in ausgewählten europäischen Staaten außerhalb der Europäischen Union'. Österreichisches Institut für Familienforschung *Arbeitspapier No. 30*, 2002 (Wien: ÖIF, 2002)

DREES, 'Les assistantes maternelles: une profession en développement', *Études et Résultats*, No. 232 (2003a)

DREES, 'Les modes d'accueil des enfants de moins de 6 ans', *Études et Résultats*, No. 235 (2003b) 1–12

DREES, 'L'accueil collectif et en crèches familiales des enfants de moins de 6 ans en 2003', *Série Statistiques*, No. 79 (2005)

G. Erning, K. Neumann and J. Reyer (eds), *Geschichte des Kindergartens. Band II: Institutionelle Aspekte, Systematische Perspektiven, Entwicklungsverläufe* (Freiburg im Breisgau: Lambertus, 1987)

G. Esping-Andersen, *The Three Worlds of Welfare Capitalism* (Princeton: Princeton University Press, 1992)

EURYDIKE, *Key Data on Education in Europe* (Luxemburg: EUROSTAT, 2005)

B. Fux, 'Which models of the family are encouraged or discouraged by different family policies?', in F.-X. Kaufmann, A. Kuijsten, H.-J. Schulze and K. P. Strohmeier (eds), *Family Life and Family Policies in Europe. Volume 2: Problems and Issues in Comparative Perspective* (Oxford: Oxford University Press, 2002), 363–419

J. C. Gornick, M. K. Meyers, and K. E. Ross, 'Supporting the employment of mothers: Policy variation across fourteen welfare states', *Journal of European Social Policy*, 7 (1997) 45–70

B. Holzer, *Die Institutionalisierung von Kinderbetreuungseinrichtungen für Kinder im Vorschulalter. Eine historisch-vergleichende Untersuchung sozialer Dienste in der Europäischen Union am Beispiel von Deutschland und Großbritannien,* Diplomarbeit, Faculty of Social Sciences, University of Mannheim (1998)

J. Lewis, 'Developing early years child care in England, 1997–2002: the choices for working mothers', *Social Policy and Administration,* 37 (2003) 219–238

G. Neyer, 'Family policies and low fertility in Europe', Max-Planck-Institut für Demographische Forschung, *Arbeitspapier No. 21,* 2003 (Rostock: MPI, 2003)

OCDE, Direction de l'Éducation, *La politique d'éducation et d'accueil des jeunes enfants en France* (Paris: OCDE, 2004)

OECD, *Starting Strong. Early Childhood Education and Care* (Paris: OECD, 2001)

OECD, 'Low fertility rates in OECD countries: facts and policy responses' (by Joëlle E. Sleebos), *OECD Social, Employment and Migration Working Papers,* No. 15, 2003 (Paris: OECD, 2003)

OECD, Can parents afford to work? Child care costs, tax-benefit policies and work incentives (by H. Immervoll and D. Barber), *OECD Social, Employment and Migration Working Papers,* No. 31, 2005 (Paris: OECD, 2005)

G. Pascall and N. Manning, 'Gender and social policy: comparing welfare states in Central and Eastern Europe and the former Soviet Union', *Journal of European Social Policy* 10 (2000) 240–266

A. Pfenning and T. Bahle (eds), *Families and Family Policies in Europe. Comparative Perspectives* (Frankfurt am Main: Lang, 2000)

S. Rokkan, *Staat, Nation und Demokratie in Europa. Die Theorie Stein Rokkans aus seinen gesammelten Werken rekonstruiert und eingeleitet von P. Flora* (Frankfurt: Suhrkamp, 2000)

T. Rostgaard, 'Family support policy in Central and Eastern Europe – a decade and a half of transition', *UNESCO Early Childhood and Family Policy Series No. 8,* 2004 (Paris: UNESCO, 2004)

Statistisches Bundesamt, *Kinderbetreuung in Deutschland. Einrichtungen, Plätze, Personal und Kosten, 1990–2002* (Wiesbaden: Statistisches Bundesamt, 2004)

UNICEF (ed.), *Women in Transition* (Florence: UNICEF, 1999)

Data links on the web

Eurydike: http://www.eurydice.org/portal/page/portal/Eurydice/EuryPresentation

UNICEF transMONEE database on new EU member states: http://www.unicef-icdc.org/resources/

Clearinghouse On International Developments in Child, Youth and Family Policies at Columbia University: http://www.childpolicyintl.org/

2
How and Why Belgium Became a Pioneer of Preschool Development

Harry Willekens

1 The research question

Belgium, together with France, was the pioneer of preschool development in the world. In 1900, 49% of three- to five-year-olds were registered in kindergartens; in 1910 the registered proportion within this age group already amounted to 60%. Registration went up dramatically after World War II to reach nearly 100% from 1970 onwards. The main change which occurred after that was that preschools were also opened for children aged only two to two and a half (Depaepe, De Vroede, Minten and Simon, 1998a, pp. 191–192). Registration and attendance are, of course, two different matters, and we know little of attendance for the period before 1960; it is possible that some parents who had registered their children only brought them to the kindergarten for a few hours a day, a few days a week or certain periods of the year. Even so, registration figures were much higher than in most other industrially developed countries, where they remained negligible until the second rise of female labour market participation from the 1960s onwards. Moreover, from early on, there were many kindergartens providing full-day care and education. All of this contrasts sharply with the provision of public child care for babies and toddlers, where – as in most other European countries – only a minimal supply existed until recently. In 1990, there were publicly subsidised child-care places for only 11.5% of children aged under three years and over three months. In 2002, this had gone up to 20.1% (Van Dongen, 2004).[1]

Belgium and France were also pioneers in another than the merely quantitative sense. In these countries, from the last third of the

nineteenth century onwards preschool institutions were generally conceived as preparatory to school, that is, neither simply as care facilities
for the children of working mothers nor as pedagogical projects of a
qualitatively different nature from school.

At present, preschool for all has become the norm in many countries,
and public care for the under-threes has taken off much more in countries such as Denmark (see Borchorst's contribution to this volume)
than in Belgium; but until the 1970s – that is, for nearly a century – the
widespread development of preschool institutions was a unique feature
of the educational landscape in Belgium and France. This article focuses
on the question of why this was so in the Belgian case. The question
is the more pressing because the early rise of preschools would at first
sight appear to constitute an anomaly in the whole of the Belgian social
picture. Belgium was, until recently, a homogeneously Catholic country
in which the Church exerted a strong influence on social and family policies – and the Church, of course, promoted the ideology of the
role of the mother as primary caretaker and was generally wary of state
intervention in the family. The Belgian state was a laggard in nearly everything having to do with education and child protection. Compulsory
education (at school or, exceptionally, at home) was first introduced
with a law of 1914, which did not come into force until 1919. Before that
time, most children had already been registered at school, but absen-
teeism was regarded as a big problem and most of those who attended
remained at school for no more than three or four years (Wynants and
Paret, 1998). According to an international survey conducted in 1905,
Belgium had one of the highest illiteracy rates in Western Europe (Penn
Hilden, 1993, pp. 316–317). The first law on child labour dates only
from 1889 and was the reaction to a crisis into which the regime had
been thrown by a violent strike movement in 1886; even so it prohibited child labour only under the age of 12, restricting it to 72 hours a
week for those under 16. The prohibition of child labour was extended
to those younger than 14 in 1914 (Chlepner, 1983, pp. 214–216). The
first general law on child protection dates from 1912, but this was in
fact a law protecting *society* against juvenile delinquents. It enabled the
newly founded juvenile courts to issue educational or restraining orders
regarding persons under 16 who had committed an act which would
have been criminal had they been 16 or over and thus closed the gap
in the legal system resulting from setting the age of penal responsibility at 16. It did not provide for the protection of youngsters who
had not themselves become delinquent, but were just the victims of
others' behaviour; for a general law organising that protection Belgium

had to wait until 1965. Nor is Belgium known for any pioneering work in the field of women's emancipation: nearly all the legislation in this field (anti-discrimination law, the introduction of gender neutrality in social security law, parental leave) was – often with considerable delay – introduced at the instigation of the European Union.

We have here a country in which, until recently, neither child protection nor women's emancipation enjoyed any priority on the social or political agenda; and yet it was a pioneer of preschool development. How is this to be explained?[2] To work towards an explanation, I will first tell the story of how preschools were established and developed in Belgium. This story will enable us to discard some explanatory hypotheses which obviously do not fit the Belgian facts and to develop other hypotheses which will then be tested by a comparison with France.

2   The story of preschools in Belgium

A small number of day-care centres for children under school age already existed in the southern part of the Low Countries before Belgian independence in 1830. Some of them were organised by municipal, others by Church authorities – a distinction which, however, for a long time remained without practical import, because most members of the board of directors and most workers of even the municipal care centres belonged to religious orders. In 1842, the first Belgian law on public education below university level introduced public subsidies for the municipal kindergartens, but no special rules were given as to which goals the kindergartens should pursue or how kindergartens should be organised or managed (Depaepe, De Vroede, Minten and Simon, 1998a, pp. 196–199). There is perhaps not much to wonder about here, for the basic idea underlying the care centres, as they were then, was that children ideally should stay with their mother. The care centres were only there as a lower-quality solution for the protection of those children whose mothers worked and could not take care of them.

Historians of pedagogy date the fundamental ideological break with this conception to the establishment of a froebelian kindergarten in Elsene in 1857, the first Belgian kindergarten with the ambition of stimulating the children's cognitive, social and emotional development rather than just 'keeping' them (Depaepe, 1990, pp. 17–19). It is in fact highly doubtful whether either the ideas of Fröbel – who from then on came to be cited continuously and ritually in the relevant Belgian literature – or the practice of the Elsene kindergarten had much of a conceptual influence on the changes occurring in the Belgian preschools during the following decades. The German philosopher and pedagogue Fröbel was a Romantic thinker, whose basic pedagogical idea was that children have to develop their manifold innate faculties so as to fully become part of the cosmic whole. The ideal way to accomplish this is through creative play. Fröbel devised a number of material objects, songs, techniques of play etc. to facilitate children's integration into cosmic totality, but leaving lots of space for children's own creativity was an essential element of his method (Fröbel, 1973/1826). These ideas could hardly have been further removed from the dominant ideologies of nineteenth-century Belgium: a materialist liberalism combined with the acceptance of Church doctrines in questions of family morals. By the standards of these ideologies, Fröbel's philosophical ideas were too hazy and his practical pedagogical precepts tended to undermine discipline; and his basic notion that all of us in a sense *are* the universe was unabashedly pantheistic and therefore blasphemous. All that stuck from Fröbel was that children below school age should be educated too, and it was this idea that spread in the Belgian preschools until it had become self-evident by the late nineteenth century. But the idea triumphed in a perverted way, for children were not supposed to be educated by giving free rein to their creative impulses, but by discipline and by imitating the example of their elders (Depaepe, 1990).

Despite this break in the underlying philosophy, preschools remained a more or less marginal phenomenon until the school struggle between the state and the Catholic Church exploded in 1879. Although this conflict was not directly over preschools, its outcomes were in my opinion decisive for Belgium's role as a preschool pioneer, and I therefore need to give some more background information regarding this conflict.

Belgium's liberal constitution of 1831 posited the separation of church and state (Articles 15 and 16), but also, in its Article 17, guaranteed the freedom of every Belgian to establish a school. The principle of the separation of church and state was, of course, inspired by the constitutions of the French Revolution, but had a different meaning in the peaceful context of nineteenth-century Belgium than in France, where it had been accompanied by massive expropriations of the Catholic Church by the state (Soboul, 1972). Whereas in France the separation principle meant that the state was henceforth independent of the Church and that state rules had priority over those of the Church, in Belgium it was also welcomed by the Church, because it was seen as a guarantee for state respect of Church autonomy and for a free space in which the Church could develop all kinds of activities at the intermediate level, especially as regards charity and education. The potential for Church activities was reinforced by Article 17 of the Constitution: although this legal principle allowed *anyone* to found schools, in practice it massively favoured the Church, which was the only organisation to have the infrastructure and the know-how to establish and manage schools on a grand scale. The position of the Church in the field of education was further strengthened by the first Belgian school law of 1842. This law obliged each municipality to establish a primary school *if no school had already been established by private initiative*. Primary schools were subsidised out of the public purse, regardless of whether they were private or run by the municipality; and the schools' curriculum was largely left to the discretion of their directors (Depaepe, De Vroede, Minten and Simon, 1998b). The result was that the state paid for the Catholic schools without having an influence on what they did.

In 1879, the liberal government under Prime Minister Frère-Orban decided to do away with all of this. Under the new law, every municipality had to have its own school, which could only employ teachers with a degree from a state higher school; the municipalities were forbidden to take over a private school as the new municipal school. Public schools had henceforth to be ideologically neutral and religion was no longer to be taught as a compulsory subject. Private schools were no longer subsidised (Depaepe, De Vroede, Minten and Simon, 1998b). The Belgian episcopate reacted by organising petitions and demonstrations and by excommunicating all the teachers working in municipal schools, as well as the students in state-organised teacher training. Parents were admonished to withdraw their children from public schools so as to 'save their souls'. New Catholic schools (and kindergartens) were established at an astonishing speed. The result was that the municipal schools in the deeply Catholic Flemish part of Belgium – many of them newly founded under the 1879 law – were left without teachers and pupils: the teachers had resigned out of fear of excommunication (and had found new jobs in the new Catholic schools), and the pupils had fled because their parents were told by the priests they should do so (Lory, 1985). The school struggle also led to a unification of Catholic political forces, which until then had been divided between liberal Catholics, who had tended to cooperate with the liberals, and the conservative 'Ultramontanians' who looked *ultra montes* (over the Alps, that is to the Pope) for their political instructions (Righart, 1986, pp. 132–188). Unified, the Catholics managed to win the 1884 national elections and were now in a position to turn back the educational reforms of the Frère-Orban government. In a first move, the municipalities were given full financial responsibility for schools *and* they were allowed to adopt private, that is, Catholic, schools as municipal schools. Since the municipalities, especially in rural areas, were mostly governed by Catholics and the municipalities had difficulties meeting their (partly new) financial responsibility, they tended to opt for adopting an existing school rather than the generally more expensive alternative of establishing a new school in addition to the existing Catholic school. From 1894 onwards, subsidies for private schools were gradually reintroduced (Depaepe, De Vroede, Minten and Simon, 1998b).

There are two points of relevance for the history of Belgian preschools in this story of the school struggle. First, the school struggle gave an enormous impetus to Catholics to found new schools and preschools; this in its turn stimulated liberal and later socialist municipal governments to establish preschools of their own, so as not to leave children entirely to the Church. Second, the school struggle brought together Catholics of quite different social and political views and thus integrated those who would otherwise have cooperated with liberals (or, somewhat later, socialists) within a unified Catholic movement, which remained cohesive in later years. After many more bends of the road had been taken to integrate the Catholic workers' movement, this led in the early twentieth century to the emergence of a Catholic political party, Catholic trade unions and employers' organisations, Catholic sickness insurance organisations, in short to the creation of a Catholic 'pillar' of society, which, from about 1920 onwards, tended to structure nearly the whole life of its individual members. This Catholic pillar found its counterpart in the socialist pillar, which emerged around the same time (Huyse, 1983; Righart, 1986). I will come back to the significance of this for our subject when considering possible explanations for Belgian early preschool development.

After the school struggle, the number of preschool establishments and the proportion of preschool attendance boomed. Registration in kindergartens went up to 60% of the relevant population in 1910 – a level which was then maintained during the interwar period. Preschool attendance had now become ideologically acceptable throughout all social strata. The prevailing idea from this time on was that babies and toddlers should remain with their mothers, but that from a certain age preschool attendance comes to supplement maternal love and is highly recommendable or even necessary as a transition between infancy and school. Preschool was perceived as *education* – hence as an activity preparatory for school – in an atmosphere still characterised by play and affection; the exclusively female preschool teachers were seen as quasi-maternal figures who were supposed to try to emulate a mother's relation to the children (Depaepe, 1990). That kindergartens were meant to be preschool institutions becomes clear when consulting *L'école gardienne*, the journal of the kindergarten teachers, which was published starting in 1899. This journal published theoretical articles on questions of pedagogy, but also focused on detailed curricula for the kindergarten: intellectual and physical exercises, songs, stories, poems etc. were planned for the year, the month, the week and even the day of the week. Nobody seems to have minded the fact that the rigidity of these precepts stood in marked opposition to the ideas of the theoreticians in the same issues. The practical part of the monthly was regularly translated into Flemish, the only language most of the preschool teachers in the north of the country could read; the theoretical articles were published only in French. From about the turn of the century, it seems to have become self-evident that sending children to a preschool was a good thing, because it prepared them for school (never mind that most then only went to school for a limited number of years and that many entered the world of labour from the age of 12). No social or political debate whatsoever is to be found on this issue. The only point which was – bitterly – debated was whether children should attend Catholic or municipal preschools. The Catholics accused the communal preschools in the larger towns – those in the smaller municipalities were under Catholic control anyway – of breeding atheism and undermining discipline, but in fact there seems to have existed a consensus among all those concerned – whether Catholic or anti-clerical – that one of the main goals of public child care for the under-sixes was to prepare the children for real life and to teach them the work and time discipline they would need to take their place in society (Depaepe, 1990).

After World War II, preschool registration went up steeply once again to reach 91% of the relevant population by 1961; from 1970, nearly the whole population was covered. Since then, preschools have increasingly admitted children aged two and a half and even two.

If we look at the whole pattern of development, it is striking that there are no real breaks or turns in this development since the late nineteenth century: preschool attendance was always high and – with the exception of a stagnation between the World Wars – went up continuously until it reached its full potential at a fairly early point in time; preschools have always been organised in competition between the Church and the communities; and despite (or because of?) this competition, all providers of public preschool education – with the exception of very few 'alternative' kindergartens, which really tried to work according to the ideas of, for example, Fröbel or Montessori – shared the same conception of what preschools are good for.

3   How to explain the early rise of preschools in Belgium

The preceding story enables us to rule out some hypotheses concerning the early flourishing and unstoppable rise of preschools in Belgium and to consider others.

The most banal hypothesis would be that the establishment of preschools was a reaction to the rise in mothers' participation in the labour force. This is surely a powerful hypothesis for those countries where preschools were essentially a phenomenon of the past few decades. For Belgium, this hypothesis is untenable. There is a massive discrepancy between the nearly continuous growth in preschool registration and the curve of women's labour market participation. A causal connection between the development of preschools and the need to reconcile paid work with family responsibilities may be found at the beginning of the period we have looked at and at its end, but not during the crucial period in which the Belgian preschool system developed and attendance became general. As we have seen, the first Belgian public child-care centres of the early nineteenth century were a response to industrialisation, to the fact that mothers working in industry, in contrast to peasant mothers, cannot mind their children while on the job. The (modest) growth in public child care for children too young to attend preschool has been a phenomenon of the last few decades and has likewise been explicitly motivated by the needs of working mothers and their children. But what about the long century in between? The first formidable growth spurt of the Belgian preschools partly coincided with the very favourable economic conditions which existed from the mid-1890s to the eve of World War I (Arrighi, 1994). But the expansion of preschools had already started before that, during the era known by economic historians as the Great Depression, and the growth in wealth during the *Belle Epoque* had double-edged implications for women's work force participation, for this was a time when it became possible for the better-off proletarian families to opt for the breadwinner–housewife model practised by the bourgeoisie (Seccombe, 1993). Although the accuracy of the data for this period is contested, a comparison between the results of the 1910 census and research done during the 1890s does suggest that women's labour market participation had already decreased somewhat by 1910 (Penn Hilden, 1993, pp. 180–181). Between 1910 and

1960, the female proportion of the work force went *down* from approximately 40% to 26%, whereas preschool registrations went *up* from 60% to 91%. Moreover, the decrease in the female work force was to a large extent caused by women's growing habit of leaving the labour force permanently after the birth of a first child (Degimbe and Simon, 1991). In other words: as fewer women and especially mothers participated in the labour market, more children went to preschools. Female labour market participation started to rise again from the early 1960s onwards (Bahle et al., 2002, p. 29), but at that time nearly all children *already* attended a preschool. The availability of places in preschools undoubtedly facilitated the later rise of mothers' employment, but was certainly not caused by working mothers' needs.

Neither is it plausible that ideological views of the family and of the relation between the state and the family could have played the decisive role in the early development of Belgian preschools. Until the advent of feminism in the late 1960s, the ideology of the mother as the child's natural caregiver remained practically uncontested in Belgium – this despite the high labour market participation of mothers in the period before World War I. The family was considered to be a sphere in which the state should refrain from interfering – as can be gathered from the fact already mentioned that the usual state interventions in family autonomy (compulsory schooling and child protection laws) came later in Belgium than in comparable countries. Belgian kindergartens were successful *despite* these ideologies, which at first sight should have predisposed Belgian parents to keep their children *out of* the preschools – and *because* the preschools, exclusively staffed by women perceived as motherly figures, projected an image of being something like substitute families. The ideology of republicanism has sometimes been made responsible for the early development of preschools in France (Letablier and Jönsson, 2003; Morgan, 2002–2003) – the underlying idea being that all those living in France should, from an early age, be educated as citizens of the republic, so as to keep them away from reactionary ideological influences, such as those of religion. But nothing could be further removed from the Belgian ideological atmosphere, which, starting with the 1830 revolution against the Dutch state, out of which Belgium as a political entity was born, has always been characterised by a distrust of the state and by the general idea that human relations work best without rules imposed from above.

One could of course try to explain the growth of the Belgian preschools by the Belgians' *pedagogical* ideology: people sent their children to preschools because they believed this to be a good way to prepare them for school and later life. There can be no doubt that this belief was widespread and, given that preschool attendance has always been voluntary and that the Belgians would have tended to resist compulsory rules anyway, that it explains the demand side of the Belgian development of preschools. Without the trust of parents – many of them housewives who could have cared for their children themselves – preschools could not have thrived as they did. But it remains something of a mystery why the belief in the beneficial effects of preschool attendance should have been so much stronger in Belgium than in other countries. In judging the explanatory weight of the Belgians' pedagogical ideology one should also keep in mind that the relation between supply and demand is considerably more complex for educational services than, say, for bread. The supply of education – or, for that matter, of all kinds of welfare services – is not just a response to demand; it generates demands which would not (or even could not) have arisen *but for* the supply. It is hard to imagine that parents would clamour for Latin courses if no Latin had ever been taught in Belgian schools; but, since it has traditionally been taught to those preparing for higher education, many Belgian parents even today still want their children to enrol in Latin courses at school. That is to say that the undeniable fact of widespread demand for preschool places in Belgium from the late nineteenth century onwards does not yet tell us much about the extent to which Belgian preschool development was *caused* by this demand. It is perfectly possible that the demand was itself no more than a reaction – though a reaction itself calling for an explanation – to the rise in the supply. And even if the demand had existed independently of the supply, it would in itself have been insufficient to explain the supply; for the supply was largely free, that is, the costs were not borne by the users, but by the providers, and the supply therefore cannot be explained by market forces.

A popular explanation for most of the peculiarities of Belgian society and politics is pillarisation, the freezing of social interests and conflicts within sets of intertwining organisations. A pillar is something which structures the life of those who belong to it from the cradle to the grave. For most of the twentieth century, it was true of most Belgians that they started life as the children of parents belonging to either the Catholic or the socialist pillar and then remained within this pillar until their death. This means that the child of Catholic parents would attend a Catholic kindergarten, a Catholic school and a Catholic university, would become a member of a Catholic youth organisation, a Catholic sports club, a Catholic trade union or professional organisation and the Catholic sickness insurance fund, would end up in a Catholic old people's home and be buried according to Catholic rites – and vice versa for a child born in a non-Catholic home, which would have had his or her life organised within the socialist pillar. Switching was not easy, living outside the pillars even more difficult. Any benefits which were in the power of the public authorities to bestow (first of all: jobs) were divided among the pillars according to unspoken but known quotas. This curious mode of organising social life also existed in other countries, such as the Netherlands and Austria (Righart, 1986; van Kersbergen, 1995), but apparently nowhere else did it exert the pervasive force it developed in Belgium. Since it is in the interest of pillars to supply encompassing services to their members, pillarisation was obviously propitious to the flourishing of preschools, and it is hence sometimes invoked as (part of) an explanation for the development of preschools. The problem with such an explanation is simply that the timing is wrong. The pillars did not find their fixed structure until the 1920s (Righart, 1986) and, as we have seen, by that time the critical phase in the formation of the Belgian preschool system was already over. What pillarisation accomplished was to further stabilise the system, to protect preschools from the financial pressure they might otherwise have come under during the economic crisis of the 1930s.

All of the foregoing hypotheses are unconvincing, at least as far as the *supply* of preschools is concerned. The only convincing hypothesis to explain *that* is that building and filling preschools proved to be an efficient way to carry on the fierce competition between organised Catholics and non-Catholics. In the beginning, this was a struggle between state and church; but, as we have seen, this struggle was decided soon in favour of the Church, which was able to repel the radical–liberal assault on its privileges and to a large extent have its educational initiatives subsidised by the state. Since the state partly paid for the Church's activities, it would be odd to look upon the two as competitors. The true competition was between the Church and the anti-clerical political parties and tendencies (first liberals, then socialists) running the communities (which established and ran the preschools). Preschool education was the very first point in the individuals' life-cycle at which both the Church and anti-clerical forces could directly intervene to attach those individuals to the movement. Since preschools apparently offered something which parents were glad to make use of, there was an incentive for both sides to enlarge the supply. Once this dynamic had started, it would have been held up only if some organised social actor had undertaken something to reverse it – that is, had been prepared to enter a struggle and to incur the costs necessary to fight this battle. There was no such actor.

At this point, it may be instructive to compare Belgium with France, the other country in which preschools began to develop very early. In comparative overviews of family policy models, the two countries are often grouped together (see e.g. Bahle in this book), and the similarity of their pioneering efforts in the matter of preschools might appear to confirm the good sense of proceeding in this way. In fact, the *only* thing they have in common as far as preschool developments are concerned is that in the 1870s–1880s an intensive struggle over schools took place between state and church (Grew and Harrigan, 1985, pp. 231–242) and that this struggle apparently gave a strong boost to preschool growth. Everything else which, in the literature on France, is invoked as a possible cause for the progressivism in the matter of preschool development is *not* to be found in the Belgian case. If we are to believe a certain literature, it was the *victory* of the French state over the Church which was decisive for the early development of preschools. This victory was made possible by the radical interpretation of the principle of the separation of church and state and was stabilised by the centralisation of decision-making competences in the school system, which enabled the state to keep the conservative forces dominating the local authorities in the countryside at bay, and by the fact that, contrary to what happened in other Catholic countries, no viable Christian-Democrat political party ever emerged in France (Letablier and Jönsson, 2003; Morgan, 2002–2003). The expansion of preschools was reinforced by pronatalist concerns, which obviously induced the state to provide services for families with children. In Belgium, the interpretation of the separation of church and state was – as explained above – much more moderate, the school struggle was won by the *Church*, the preschool system was pluralistic and decentralised, the Christian Democrats were in government for most of the twentieth century, and pronatalism was a negligible strand in family policy debates. In other words: all the features of the French development which enabled the state to triumph over conservative forces were *reversed* in Belgium, and nevertheless the growth of preschools was even much more pronounced in Belgium than in France, where in 1970 only about three-quarters of three- to six-year-olds attended preschool (Morgan, 2002–2003, p. 273), as opposed to nearly all in Belgium. This comparison very strongly suggests that the factors mentioned above which contributed to the French state's victory over the Church were *not* causal in bringing forth the rise of preschools. For the decisive cause, we should look at what France and Belgium had in common – and this was *only* the struggle over the public power to socialise young children. This competition was stronger in Belgium than in France, because the financial conditions under which the parties had to compete were less unequal in Belgium: whereas Catholic preschools were co-financed out of the public purse in Belgium, they could count on no such subsidies in France. From this perspective, the greater availability of preschool places in Belgium becomes perfectly comprehensible: if competition was the clue to the early development of preschools, then the fiercer the competition the more development of preschools one should expect.

4   Conclusion

Belgium's pioneering role in the development of preschools has been a kind of accident of history. Nothing seemed to predispose the country for such a role. The development of preschools had very little to do with either the reconciliation of paid work and work in the home or with any ideology of public responsibility for the education of young children. It was an offshoot of the struggle between the Catholic Church and anti-clerical forces and appears at odds with the conservative familialism which has permeated social and family policy during most of Belgium's history. The development of preschools in Belgium is also a prime example of the path-dependency of the life of institutions. At the end of the nineteenth century, preschools could hardly have claimed to be functionally necessary for production relations, for social cohesion or for any other social goal. But, once the preschool system was put in place and had been favourably received within broad layers of the population, it just went on expanding until it covered the whole of the population. The more it became settled, the more effort would have been required to turn it from its course; but since the relevant social actors had an interest in its perpetuation, there was nobody to make such an effort.

Notes

1. Sometimes much higher figures can be found. If *nonsubsidised* childminders are added to the count, the proportion of available places for 2002 is around 30% of the relevant population (Van Dongen, 2004). But I do not see how such a mode of calculation could be justified: nonsubsidised childminders are *private* solutions – just as au-pair girls or grandparents.
2. In this article, I will concern myself *only* with the explanation of developments for the 3–5-year olds, for the simple reason that it is only in this respect that Belgium distinguishes itself from the European mainstream.

Bibliography

G. Arrighi, *The Long Twentieth Century* (London: Verso, 1994)

T. Bahle, B. Fix, P. Flora, F. Kraus, F. Rothenbacher and H. Willekens, *Family Change and Family Policies: Belgium* (Mannheim: MZES, 2002)

B. Chlepner, *Cent ans d'histoire sociale en Belgique* (Brussels: Editions de l'Université de Bruxelles, 1983)

N. Degimbe and A. Simon, 'Travail féminin: taux d'activité et temps partiel', *Revue du travail* (1991) 12–20

M. Depaepe, 'De eeuw van het kind in historisch-pedagogisch perspectief', in H. Cammaer and E. Verhellen (eds), *Onmondig en onvolwassen* (Leuven: Acco, 1990), 16–29

M. Depaepe, M. De Vroede, L. Minten and F. Simon, 'L'enseignement maternel', in D. Grootaers (ed.), *Histoire de l'enseignement en Belgique* (Brussels: Crisp, 1998a), 190–217

M. Depaepe, M. De Vroede, L. Minten and F. Simon, 'L'enseignement primaire', in D. Grootaers (ed.), *Histoire de l'enseignement en Belgique* (Brussels: Crisp, 1998b), 111–189

F. Fröbel, *Die Menschenerziehung* (Bochum: Kamp, 1973, originally 1826)

R. Grew and P. Harrigan, 'The catholic contribution to universal schooling in France, 1850–1906', *Journal of Modern History*, 57 (1985) 211–247

L. Huyse, 'Breuklijnen in de Belgische samenleving', in L. Huyse and J. Berting (eds), *Als in een spiegel? Een sociologische kaart van België en Nederland* (Leuven: Kritak, 1983), 9–25

M. Letablier and I. Jönsson, 'Kinderbetreuung und politische Handlungslogik', in U. Gerhard, T. Knijn and A. Weckwert (eds), *Erwerbstätige Mütter – ein europäischer Vergleich* (Munich: Beck, 2003), 85–109

J. Lory, 'La résistance des catholiques belges à la « loi de malheur », 1879–1884', *Revue du Nord*, 67 (1985) 729–747

T. Luykx, *Politieke geschiedenis van België* (Amsterdam: Elsevier, 1969)

K. Morgan, 'The politics of mothers' employment. France in comparative perspective', *World Politics*, 55 (2002–2003) 259–289

P. Penn Hilden, *Women, Work and Politics. Belgium 1830–1914* (Oxford: Clarendon, 1993)

H. Righart, *De katholieke zuil in Europa* (Meppel: Boom, 1986)

W. Seccombe, *Weathering the Storm. Working-Class Families from the Industrial Revolution to the Fertility Decline* (London: Verso, 1993)

A. Soboul, *Précis d'histoire de la Révolution française* (Paris: Editions sociales, 1972)

W. Van Dongen, *Kinderopvang als basisvoorziening in een demokratische samenleving* (Brussels: CBGS, 2004)

K. Van Kersbergen, *Social Capitalism. A Study of Christian Democracy and the Welfare State* (London: Routledge, 1995)

P. Wynants and M. Paret, 'École et clivages au XIXe et XXe siècles', in D. Grootaers (ed.), *Histoire de l'enseignement en Belgique* (Brussels: Crisp, 1998), 13–84

3
Public Child Care and Preschools in France: New Policy Paradigm and Path-dependency

Claude Martin and Blanche Le Bihan

In France, childhood was considered quite early to be a 'common good' and a source of human capital, mainly because of the demographic challenge that the country was facing at the beginning of the twentieth century. At that time, children were the expected results of a probirth family policy. Then new social problems emerged, new public debates took place and new political measures were implemented throughout the century. Indeed, family policy is not restricted to child care. It also includes many other issues: civil law, women's rights, social and gender equity, support for disadvantaged households, same-sex couples, etc. Depending on the priorities, different periods can be identified (Commaille and Martin, 1998). But if we consider public child-care policies specifically, what about these changes? How can they be defined? Do they correspond to what Peter Hall calls 'third-order change', marked by radical changes and associated with 'paradigm shift'? Or to 'normal policymaking', that is, a process that adjusts policy without challenging the main objectives of a given policy paradigm, which defines first- and second-order change (Hall, 1993)? In this perspective, can these changes be defined as a 'path dependency process' (Pierson, 2004)?

In this chapter, we argue that incrementalism is a major component of the evolution in this public policy sector since World War II, but also that, during the 1990s, the move towards reconciling work and family responsibilities and the introduction of an objective of 'free choice' for parents in a context of severe unemployment can be analysed as a shift in public child-care policy. Indeed, at that period, not only did the policy setting change, but the hierarchy of goals and use of instruments also shifted radically. Organised interests, political parties and policy experts were all involved in this change. Yet, if we consider a specific aspect of child-care policy in France – preschool – continuity is a main dimension of the evolution since the end of the nineteenth century. Indeed, the roots of an institution do not disappear, and the choices made at the beginning of the twentieth century still have an impact on today's policy. In fact, at each different period, new objectives have been added on top of the old ones.

The question of change in this public policy domain is thus complex. Public child care offers a very interesting angle to understand it, as it seems to be at the root of the French welfare system and, after a long period of adjustments and marginal adaptations, has again become a public challenge. But we have to keep in mind the gap between the role of preschool and the development of new instruments and even new arguments, not to mention new paradigms for organising and implementing these instruments.

1   Public child care as an element of a larger domain: family policy

In France, child-care policies have traditionally been integrated within a larger public policy domain: family policy. So it is sometimes difficult to isolate public child-care policies from this larger explicit domain of public intervention. Looking back helps to understand the crucial problem of defining these domains. Public child-care policies are part of family policy, but not all of it, as family policies also include civil law concerning the family as an institution (marriage, divorce, parental authority, etc.), family allowances, housing benefits, means-tested benefits for poor households and child-care allowances and services. At the same time, preschool, which is undoubtedly a crucial part of the French public child-care system, is often considered part of another sector of public intervention: education. When considering public child-care policies, we have to keep this jigsaw puzzle in mind.

French family policy is indeed generally considered one of the most explicit and intensive in Europe. It has even been said that family issues could be the basis of the French social security system, just as poverty was a cornerstone of the Anglo-Saxon welfare state, and workers' status that of Germany's *Sozialstaat* (Merrien, 1990). This is why family benefits were first regarded as an extension of the 'family wage' and, in a way, as one of the main pillars of the French social welfare system (Friot, 1998).

But family became a state concern (*une affaire d'Etat*) mainly because of a demographic challenge. The legitimacy of the state to intervene in private life is directly connected to this issue: renewal of the generations. Low fertility during the nineteenth century and the trauma of World War I explain the strong pronatalism in France. Thus children early on came to be regarded as a 'public good', justifying public intervention in order to guarantee economic and social development. Promoting fertility and guaranteeing proper socialisation of children as future citizens have been explicit public issues in France for more than a century.

In the early twentieth century, all the conditions were in place to promote fertility *and* family as public concerns: the demographic deficit; a strong public debate combining different traditions of thinking (familism, probirth hygienism, libertarian antistatism); social movements to promote the family institution and fertility;[1] some experiments such as the family premium in 'patriarchal industries' and for civil servants at the end of the nineteenth century; the institution of mutual aid funds (*les caisses de compensation*); and the development of preschools since the end of the nineteenth century.

These different elements explain the *décrets-lois* of 1938 and 1939 which institutionalised French family policy as a probirth policy. Even the Vichy government (1940–1944) did not fundamentally affect this basic 'natalism', despite the strengthening of a familist ideology, that is, the development of a political rhetoric, of conservative normative statements concerning family institution, mothers' role, rights and obligations, etc. The French Social Security Act in 1946 finalised this process of institutionalisation by creating a 'family branch' of our Bismarckian welfare system. Since then, child-care issues have been blended in with family policy, which became an explicit and independent sector of public policies and an element of the French public administration.

Family policy goals changed significantly between the end of the Third Republic (*Code de la famille* in 1939) and the 1990s, turning away from this probirth perspective and towards a distributive (universal and horizontal) and then redistributive (selective and vertical) perspective. Looking back, it is therefore tempting to consider different phases in this story, with important turning points and policy shifts concerning family policy as a whole:

- 1945–1965: The 'Golden Age' of French family policy, with strong incentives to promote fertility and compensate for the cost of raising children. This period was characterised by a universal and intense family policy, which in the mid-1950s represented more than half of social security expenditures, and the strong development of preschools.

- 1965–1985: During this phase, new issues appeared on the family policy agenda. First, between 1965 and 1975, 'women's rights' claims led to fundamental reforms in civil law concerning marriage (the reform of the marital property regime in 1965 and 1985), parental rights and obligations (1970), parent–child relations (1972), divorce (1975), sexuality (1975, abortion). Second, between 1975 and 1985, the equity issue gained attention with the 'rediscovery of poverty in a rich country', as Lionel Stoléru (1977) describes; means-testing of family allowances was developed in order to support disadvantaged households. During this phase, marked by important policy shifts in family policy overall, childhood, fertility and child care did not disappear as public concerns, but became relatively secondary in the family policy debate. Yet these new political goals had an impact on the political measures introduced later in this public sector.
- Many experts have argued that a real turning point in public child-care policy came in the mid-1980s and early 1990s (Fagnani, 1997; Fagnani and Grignon, 1997; Martin, 2000; Martin et al., 1998). As unemployment still represents the main political issue in France, despite many different attempts to reduce it, the different governments (right-wing or left-wing) have used child-care policies as an indirect way to manage this problem.

During the 1990s, European institutions probably also played an important role by promoting the reconciliation of work and family life in the different member states. Initially centred on gender equality issues (equal pay and equal opportunity since the Rome Treaty, 1957), the different EU recommendations during the 1990s[2] turned towards reconciliation or work/life balance in order to promote female employment (Lewis, 2006).[3] Other signs of this political rationale include integrating the issue of reconciling work and family life in the EU's evolving employment strategy since 1998, for example with the adoption at the Lisbon Council of the objective to reach 60% female employment. This does not necessarily mean that the French turning point could be the result of these EU recommendations, but we argue that this policy shift has a larger frame of reference at the European level.

Can this evolution be understood as the result of a new paradigm? Changes indeed took place in the 1990s at the European and national level: tackling unemployment, facilitating a balance between work and family responsibilities and introducing 'free choice' are now the main components of child-care policy measures.

2 A new policy paradigm in the field of child care? Promoting employment and 'free choice'

Apart from preschools, since the 1970s, public child-care policy has evolved around three main instruments: first, collective child-care institutions (crèches), with the idea that these could prepare children for preschool and then for school; second, specific benefits to help parents find and pay for professional child care, with some guarantee of quality; and third, parental leave.

In the 1970s and early 1980s, the logic was mainly that of professionalisation and quality and the policy was based on the first two instruments presented above. Indeed, the family fund (*branche famille*) of the social security system and public authorities made real efforts on behalf of an active child-care policy, in particular care for children under three (Norvez, 1990).[4] Together with the extension of women's full-time employment, a series of measures were introduced in the 1970s in order to promote the creation of different types of collective day care (collective crèches, familial crèches, mini-crèches, *haltes-garderies*). In 1977, public authorities also implemented an official professional status for child-care providers and created the first unpaid parental leave (*congé parental*).[5]

The development of public child care became a priority during the first term of President Mitterrand (1981–1988). As a candidate in 1981,[6] Mitterrand had promised to increase the number of places in collective crèches or day care. The office of state secretary for the family was created in 1981, and the first office-holder rapidly convened a group of experts to provide proposals for a policy on early childhood. The Bouyala-Roussille report *L'enfant dans la vie*, published in 1982, proposed developing contracts (*contrats crèches*) between municipalities and *Caisses d'allocations familiales* to increase the number of places in collective child care for children under three (collective, familial and parental crèches). At the same time, the new laws concerning decentralisation gave municipalities overall responsibility for administering child care and many of them set up an early childhood office (*service petite enfance*).[7] But this incentive provided by the contracts between CAF and municipalities was not sufficient. The goals were never reached: despite an initial objective of 100,000 new places, by 1988 only 20,000 had been created.

During this period, the second child-care policy instrument was also developed: a benefit for the payment of childminders (*prestation spéciale assistante maternelle*, PSAM). The objective was to cover part of the cost of employing a registered child-care provider and therefore to encourage the development of individual care for children.

To some extent, the following years (1985–1995) could be considered a continuation of past trends (increase in and diversification of the supply of child care). But the progressive reforms implemented during this period and the attention given to the third instrument identified above, parental leave, could be better interpreted as a policy shift. Child-care policy measures indeed became a tool to promote women's labour market participation (Fagnani, 1995; Martin et al., 1998) in two ways: first, reducing female unemployment by creating a flat-rate parental leave; second, by promoting female employment in child care and household services and helping to balance work and family obligations for working mothers. Both instruments were adopted to provide 'free parental choice'. Different means were used to achieve these employment effects.

In 1985, a new parental leave benefit was created (*Allocation parentale d'éducation*, APE) to help reconcile work and family life of parents (in fact mothers) with young children. APE was a flat-rate, non-means-tested benefit for economically active parents with at least three children, the youngest of whom had to be under three. The benefit could be received up to the third birthday of the youngest child. In fact, 95% of recipients were mothers (mainly young mothers) in low-paid jobs or unemployed.[8] These characteristics might have explained their difficulties in re-entering the workforce after the leave ended.

A bigger step in the same direction was made in 1994, with the extension of the APE to families with two children. Only a parent who could demonstrate a minimum of two years of labour-market activity during the past five or ten years (depending on the number of children) was eligible for APE. This reform had an important impact on the employment rate of mothers of two children, which fell from 70% to 55% (Algava and Bressé, 2005; Piketty, 2005). In other words, between 1994 and 1997, around 150,000 mothers of two children (at least one of them under age three) left the labour market, mainly the less qualified (Piketty, 2005). The unemployment rate of these mothers also dropped dramatically from 11% to 5%. As a result, between 1994 and 2001, public expenditure on this benefit increased by 213%.

In practice, APE was a long, low-paid parental leave benefit taken up mainly by people on low incomes, most often unemployed or with precarious and unsatisfying jobs. In fact, women made a trade-off between this allowance and a low wage or unemployment benefit (Afsa, 1996; Algava and Bressé, 2005; Fagnani, 1995, 1996; Piketty, 2005). Re-entering the labour market remained a problem because a break of several years generally hindered recipients from reintegrating and might aggravate the unemployment trap. Even if some of them did find jobs, their working conditions were precarious (more short part-time jobs and short-term contracts). The gendered impact of APE was thus real since most recipients were female. It reinforced assigned gender roles within households and in the labour market (Fagnani, 1996).

Child-care policy changed dramatically also in terms of services offered. First, overall expenditure shifted from crèches to cash benefits. The number of places in crèches has indeed shrunk dramatically since the mid-1990s. Whereas mean growth between 1985 and 1996 was 5,000 additional places per year, between 1996 and 1999 this slowed to 1,500 new places per year. In the period 1999–2005, only 3,173 new places were created, which means an average of 530 new places per year or an annual mean growth of 0.38%. Between 2000 and 2004, the number of places in crèches shrank by 1,600 (Bailleau, 2007; Périvier, 2003).

By contrast, financial support to families using individual child care increased, first through the allowance for child care in the home (*allocation de garde d'enfant à domicile*, AGED), created in 1987 for parents hiring a domestic employee (without any criteria of qualification) to care for their children under age three. The incentive was a tax credit covering a large part of the cost. The maximum tax credit for an employee in the home was raised in 1994 from 13,000 francs (€1,900) to 45,000 francs (€6,700). The same year, AGED was extended to families with a child between three and six. Since both advantages could be cumulated, the total subsidy could cover 70% of the cost of a full-time employee. Consequently, the number of AGED recipients more than doubled between 1994 and 1996, from 25,000 to 54,000 (Fagnani and Rassat, 1997).

Second, the status of childminders (*assistante maternelle*) was improved and a new allowance was introduced in 1991 (*aide pour l'emploi d'une assistante maternelle agréée*, AFEAMA), to replace the previous PSAM and provide additional financial support to families employing a registered childminder (Martin et al., 1998). This new benefit covered about 40 % of the total cost of childminders and was a disincentive to hiring unregistered child-care providers, who before the reform were nearly as numerous as registered ones. Moreover, registration procedures were simplified in order to boost the number of registered childminders. Both measures were part of the effort to increase the number of jobs created at local community level, for example, domestic work, childminding, caring for elderly people, etc. Between 1994 and 2001, public expenditure on AGED increased by 54% and on AFEAMA by 177% (Leprince and Martin, 2003).

In January 2004, these different allowances (AGED, AFEAMA and APE) were replaced by the *prestation d'accueil du jeune enfant* (PAJE), which improves on the earlier allowances. PAJE is composed of different elements: a universal basic allowance up to the child's third birthday, conceived as a financial supplement for child care (*complement du mode de garde*, CMG) for the parents of children under six who want to work, and a supplemental allowance aimed at enabling 'freedom of choice' (*complement de libre choix d'activité*, CLCA) for parents who want to reduce their working hours or stop working entirely to take care of their children up to their third birthday. CLCA may be paid after the first birth for six months following the maternity leave. For a second or additional child, it can be paid up to the third birthday of the youngest. This allowance allows people to stop working or to work part-time with a partial allowance. In July 2006, a new allowance was added, with the same objective but for families with at least three children (*complément optionnel de libre choix d'activité*, COLCA). It is €230 more than CLCA and is paid for only one year, based on the parents' income, the age of the child and the type of child care. In 2006, CLCA and COLCA covered a total of 572,000 recipients.

This 2004 reform, which replaced all the former child-care allowances with a single benefit (PAJE), did not fundamentally change the economic rationale, except in terms of vocabulary (with its 'free choice' rhetoric). But, compared with the previous period, regulation is radically different: the main rationale, which is economic in nature, has marginalised other goals, like quality of services, child development, equity, etc. In an employment policy perspective, collective child care is too expensive in comparison with individual child-care arrangements, notably because of its higher requirements in terms of quality of services (infrastructure, cost and qualification of employees, guaranteed wages, stability of the employment contract, etc.). By strongly promoting individual child care in the home (of the child's parents or of the child-care provider), they have undermined previous efforts to develop collective child care, at least in certain areas.

While the supply of formal child care has undoubtedly increased and become more diverse, giving women more choices, the greater diversification of facilities is in practice more and more socially strati-fied. Indeed, the diversity of child care and the 'free choice' system do not concern all families. Measures taken since the 1990s are mainly related to formal individual child care (employee at home, registered child-care providers) and thus cannot be used by low-income fam-ilies who still largely resort to either informal child-care arrangements or highly subsidised collective child care (Ruault and Daniel, 2004). Moreover, low-income parents also receive more encouragement than in the past to care for their children themselves (see Bressé and Galtier, 2006).

3 Preschools: a path-dependent process

The picture would be incomplete without mentioning the crucial role of preschool in France. Turning to this last instrument alters our diagnosis or, more precisely, completes it. When it is taken into account, child-care policy in France also seems very typical of a path-dependency process.

The history of preschools in France is probably one of the longest in Europe (with Belgium) (Norvez, 1990). Since 1887, a decree (*décret* of 18 January 1887) prepared by Pauline Kergomard has defined the objec-tives of these institutions created for children more than two years old: 'Preschools are institutions of primary education, where the children of both sexes receive in common the care necessary for their physical, moral and intellectual development.' The main objective was initially a social one, and preschool was regarded both as a shelter and as a place where children could acquire elements of education which could be missing because of the absence of the working mother.

This institution developed rapidly between 1875 and 1900 (for more details, see Norvez, 1990). In 1901, 754,000 children were already being taken care of in 6,000 private and public institutions. The closing of the private and religious institutions in 1903 (60% of total preschools at the time) put an end to this development and led to a deep crisis. In 1938–1939, the number of children in preschools was less than 400,000 (16% of all children under six) and only 290,000 at the end of World War II in 1945.

Starting in 1946, a period of institutionalisation of family policy brought a new increase in the number of children enrolled in preschools: between 1945 and 1951, it more than doubled and reached 800,000 in 1959, or 40% of children between age two and five, and already 90% of five-year-olds. This growth continued during the 1960s and 1970s: in 1976–1977, the number of children in preschools reached 1.9 million, almost all in public institutions. At that time, all the four- and five-year-olds had a place in a preschool. At the beginning of the 1980s, 90% of three-year-olds and already 30% of children aged 30 months attended preschool. The decrease in fertility slowed this evolution, but preschool was completely established as a public, almost free of charge, answer to parents' needs. The relative reduction in the number of pupils offered an opportunity to improve the quality of the service. Indeed, the average number of pupils by class fell noticeably from 32 in 1978 to 29 in 1985. At the end of the 1980s, 2.5 million children were attending preschool.

The history of this public policy is strewn with different controversies. At the very beginning, a lot of actors involved in the policy process insisted on the need to make a distinction between preschool and school. The main objective of preschool was to prepare children for school, for learning, in other words, to 'teach them to learn' and to 'teach them to be', through play, manual and physical activities, but also to give them some initial elements of moral education and hygiene. Preschool was also considered a way to socialise parents (mainly the more disadvantaged, of course), in particular in terms of health prevention and morality. In this perspective, it was more a place of 'education' (in the broadest sense of the term) than a school, which is more specifically devoted to learning, training, knowledge acquisition and performance.

With the progress of developmental psychology, the role of preschool has gradually evolved: it has come to be considered a way to develop the child's personality and self. In the 1980s, it therefore seemed the best way to improve school performance and reduce inequalities. Despite the results of many evaluations during the 1970s concerning the capacity of preschool to reduce inequalities in schools, this belief is still very strong among professionals and teachers. But some critics suggest that preschool reinforces the influence of parental socialisation and is better adapted to selecting the best pupils.

Once these different conceptions of preschool had developed, the public debate was relatively stable throughout the twentieth century. Perceived as a tool for forming French citizens, preschool has a strong legitimacy in public opinion. The main question today concerns the relevant age to begin preschool, and the most important criticism concerns two-year-olds: many psychologists, linguists and paediatricians consider age two definitely too early for a child to attend such a collective institution. In 2002, 35.5% of children under three were enrolled in preschool, with huge regional variations (from 5% in the *département* of

Haute Savoie to 75% in the *département* of the Morbihan in Brittany). Preschool access for under-threes was first justified on social grounds and aimed at socialising children from underprivileged households. But, in practice, it serves mainly the more affluent social groups. In fact, preschool is used by dual-career couples as child care to help reconcile work and family responsibilities.

An official report by the *Haut Conseil de l'Education* on primary school published in 2007 criticises preschools for not achieving the aim of preparing children for primary school in terms of language acquisition. In this way, according to the report, preschool could be considered partly responsible for the failure of some children in primary school.

In summary, preschool has long been recognised in France as an element of public child-care policy. Even the arguments concerning the appropriate age to start preschool and those related to preschool's capacity to prepare children for school or to reduce social inequalities have been developed since the beginning of the twentieth century. The different reforms of this instrument therefore appear more as marginal adaptations than real changes, at least so far. A turning point in this policy field seems very unlikely and path-dependency is the more appropriate way to understand the evolution of preschool since the beginning of the twentieth century.

4 Conclusion

Public policy on child care in France has been going through a complex process of change, combining path-dependent evolution and a major turning point in the 1990s. Indeed, on the one hand, preschool appears to be a long-standing policy which is very popular among French citizens. Despite the many criticisms and controversies, the analysis shows that no fundamental reforms have been implemented for a long time. On the other hand, child-care policies relying on cash benefits, direct services to households and parental leave benefits demonstrate that a clear turning point was taken during the 1990s. This evolution, amounting to a paradigm shift, largely corresponds to the situation in many European countries.

In the French case, the intensity of this change depends on the priority given to employment policy by the successive governments during the last decade. Indeed, the question of employment became a main reference and reforming child care policies a way to manage the labour market: either by pushing some low-skilled and/or unemployed mothers out of the labour market to care for their own children; by facilitating the work–family balance for educated mothers with higher-paying jobs; or finally by creating jobs in the field of child care for many other women looking for professional employment. This employment objective and the solutions adopted put aside the questions of quality of care, well-being of children and gender equity. These issues are secondary compared to the question of access to work, promotion of work, creation of jobs, etc.

Comparing the French U-turn on child-care policies with the EU situation, common arguments can be identified. One of these is the language of 'social investment' affecting all the EU member states, with some national specificities. Indeed, some European experts emphasise the need for a 'social investment strategy centred upon childhood' (Esping-Andersen, 2002). To face the challenge of social inequalities, Esping-Andersen advocates a prevention strategy (investment in the child), rather than a curative strategy (passive adult-oriented social policies): 'Since the possibilities of employment and a professional career depend to an ever greater extent on the individual's acquisition of learning skills, this must be taken as the starting point. The mobilisation and adaptation of the adult is realistic and profitable provided he or she is already in possession of a minimum of learning capacity... Policies that aim at guaranteeing a second chance are far more costly and far less efficient than those that aim at improving the well-being of the very young.' (Esping-Andersen, 2002, pp. 49 and 55). In this social investment strategy, women and children are considered on the basis of their maximum productivity potential. Consequently, top-quality public child-care services should be developed and the employment of mothers should be promoted in order to ensure better economic and social living conditions for their children and to avoid poverty.

This 'social investment strategy' is directly connected with 'activating social policies' which are aimed at integrating the entire population into the labour market. These strategies represent new priorities and measures for restructuring welfare regimes. Nevertheless, this economic rationality and the new paradigm it constitutes have limits. First, it does not mean that the main objective may be full individual citizenship (Lewis, 2006). As Olk suggests: 'The central goal is not the strengthening of the power position of women vis-à-vis men, but women are important because of their economic potentiality, which can be activated by an intensified participation in the labour market. And with regard to children, it is not the creation of a "good childhood" in the here and now, but rather mobilizing children as productive workers of the future. It is not the citizenship rights of women and children which are at the centre but the role of women and children as invest-ment goods in a social investment regime... The child is not "being a citizen", but rather a "citizen-in-becoming". And the citizen status is reduced to the economic dimension of the productive citizen-worker-of-the-future, and weakens the political and social dimension of full citizenship.' (Olk, 2006).

Second, the development of this new welfare architecture (inform-ing social policy and social investment strategy), with the objective of enhancing both parents' participation in the labour market, may result in forcing these workers to accept any employment, even if it leads to worse living conditions and to less time spent with their children. The development of atypical working hours and the resulting difficulty of finding care for children early in the morning, late in the evening, on the weekend or even at night is in that sense a major concern for the European objective of balancing work/life obligations.[9]

Notes

1. The state recognised various family associations (Catholic and secular, right- and left-wing) as social partners with the Loi Gounot in 1942.
2. Maastricht Treaty (1992); recommendation of the EU Council on child care (1992), Council directives on parental leave (1996) and part-time work (1997).
3. For the impact of the EU on the UK situation, see Lewis (2007a, 2007b).
4. For decades, the care issue has been radically different for three- to six-year-olds: already in the 1970s they were largely cared for in public preschools that cost almost nothing (*écoles maternelles*), as we will discuss later. For a discussion of this period, see Martin, Math and Renaudat (1998).
5. An unpaid parental leave with legal guarantees, which is part of the labour legislation (*code du travail*).
6. See F. Mitterrand, 'Les 110 propositions pour la France' and Jenson and Sineau (1995).
7. It is important to note that, in contrast to the *écoles maternelles*, there is no legal obligation for a commune or any other body to create child-care facilities.
8. Only 4% of leave days were taken by fathers.
9. The development of atypical working hours is one challenge parents are currently facing (see Le Bihan and Martin, 2005).

Bibliography

C. Afsa, 'L'activité féminine à l'épreuve de l'allocation parentale d'éducation', *Recherches et Prévisions*, 46 (1996) 1–8

E. Algava and S. Bressé, 'Les bénéficiaires de l'allocation parentale d'éducation: trajectoires d'activité et retour à l'emploi', *Etudes et résultats DREES*, 399 (2005)

G. Bailleau, 'L'accueil collectif et en crèche familiale des enfants de moins de 6 ans en 2005', *Etudes et résultats DREES*, 548 (2007)

N. Blanpin, 'Accueil des jeunes enfants et coûts des modes de garde en 2002', *Etudes et résultats DREES*, 422 (2005)

P. Bloche and V. Pécresse, *L'enfant d'abord. 100 propositions pour placer l'intérêt de l'enfant au cœur du droit de la famille.* Rapport parlementaire no. 2832. Assemblée nationale (Paris: Assemblée Nationale, 2006).

N. Bouyala and B. Roussille, *L'enfant dans la vie – Une politique pour la petite enfance,* rapport au secrétaire d'Etat à la Famille (Paris: La Documentation Française, 1982)

S. Bressé and B. Galtier (2006), 'La conciliation entrer vie familiale et vie professionnelle selon le niveau de vie des familles', *Etudes et résultat DREES,* 465 (2006)

J. Commaille and C. Martin, *Les enjeux politiques de la famille* (Paris: Bayard, 1998)

G. Esping-Andersen, 'A child-centred social investment strategy', in G. Esping-Andersen, D. Gallie, A. Hemerijck and J. Myles, *Why We Need a New Welfare State* (Oxford: Oxford University Press, 2002), 26–67

J. Fagnani, 'L'allocation parentale d'éducation: effets pervers et ambiguïtés d'une prestation', *Droit social,* 3 (1995) 287–295

J. Fagnani, 'Retravailler après une longue interruption le cas des mères ayant bénéficié de l'allocation parentale d'éducation', *Revue Française des Affaires Sociales,* 3 (1996) 129–152

J. Fagnani, 'Recent changes in family policy in France: Political trade-offs and economic constraints', in E. Drew, R. Emerek and R. Mahon (eds), *Women, Work and the Family in Europe* (London: Routledge, 1997), 58–65

J. Fagnani and M. Grignon, 'La politique familiale en France depuis les années quatre-vingt : des préoccupations natalistes aux politiques de l'emploi', in F. Ronsin, H. Le Bras and E. Zucker-Rouvillois (eds), *Démographie et Politique* (Dijon: Editions Universitaires de Dijon, 1997), 115–125

J. Fagnani and E. Rassat, 'Les bénéficiaires de l'AGED: où résident-ils ? Quels sont leurs revenus ?', *Recherches et Prévisions,* 47 (1997) 79–87

B. Friot *Puissances du salariat. Emploi et protection sociale à la française* (Paris: La dispute, 1998)

Haut Conseil de l'Education, *L'école primaire. Bilan des résultats de l'école* (Paris: La Documentation Française, 2007)

P. A. Hall, 'Policy paradigms, social learning, and the State. The case of economic policymaking in Britain', *Comparative Politics,* 25 (1993) 275–296

J. Jenson and M. Sineau, *Mitterrand et les françaises. Un rendez-vous manqué* (Paris: Presses de la fondation des sciences politiques, 1995)

B. Le Bihan and C. Martin, 'Atypical working hours: Consequences for childcare arrangements', *Social Policy and Administration,* 38 (2004) 565–590

F. Leprince and C. Martin, *L'accueil des jeunes enfants en France: état des lieux et pistes d'amélioration.* Rapport pour le Haut conseil de la population et de la famille (Paris: La Documentation Française, 2003)

J. Lewis, 'Work/family reconciliation, equal opportunities, and social policies: the interpretation of policy trajectories at the EU level and the meaning of gender equality', *Journal of European Public Policy,* 13 (2006) 420–437

J. Lewis and M. Campbell, 'UK work/family balance and gender equality, 1997–2005', *Social Politics,* 14 (2007a) 4–30

J. Lewis and M. Campbell, 'Work/family balance policies in the UK since 1997: A new departure?', *Journal of Social Policy,* 36 (2007b) 365–381

C. Martin, 'Familienpolitische Reformen in Frankreich zwischen den Jahren 1981 und 1997: Kontinuität oder Pfadwechsel?' (Family Policy reforms in France between 1981 and 1997: Actors and turning points?), *Zeitschrift für Familienforschung,* 3 (2000) 5–20

C. Martin, *La parentalité en question. Perspectives sociologiques.* Rapport pour le Haut Conseil de la Population et de la famille (Paris: La Documentation Française, 2003). Retrieved 13 October 2008 at http://www.ladocumentation-francaise.fr/rapports-publics/034000552/index.shtml

C. Martin, A. Math and E. Renaudat, 'Caring for very young children and dependent elderly people: Towards a commodification of care', in J. Lewis (ed.), *Gender, Social Care and Welfare State Restructuring in Europe* (Aldershot: Ashgate publishers, 1998), 139–174

F.-X. Merrien, 'Etats-providence: l'empreinte des origines', *Revue française des affaires sociales,* 3 (1990) 43–56

A. Norvez, *De la naissance à l'école. Santé, modes de garde et préscolarité dans la France contemporaine,* Cahier no.126 (Paris: PUF-INED, 1990)

T. Olk, 'Children in the "social investment strategy"'. Paper presented in the Wellchi network Conference. European Commission, University of Hamburg (Hamburg, 2006)

H. Périvier, 'La garde des jeunes enfants: affaires de femmes ou affaire d'Etat?', Lettre de l'OFCE, no. 228 (2003)

P. Pierson, *Politics in Time. History, Institutions, and Social Analysis* (Princeton and Oxford, Princeton University Press, 2004)

T. Piketty, 'Impact de l'Allocation parentale d'éducation sur l'activité féminine et la fécondité en France', in C. Lefèvre (ed.), *Histoires de familles, histoires familiales. Les Cahiers de l'INED,* 156 (2005) 79–109

E. Plaisance, *L'enfant, la maternelle, la société* (Paris: PUF, 1986)

M. Ruault, A. Daniel, 'Les modes d'accueil des enfants de moins de six ans', *Etudes et résultats,* 235 (2004)

C. Sauviat, 'L'accueil ou la garde d'enfants: des marchés de service façonnés par les contextes nationaux. Suède, Etats-Unis, France', IRES, Document de travail no. 96.03 (Paris, 1996)

L. Stoléru, *Vaincre la pauvreté dans les pays riches* (Paris: Flammarion, 1977)

4

Child Care in Spain after 1975: the Educational Rationale, the Catholic Church, and Women in Civil Society[*]

Celia Valiente

1   Introduction

In Spain today, preschool attendance rates are among the highest in the European Union (EU) for children aged three, four and five (96 percent, 100 percent, and 100 percent respectively). In contrast, Spanish child-care attendance rates are comparatively low for children aged two and under. Why is Spain at the vanguard of the European Union (EU) regarding preschool attendance rates for children aged three, four and five years? After briefly describing in the first section of this chapter the main Spanish preschool policies since 1975, in the second section I present the analytical framework to answer this question. In the third, fourth and fifth sections, I explain that in Spain most child-care provision has historically been part of education policy. Between the mid-1930s and 1975, Spain was governed by a right-wing authoritarian regime headed by General Francisco Franco. A transition to democracy and a stable democracy followed the dictatorship. After 1975, policy-makers continuously expanded the programmes that were already in place: public preschool services for children under the age of mandatory education (six years). In postauthoritarian Spain, the context was favourable for the increase in public preschool supply because the Catholic Church, which is a principal actor in education, is interested in the expansion of preschooling, provided that part of it is private and subsidised by

72

the state. The major presence of women in civil society and the increasing strength of the women's movement mean that women now form a visible electorate that politicians usually take into consideration. As a result, policy-makers tend to support policies that could be seen as favourable to women, such as an expansion of public child care.

Finally, in the sixth section of this chapter, I argue that preschool is not child care, and therefore, in Spain, working parents cannot rely only on preschool to combine work and family. I also identify two major barriers to an expansion of care in centres for the under-twos: societal views about the best care options for infants and toddlers, and a pool of grandmothers and immigrants who take care of very young children at home. Secondary literature and published primary data are the main sources of this chapter.

2 Analytical framework

Social policy is usually expanded and more infrequently restricted. This dynamic is captured by a concept used by social scientists: path-dependency (Pierson, 2000; Rose, 1990). According to path-dependency analyses, in a given policy area several courses of action are possible while politicians are initially trying to solve a problem. But once a course of action (or path) is chosen, it is easier for policy-makers to advance a bit farther along the path than to start a completely new course of action. Several reasons explain the continuity of any given policy along the same path, among others that some individual and collective actors are interested in maintaining the status quo. These actors are the recipients of the social programme and the bureaucrats who administer it. Because these individual and collective actors share a specific goal (the maintenance and even expansion of the social policy), they can mobilise with relative ease to achieve this goal. At some point in time, dismantling the existing policy and/or initiating a new course of action may be almost impossible.

At least three insights of the path-dependency literature are worth noting. First of all, time matters, and past decisions have consequences on future decisions. Thus, while studying policy-making at any given moment, it is also necessary to analyse the actions of former politicians in the same policy area. Second, although policy-makers at any given point in time tend to follow the same path as their predecessors, the results of policy-making may be different at different times. For instance, politicians may initiate a social policy that covers only a limited category of beneficiaries. Decade after decade, subsequent politicians include more categories of beneficiaries within the social scheme. Eventually, the whole population may be covered by such a scheme. Thus, a programme for only a small fraction of the population may evolve after a long period of time into a very different programme, such as a universal service. Third, context matters too. Some contexts are more favourable than others to an intense expansion of pre-existing policies, for instance, if numerous actors are interested in such an expansion, and no major actor wants to dismantle the pre-existing policy.

With respect to the more specific comparative literature on welfare states, in general and with important exceptions, researchers have not studied education policy. Recently, education has been included in some welfare state studies (see, for instance, Esping-Andersen, 2007). This is the approach used in this chapter. Like other social policies, education may (or may not) help to erode social inequalities. Therefore, there is no reason to ignore education in studies of social policy-making.

The literature on the origin and development of welfare states in Western countries has usually privileged the study of socioeconomic development and class politics as primary forces causing the establishment and expansion of social policy (Castles, 1994, p. 19; Daly, 1999, p. 106; van Kersbergen, 1995, p. 1). The role played by organised religion in social policy-making has received less attention. In Western countries in modern times, states and churches have fought for control of the education system. Therefore, the study of organised religion is especially important to understanding education policy.

Spain is a culturally homogeneous Catholic country. After the expulsion of Jews in 1492 and of Muslims soon afterwards, no significant religious community other than the Catholics has been openly active in Spain in the last four centuries. The majority of adult Spaniards consider themselves Catholic (77.6 percent in July 2007).[1] Although the number of practising Catholics is much lower than the number of self-declared Catholics, it is significant: 15.8 percent of those self-declared Catholics or believers of other religions affirmed that they attended religious services (excluding social events such as weddings, first communions, or funerals) almost every Sunday or religious holiday, and 2.2 percent attended on various days during the week (Centro de Investigaciones Sociológicas, 2007). Part of the literature on the origin and development of welfare states identifies Christian democratic parties as principal actors in the translation of Catholic social doctrine into actual social policy-making (Morgan, 2006; van Kersbergen, 1995).[2] However, in postauthoritarian Spain, the church has no direct political representation, because no major Christian democratic party or trade union exists (Casanova, 1993).

The literature on welfare states in the Western world argues that the influence of Catholicism on social policy-making has been very complex. A correlation has been found between Catholicism and the level of expenditure on social security transfers at some points in history (Castles, 1994, pp. 24–26). Catholicism indirectly influences the type of social policy, because Catholic social doctrine manifests at least three marked preferences regarding the sort of social policy to be established. Firstly, social provision should be implemented by organisations of civil society (especially those of the Catholic Church). Secondly, social provision should preserve status differences in society, for instance, because of the existence of different schemes for different types of workers. Thirdly, social provision should help families care for their members basically by providing them with income in case the head of the family is unable to earn a sufficient wage in the labour market, rather than replacing families in their caring functions by providing them with caring services. Regarding social policies that particularly affect women, the Catholic hierarchy has historically supported the view that married women's place is mainly in the home taking care of their relatives. Thus, social policy should not interfere but reinforce the performance of this role (Castles, 1994; Daly, 1999; Morgan, 2006; van Kersbergen, 1995).

3   Child-care policies in Spain after 1975

Child care can be thought of as a labour-market, gender-equality or education policy. In Spain before and after 1975, education has been the predominant rationale. Since 1975, the main child-care policy has been an ever increasing supply of public preschool programmes for children under the age of mandatory schooling (six). These programmes are free of charge, full-day, and administered within the policy area of education authorities. The absolute number and proportion of children who attend preschool programmes in public centres has increased intensively since 1975. While this type of centre was attended by 347,026 children younger than six in academic year 1975–1976, this figure had nearly tripled (991,626 children) by academic year 2006–2007. Seen from another perspective, in academic year 1975–1976, more than a third (38 percent) of children enrolled in preschool education attended public centres. In academic year 2006–2007, this proportion was nearly two-thirds (64 percent). The expansion of the supply of places in public child care has taken place in a context characterised by the existence of a private sector. In academic year 1975–1976, the number of children enrolled in preschool education who attended private centres was 573,310, while in academic year 2006–2007 the figure was 546,341.[3]

In part as a result of the policy just described, Spanish preschool attendance rates (in public and private centres) for three-, four-, and five-year-olds are among the highest in the EU at 96 percent, 100 percent and 100 percent respectively (Ministerio de Educación y Ciencia, 2006; provisional data for academic year 2006–2007). In academic year 2002–2003, four EU countries (Belgium, France, Italy and Spain) had 100 percent of four-year-old children enrolled in pre-primary or primary education, while the EU-25 average was 14 points lower (86 percent). In the same academic year, the Spanish participation rate of three-year-old children in pre-primary or primary education (95 percent) was exceeded only by those of Belgium, France and Italy (100 percent in each of the three countries), and was 27 points higher than the EU-25 average (68 percent) (Andrén and Schmidt, 2005, pp. 8–9). Conversely, the proportion of Spanish children aged two or younger cared for in public or private centres is comparatively low: 4 percent for children younger than one year, 16 percent of children aged one year, and 30 percent for those two years old (academic year 2005–2006; Ministerio de Educación y Ciencia, 2007).[4]

In democratic Spain, besides the pronounced expansion of the supply of public preschool programmes, the other most important change in the area of child-care policy has been territorial decentralisation. Under Franco, the state was highly centralised, but during the transition to democracy a broad process of devolution of powers from the central state to the regions (less so to municipalities) was set in motion. Since the early 1980s, some regional governments have been acquiring responsibilities previously assigned to the central state (for instance, education). The process of devolution of full responsibilities for education to all regions was completed in 2000.[5]

4   The educational rationale of Spanish child-care policy

As already noted, in Spain, child care has always been mainly an education policy independent of the political regime governing the country. In Franco's Spain, the gender equality argument was out of the question, since the regime actively opposed the advancement of women's rights and status. Divorce was abolished and the selling and advertising of contraceptives were criminalised. Abortion was defined as a crime subject to a prison sentence. According to the official doctrine of the dictatorship, the ideal family was a hierarchical unit, because the authority within it rested with the father, who was supposed to be its sole (or at least its main) supporter. Motherhood was defined not only as the main family duty of women but also as women's main obligation towards state and society. The role of mothering was perceived as incompatible with other activities, such as waged work. During the first phase of the Franco regime (between the second part of the 1930s until the late 1950s – early 1960s), the state took measures to prevent women's labour outside the home. For example, a married woman needed her husband's permission before signing a labour contract and engaging in trade. During the second phase of the Franco regime (between the late 1950s – early 1960s and 1975), policy-makers approved some liberalisation measures related to women's status, such as the abolition of some obstacles regarding paid employment (for instance, banning married women from working and prohibiting women from practising some law professions) (Morcillo, 2000; Nash, 1991).

Regarding children under the age of mandatory education, when Franco died in 1975, the central state already had a preschool policy within the policy area of education. A principal institution to formulate this policy was functioning: the Ministry of Education. (Limited) premises and staff to implement this policy also existed: preschool teachers and classes for children under the age of six in public schools. The path-dependency approach to policy analysis suggests that, after 1975, central state policy-makers (and later regional authorities) found it easier to expand what was already in place than to invent a completely new policy from scratch. In fact, since the transition to democracy, the supply of places in public preschool centres has been expanded by parties of different ideological colours while in office at the central state level (although for different reasons): the centre-right coalition of parties Union of the Democratic Centre (*Unión de Centro Democrático*, UCD) up to 1982, the social-democratic Spanish Socialist Workers' Party (*Partido Socialista Obrero Español*, PSOE) between 1982 and 1996, the conservative People's Party (*Partido Popular*, PP) between 1996 and 2004, and again the PSOE since then. In the 1970s and 1980s, public preschool places were provided especially for children aged four and five, while in the 1990s and after 2000 these places were also increasingly given to children aged three.

Governments formed by the UCD, PSOE and PP have understood preschool services as a necessary step for Spain to catch up with surrounding countries since most EU(-15) member states are economically more developed. All three governing groups have thought that one of the reasons for Spain's relative backwardness was an education deficit. The social-democratic PSOE promoted public preschool mainly to diminish class inequality. Historically, access to nonmandatory education was sharply differentiated by class (de Puelles Benítez, 1999, pp. 368–369; McNair, 1984, p. 47; Medina, 1976, pp. 123, 130). The conservative PP maintained and increased the supply of publicly supported preschool. In the context of strong electoral competition from the PSOE, the conservatives did not want to be seen by the electorate as a party that defended the interests of affluent citizens who tend to use private child-care and preschool programmes (Valiente, 2002, p. 63; 2003, p. 289). For the same reasons, regional governments of different ideological colours continued to expand public preschool programmes when powers on education were transferred from the central state to the regions.[6]

5   The Catholic Church

The Catholic Church is a key player in education, controlling the majority of private centres (but not all). Private centres provide educational services to approximately a third of non-university students (Ministerio de Educación y Ciencia, 2006, p. 3). In general, the Catholic Church is interested in the expansion of education, provided that a substantial part of it is private and subsidised by the state.

Most private provision of non-university education is subsidised by the state. In academic year 2004–2005, 84 percent of non-university students in private education were pupils of subsidised centres (*centros privados concertados*). In the same academic year, 72 percent of non-university students in subsidised private education were pupils attending religious centres. In exchange for state funding, subsidised private centres must use the same criteria as public centres to select students if the number of applicants exceeds the number of places; they must also supply education free of charge (this does not include extracurricular activities, school meals, or textbooks); and they must allow parents, students and school staff to participate in school decision-making. State subsidies are a very important source of income for providers of subsidised private education. On average, in academic year 2004–2005, the state covered 75 percent of current expenses of subsidised private centres (Instituto Nacional de Estadística, 2007a, p. 4). Up to the 1990s, the state subsidised mainly private mandatory education, but since then the state has increasingly subsidised private preschool education as well.

In sum, in postauthoritarian Spain, the Church has continuously demanded (and obtained) subsidies for its private education provision, including preschool services. In this way, two of the preferences of social Catholic doctrine have been satisfied. First, (part of) social policy is administered by organisations controlled by the Church, that is, confessional private schools. Second, in general and with important exceptions, access to private education is related to social class. Thus, the existence of a private education sector means the preservation of status differences within society.

In postauthoritarian Spain, the Catholic Church has also constantly demanded that the state grant religion academic status in the school curriculum (Bonal, 2000, pp. 205–206; McNair, 1984, p. 144). Contrary to expectations derived from the literature on the origin and development of welfare states, in the last three decades, the Catholic hierarchy has not vocally and continuously argued that preschool or child care is detrimental for children, or that mothers should take care of their offspring at home. It is not easy to explain why the Catholic Church has behaved in this way. Probably, the fact that the Church controlled a significant sector of non-university education made the Church hierarchy more interested in expanding this sector than in locking women and their very young children in their homes.

It is important to note that the ascendancy of the Church in politics (and society) has been severely declining at least since the transition to democracy. Spain now belongs to the group of Western countries with secularised polities (and societies). The (imperfect) separation of church and the Spanish state is reflected in the Constitution. According to Article 16, Spain is a nondenominational state based on religious freedom. Nevertheless, this very same article also states that 'public authorities will keep in mind the religious beliefs of Spanish society' (that is, Catholicism). Article 16 also refers to the desirability of cooperation between the state and the Catholic Church and the remaining denominations. The state's special treatment of the Catholic Church is mainly reflected in important state transfers, tax exemptions and financial support to most Catholic schools, hospitals, centres of social action and patronage for the arts. Thus the Catholic Church in Spain is not self-supporting but needs state money for its economic survival. The Catholic Church accepted the principle of nonconfessionality of the Spanish state and the constitutional regulation of state–church relations (Bedoya, 2006; Casanova, 1993, p. 117; Linz, 1993, p. 35).

The Catholic Church does not agree with some laws regulating moral matters, such as the laws that legalised divorce (1981), liberalised abortion (1985), or permitted gay marriage (2005), but it has not made an enormous effort to have them revoked. Resistance by Catholics to these public policies has been more moderate in Spain than in other Western countries. The Catholic Church is not involved in the main political controversies of the country (with the possible exception of the nationalist question in the Basque country) and does not control the government agenda, but is not silent on matters the Church considers important (education and moral issues such as abortion and sexuality, among others) (Linz, 1993, pp. 32–48).

The (imperfect) separation of church and state is a characteristic of the democratic regime established after the end of the dictatorship in 1975, but not of the right-wing authoritarian regime headed by Franco. During the first phase of the Franco regime, the church and the political regime supported each other. Catholicism was the official religion of the country. Freedom of worship was abolished. The state gave the church the prerogative of managing all matters regarding marriage and the separation of married couples. Catholic marriage was mandatory, with very few exceptions. The state allowed the Catholic Church to control part of the education system: a significant number of primary and secondary schools, but not most universities, which had been under state control at least since the mid-nineteenth century (McNair, 1984, pp. 18–19). In all primary and secondary schools, the state made religious teaching and religious practices mandatory and education had to conform to the teachings of the Catholic Church. The Church was given the right to inspect private and public centres (McNair, 1984, pp. 28–29). Sex-segregated schools were the norm, and boys and girls not only attended different schools but also had different curricula. The state supported the Catholic Church financially, and the Church was exempt from taxation. In turn, the Church supported the authoritarian regime, provided it with legitimacy, and declared the civil war (1936–1939) a crusade between supporters of Christianity (Franco's followers) and the unfaithful and immoral (the Republicans). Some of the administrative cadres of the Francoist state came from Catholic lay organisations such as the *Asociación Católica Nacional de Propagandistas* and later Opus Dei. Catholic hierarchies occupied a salient place in official governmental acts. State authorities *ex officio* attended religious ceremonies (Casanova, 1993, pp. 107–108; Linz, 1993, pp. 9–25).

Relations between church and state changed in the second phase of the Franco regime. Part (only a part) of the Church distanced itself from the regime, criticised the position and actions of the Church in the civil war, and even gave protection and support to political dissidents. Catholics became members of groups and parties of all ideological colours in opposition to the dictatorship. Thanks to this progressive distancing of a part of the Church from the political regime, when Franco died in 1975, the Church could align itself with other political and social forces in building a new democratic state (Casanova, 1993, pp. 114–117; Linz, 1993, pp. 25–32).

6 Women in civil society and the women's movement

Women are increasingly active in organisations of civil society, whether in women-only groups or in mixed associations. Thus, women now constitute a visible electorate that politicians often take into consideration when calculating what policies they support or oppose. As for the large presence of women in mixed associations in civil society, for example, on average, women outnumber men in the so-called third sector dedicated to social causes (Pérez Díaz and López Novo, 2003, pp. 214–217, 231–233, 241–242). The women's movement is made up of one branch which is explicitly feminist and another branch which is not. The latter is formed by housewives' organisations, widows' associations, mothers' movements, and cultural and religious associations, among others. This branch is currently thriving in terms of number of members and degree of activity (Ortbals, 2004).

The first groups of the explicitly feminist branch of the women's movement (hereafter referred to as the feminist movement) were set up in the late 1960s and early 1970s in the period of liberalisation of the authoritarian political regime. Many of the first feminists were active in the opposition to the dictatorship, where they encountered illegal left-wing political parties and trade unions. These have been the (uneasy) allies of the feminist movement ever since (Threlfall et al., 2005).

In the last three decades, the feminist movement has influenced gender equality policy-making mainly due to its involvement with left-wing political parties. Many feminists mobilised within both feminist groups of civil society and left-wing political parties. When these reached power, some of their feminist activists and leaders occupied decision-making positions in the state from which they could advance an agenda of gender equality. Alternatively, feminists within left-wing political parties endlessly pressurised male activists and leaders to take gender equality into consideration when choosing their policy objectives (Threlfall, 1996; Threlfall et al., 2005). The feminist movement has also intervened in the gender equality policy area mobilising public opinion in favour of the need to improve women's status (Trujillo Barbadillo, 1999).

Since the transition to democracy, child care has been an issue of only moderate priority for the feminist movement. Child care helps women to combine work and family. Therefore, feminists in all Western countries including Spain have demanded child-care services. But in Spain, the existence of the right-wing authoritarian regime helped move Spanish feminists away from issues such as motherhood and child care later on. After 40 years of being literally bombarded with the idea of mothering and caring as the most important task in women's lives, the last thing Spanish feminists wanted to do after the dictatorship was to pay a lot of attention to the issues of motherhood and child-rearing. Women's liberation was then understood as opening the range of concerns that define women's lives, such as waged work, political participation, or control of their bodies. This definition carefully skirts the place of motherhood and child care in the life of the newly liberated Spanish (Valiente, 2002, p. 65; 2003, p. 288).

Even though child care has not been a top priority for the feminist movement through the whole postauthoritarian period, preschool is seen by important sectors of public opinion not only as an education policy but also as a policy favourable to women. This is so because preschool is used (together with other options) by working parents to combine work and family, and an increasing number of women work for pay. Thus, an expansion of public preschool services is usually perceived by broad sectors of the citizenry as a policy that helps women. Cuts in public preschool provision would be interpreted as a policy against women and therefore out of the question in a country where women form an ever increasing part of civil society, and both branches of the women's movement are increasingly visible.

7   Limitations of preschool and future challenges

As stated earlier, in Spain, the supply of places in free public preschool was increased substantially over the last three decades. Nevertheless, the very definition of these institutions as schools rather than child-care centres has limited their utility for working parents. Preschool programmes provide solid educational services for children aged three to five years. Addressing the educational needs of young children (from all social classes) is a laudable goal, and its achievement should be celebrated. However, preschool programmes cannot be used by parents as perfect substitutes for child care, because preschool holidays are considerably longer than work holidays and preschool hours are shorter than the work hours for full-time jobs (sometimes much shorter and interrupted by a break). Even if the Spanish women's employment rate (51.6 percent) is lower than the EU(-25) average (56.5 percent), most Spanish women who work for wages (77.3 percent) have full-time jobs (third quarter 2005 data; Romans and Hardarson, 2006, pp. 3–5). Policies other than preschool education to help parents combine work and family are seriously underdeveloped in Spain (León, 2007).

At least two obstacles will hinder the expansion of child-care services in the near future for the under-threes: widespread assumptions regarding the centrality of mother-care for small children; and an important number of grandmothers and immigrants who provide child care. It is still commonly believed by both women and men in Spain that care by the mother is indispensable at least at the beginning of the child's life, and that the (full-time) employment of mothers jeopardises the upbringing of very young children. For instance, in a 2002 survey, slightly over half of the adult population of both sexes strongly agreed or agreed with the statement that a preschool child will suffer if his/her mother works (data from Morgan, 2008, p. 29).

When mothers do not stay at home day and night to take care of their children, the second preference of many parents is that another woman, often a grandmother, replaces the working mother in the home. Grandmothers are frequently available to look after their grandchildren because the majority of women in these age groups are full-time housewives, and many young parents live near their parents. Other children are also cared for by domestic workers, who also perform household duties. This option is only available to members of the upper-middle or upper classes who can afford these services. Immigrants are available to perform this type of job. On 1 January 2007, 45.12 million people lived in Spain, of whom around 10 percent were foreigners (Instituto Nacional de Estadística, 2007b; provisional data). Labour market experts estimate that approximately 600,000 people (overwhelmingly women) are employed as domestic workers in Spain (*El País* 21 May 2007, p. 102). However, the official figure is lower: in July 2007, around 271,500 people contributed to the special scheme of social security for domestic workers (Ministerio de Trabajo y Asuntos Sociales, 2007).

8   Conclusion

In this chapter, I have shown that the main child-care public policy after 1975 has been an ever increasing supply of full-day, public preschool free of charge. This policy already existed before 1975 although it was considerably less developed than it is today. As the literature on path-dependency would predict, pre-1975 public preschool provision was expanded in postauthoritarian Spain by governments of different ideological colours at the central state level and later at the regional level. In part as a result of this policy, Spain is at the vanguard of the EU regarding preschool education coverage for children aged three (96 percent), four (100 percent) and five (100 percent). In the last years of the dictatorship, the majority of children under six did not attend preschool. In academic year 1971–1972, preschool attendance rates for children aged three, four, and five were 12 percent, 42 percent, and 61 percent respectively (Pérez Peñasco, 1976, p. 224). Thus, by expanding pre-existing programmes, postauthoritarian policy-makers converted a programme of limited coverage into a nearly universal scheme.

From the literature on path-dependency, one can infer that context matters while explaining the intensity with which policy-makers continue along the same path as their predecessors. In postauthoritarian Spain, the intense expansion of public preschool services can be understood if one considers the fact that the Catholic Church is interested in the expansion of preschool services, provided that part of them are private and subsidised by the state. This policy is perceived as beneficial to women in a country where more and more women are active in civil society.

I have also identified some factors that mitigate the demand of public child care for children aged two or under. An important share of the population thinks that very young children should be taken care of at home. Mothers who do not work for wages, grandmothers and immigrants are providing this type of child care in different types of families. Cultural specificities and class differences are at play here. On the one hand, many Spanish people find it natural for grandmothers to take care of their very young grandchildren while the mothers of these children are working for pay. In other EU countries, many citizens think that family obligations should not be stretched that far (Millar and Warman, 1995). On the other hand, in Spain, families in the upper-middle and upper classes prefer their toddlers and infants to be cared for at home by domestic workers rather than in centres by professional staff, while exactly the opposite is true in other EU member states. In

Spain (and possibly other Mediterranean countries), most members of the upper-middle and upper classes feel comfortable when being served by others at home, while in other countries (for example, the Nordic states) most members of the very same classes feel quite uncomfortable and even embarrassed in the same situation. To investigate these and other cultural dimensions beneath the surface of child-care policies is one of the next steps in the research on social policy from a comparative perspective.

Notes

*This chapter contains research undertaken by the project 'Gender and citizenship in multicultural Europe: The impact of the contemporary women's movements (FEMCIT)' financed by the European Commission's Sixth Framework Program (EC contract number 028746–2).

1. In the same opinion poll, 1.4 percent of the interviewed identified themselves as belonging to other religions, 12.4 percent non-believers and 6.8 percent atheist, and 1.8 percent did not answer.
2. For a critique of the importance given to Christian Democratic parties by this literature, see Castles (1994, pp. 23–24) and Daly (1999, p. 106).
3. Calculated by Celia Valiente from data of Instituto Nacional de Estadística (1977) pp. 101–103; Ministerio de Educación y Ciencia (2006) p. 3 (provisional data for the academic year 2006–2007).
4. See comparative data in Morgan (2008), pp. 31–32.
5. Other child-care policies such as tax exemptions for child-care expenses are much less important than the supply of preschool places in public centres. Due to space constraints, only the latter is analysed in this chapter.
6. However, some regional governments were more committed to public pre-schooling than others. Due to space constraints, this paper does not analyse regional variations.

Bibliography

B. Andrén and P. Schmidt, 'Education in Europe: Key Statistics 2002–2003', *Statistics in Focus: Population and Social Conditions*, 10 (2005) 1–12

J. G. Bedoya, 'Las cuentas del catolicismo español', *El País* (30 September 2006) 43

X. Bonal, 'Interest Groups and the State in Contemporary Spanish Education Policy', *Journal of Educational Policy*, 15, 2 (2000) 201–216

J. Casanova, 'Church, State, Nation, and Civil Society in Spain and Poland', in S. A. Arjomand (ed.), *The Political Dimensions of Religion* (Albany, New York: State University of New York Press, 1993), 101–153

F. G. Castles, 'On Religion and Public Policy: Does Catholicism Make a Difference?', *European Journal of Political Research*, 25, 1 (1994) 19–40

Centro de Investigaciones Sociológicas, *Study Number 2,728, July* (2007). Retrieved 8 August 2007 at www.cis.es

M. Daly, 'The Functioning Family: Catholicism and Social Policy in Germany and Ireland', *Comparative Social Research*, 18 (1999) 105–133

M. de Puelles Benítez, *Educación e ideología en la España contemporánea* (Barcelona: Labour, 4th ed., 1999)

El País (21 May 2007) 102

G. Esping-Andersen, 'Investing in Children and Their Life Chances', Paper presented at the International Conference Welfare State and Competitivity: the European Experience and the Agenda for Latin America, Fundación Carolina, Madrid, 26–27 April (2007)

Instituto Nacional de Estadística, *Estadística de la enseñanza en España: Curso 1975–76* (Madrid: Instituto Nacional de Estadística, 1977)

Instituto Nacional de Estadística, *Notas de prensa-19 de julio de 2007: Encuesta de Financiación y Gastos de la Enseñanza Privada, curso 2004–2005* (2007a). Retrieved 27 August 2007 at www.ine.es

Instituto Nacional de Estadística, *Notas de prensa-11 de junio de 2007: Avance del Padrón Municipal a 1 de enero de 2007, datos provisionales* (2007b). Retrieved 27 August 2007 at www.ine.es

K. van Kersbergen, *Social Capitalism: A Study of Christian Democracy and the Welfare State* (London: Routledge, 1995)

M. León, 'Speeding Up or Holding Back? Institutional Factors in the Development of Childcare Provision in Spain', *European Societies*, 9, 3 (2007) 315–337

J. J. Linz, 'Religión y política en España', in R. Díaz-Salazar and S. Giner (eds), *Religión y sociedad en España* (Madrid: Centro de Investigaciones Sociológicas, 1993), 1–50

J. M. McNair, *Education for a Changing Spain* (Manchester: Manchester University Press, 1984)

A. Medina, 'Problemática de la educación preescolar en España', *Revista de Educación* 247 (1976) 111–134

J. Millar and A. Warman (eds), *Defining Family Obligations in Europe* (Bath: University of Bath Social Policy Papers 23, 1995)

Ministerio de Educación y Ciencia, *Datos y cifras, curso escolar 2006/2007* (2006) Retrieved 3 August 2007 at www.mec.es

Ministerio de Educación y Ciencia, *Estadística de las enseñanzas no universitarias: Resultados detallados del curso 2004–2005* (2007) Retrieved 3 August 2007 at www.mec.es

Ministerio de Trabajo y Asuntos Sociales, *Resumen últimos datos* (2007) Retrieved 27 August 2007 at www.mtas.es

A. G. Morcillo, *True Catholic Womanhood: Gender Ideology in Franco's Spain* (Dekalb: Northern Illinois University Press, 2000)

K. J. Morgan, *Working Mothers and the Welfare State: Religion and the Politics of Work-Family Policies in Western Europe and the United States* (Stanford: Stanford University Press, 2006)

K. J. Morgan, 'Towards the Europeanisation of Work-Family Policies? The Impact of the EU on Policies for Working Parents', in S. Roth (ed.), *Gender Issues and Women's Movements in the Enlarged European Union* (London: Berghahn, 2008, forthcoming)

M. Nash, 'Pronatalism and Motherhood in Franco's Spain', in G. Bock and P. Thane (eds), *Maternity and Gender Policies: Women and the Rise of the European Welfare States, 1880s-1950s* (London: Routledge, 1991), 160–177

C. D. Ortbals, *Embedded Institutions, Activisms, and Discourses: Untangling the Intersections of Women's Civil Society and Women's Policy Agencies in Spain* (PhD dissertation: Indiana University, 2004)

V. Pérez Díaz and J. P. López Novo, *El tercer sector social en España* (Madrid: Ministerio de Trabajo y Asuntos Sociales, 2003)

A. Pérez Peñasco, 'Educación', in Fundación Foessa (ed.), *Estudios sociológicos sobre la situación social en España 1975* (Madrid: Euramérica, 1976), 195–344

P. Pierson, 'Increasing Returns, Path Dependence, and the Study of Politics', *American Political Science Review* 94, 2 (2000) 251–267

F. Romans and Ó. S. Hardarson, 'Labour Market Latest Trends - 3rd Quarter 2005 Data: The Employment Rate Continues to Rise', *Statistics in Focus: Population and Social Conditions* 6 (2006) 1–8

R. Rose, 'Inheritance Before Choice in Public Policy', *Journal of Theoretical Politics*, 2, 3 (1990) 263–291

M. Threlfall, 'Feminist Politics and Social Change in Spain', in M. Threlfall (ed.), *Mapping the Women's Movement: Feminist Politics and Social Transformation in the North* (London: Verso, 1996), 115–151

M. Threlfall, C. Cousins and C. Valiente, *Gendering Spanish Democracy* (London and New York: Routledge, 2005)

G. Trujillo Barbadillo, 'El movimiento feminista como actor político en España: El caso de la aprobación de la Ley de despenalización del aborto de 1985', Paper presented at the Annual Meeting of the Spanish Association of Political Science and Public Administration, Granada, Spain (1999)

C. Valiente, 'The Value of an Educational Emphasis: Child Care and Restructuring in Spain since 1975', in S. Michel and R. Mahon (eds), *Child Care Policy at the Crossroads: Gender and Welfare Restructuring* (New York and London: Routledge, 2002), 57–70

C. Valiente, 'Central State Child Care Policies in Postauthoritarian Spain: Implications for Gender and Carework Arrangements. *Gender & Society*, 17, 2 (2003) 287–292

5
The Paradox of Public Preschools in a Familist Welfare Regime: the Italian Case

Eva Maria Hohnerlein

1 Introduction

The Italian welfare regime has never attempted to develop a coherent, comprehensive child-care policy. In fact, in the debates on the design, expansion and redesign of the various welfare state arrangements, child-care services – like social services in general – remained marginal. The lack of interest corresponded to the absence of any explicit family policy on the political agenda during most of the twentieth century. According to a general consensus, parents were responsible for the care and upbringing of children, and the state was not to interfere with this private sphere. Mothers were the main care providers, and the state stepped in only when children were deemed to be at risk. As a result of this cultural attitude, strongly influenced by the Catholic Church, it was generally accepted that child-care needs had to be met largely by and within the family. Care provision as an institutional *social* service is therefore still very low on average as compared with other European countries. The reliance on intrafamily care and informal arrangements (involving in particular grandmothers), the scarcity of public child care, and the low employment rate of women make Italy a typical example of what might be termed a 'familist' welfare regime.

Along with this familist attitude towards child care, Italy presents – surprisingly – a peculiar situation. On the one hand, very few children under age three have access to public child care. The incidence of places available for children up to age three reached on average 7.4% in 2000, but there are vast disparities between regions and municipalities (Centro Nazionale di documentazione e analisi per l'infanzia, 2002, p. 16). By contrast, almost 100% of children aged three to six are enrolled in the voluntary preschool system, most of them attending state-run preschools which are in effect part of the public education system.

The reason for this situation, in open contrast with a familist approach to child care, is a fundamental shift in Italian policies directed at children aged three to six: while maintaining the traditional family model, Italy decided to emphasise the right of all children to education by offering a universal, voluntary, and free system of preschools under the auspices of the Ministry of Education as a pre-primary grade of the school system. The earlier path was abandoned in 1968 when Italy adopted the Act on Establishing State Maternal Schools (Act No. 444/1968).[1] This law embodied a new approach geared towards providing a distinct educational service for children from all families instead of targeted social services in cases of 'social emergency' on the one hand, or the provision of elitist child-care services in private institutions for a selected few on the other. The new and highly controversial approach implied a special responsibility of the state for the education of all preschool children aged three to six, but it was clear that for this age group education would also have to include some type of care. As a result Italy has managed to move away from the traditional path associated with child care linked to social assistance and means-tested social services, restricted to destitute families and unevenly distributed across regions, towards a truly universal, publicly funded educational service for children. This new policy was radically distinct from the traditional targeted welfare interventions for children, as it transformed the child-care institutions into places of education and instruction (Trifiletti, 2003, pp. 117–136). Although the transition has been long and controversial, and although implementation had to overcome serious obstacles, subsequent reforms have not abandoned this path. So Act 444/1968 on establishing state preschools indeed marked a turning point, not only for the new conceptual approach of state responsibility for young children, but above all for the practical changes it brought to the lives of children and families.

2 Evolution of institutional child care before the 1968 reform

As in other countries, care policies for children originally were limited to rudimentary child welfare services aimed at children at risk: those with irregular behaviour, from poor families or living in a one-parent family in need of social and economic support.

Regulation of institutional child care preceded Italian unification. Early legislation on institutional child care, as enacted, for example, in Piemonte in 1850 or later in the new Italian state in 1862, brought child-care institutions (*asili infantili*) together with other public welfare institutions under the auspices of the Ministry of the Interior. The foremost concerns were public order and security, so provisions dealt with the safety and public health requirements of child-care institutions and a minimal supervision of such institutions limited to issues of proper administration of assets. In 1880, the state intervened with regard to professional staff qualifications in those child-care institutions that offered a pedagogical programme based on the teachings of Froebel and required a lower-grade teaching licence, the *patente magistrale di grado inferiore*. Although this requirement was extended in 1889 to the staff of all child-care institutions receiving public funds, it was widely ignored in practice. For more than a century, the state left institutional child care to the goodwill and philanthropy of private individuals, private religious entities or local authorities. Accordingly, the first Italian school law, the *legge Casati* (1859), did not refer to the preschool segment at all.[2]

At the beginning of the twentieth century, the Ministry of Education focused on establishing a (uniform) national education system and eradicating illiteracy. Not until 1911, and against strong opposition from the Catholic Church, did the central state assume direct responsibility for primary schools in most municipalities (Act no. 487/1911). It is interesting to note that the 1911 legislation on primary education contained a somewhat indirect institutional link to child care-institutions. Every municipality was required to establish a 'school welfare board' (*patronato scolastico*). The primary task of these boards was to combat truancy and encourage regular school attendance through various measures such as school meals and subsidies for school uniforms and shoes, books, and other school items. The support measures also had the task of promoting the founding of child-care institutions (di Pol, 2005, p. 204).

In 1911, Minister of Education Luigi Credaro also set up a commission to prepare a national pedagogical programme including the preschool sector. From a conceptual point of view the 'Instructions of the Minister' issued in 1914 had some innovative potential, as they addressed for the first time the issue of universal child care aimed at supplementing, not replacing, maternal care. The instructions, inspired mainly by Froebel's ideas and those of two Italian pedagogues, the Agazzi sisters, were not put into practice due to the lack of professionally trained teaching staff, up to 60% of whom were nuns. To cope with this deficit, a biannual professional training course in specialised schools for teaching staff in child-care institutions was created in 1916.

During the Fascist period the school reform law of *Gentile* (1923)[3] redefined the educational system as such and provided a three-year cycle for maternal schools characterising them as a voluntary preparatory grade for subsequent schooling. However, the provisions on maternal schools remained a declaration of principles without appropriate implementation. In fact, the lack of qualified teaching staff turned out to be a major reason why educational programmes continued to be deficient and why the focus remained on social assistance. The Ministry of Education tried to remedy this situation by introducing a two-year professional course for teaching staff of child-care institutions (in what were called *scuole di metodo*) in 1923. As the results of such a short course proved unsatisfactory, in 1933 the schools were transformed into a more demanding college of education with a three-year programme. Apart from some slight modifications, these schools remained in operation until 2001.

Before Italy's Fascist regime collapsed in July 1943, the Ministry of Education had prepared plans to put preschool education under state control. According to the charter of the (Fascist) school model of 1939, mandatory preschool attendance for two years would have been imposed as a preparatory part of elementary education. The charter also provided for a four-year 'female college of education' to prepare future mothers on the one hand and preschool teaching staff on the other, and it would have made the working conditions for preschool staff equivalent to those of elementary school teachers. The philosophy embodied in the Fascist school charter was of course severely opposed by the Catholic Church. Although never implemented because of the war and the regime's collapse, this charter was the first comprehensive attempt at a radical break with previous child-care policies, by establishing direct state responsibility for and state control over preschool children (Catarsi, 1994, pp. 200–206; di Pol, 2005, pp. 216–218).

The impact of early private initiatives

The historical antecedents of preschool education were daycare centres for children based on a social assistance approach rather than an educational one. The first Italian daycare centre was founded by the priest Ferrante Aporti in Cremona in 1828. According to his mainly philanthropic objectives, these daycare centres were created to collect, supervise, educate and nourish destitute children, such as children of widows, widowers, workers or farmers with a large number of children who were left to themselves and unable to get a proper education, partly due to extreme poverty, partly to health problems or to lack of time. In addition to simply looking after such children, Aporti also pursued educational objectives including the promotion of intellectual activities and the development of cognitive capacities. Despite a number of obstacles to realising these new concepts, such as the lack of appropriate funding and the lack of staff training, Aporti laid the foundations for the recognition of preschool institutional education and instruction in Italy and challenged the family's traditional monopoly on this task. Child-care centres inspired by Aporti's ideas spread rapidly in some of the more progressive regions in northern Italy, in particular Lombardy and Tuscany.

The new concepts represented a serious challenge to the Catholic Church. Critics maintained that these institutions would be a danger for destitute families. The underlying philosophy was attacked as being imported from abroad, inspired by Protestant and other dangerous ideas incompatible with the teachings of the Catholic Church. Neither the Church nor other public bodies believed that children from poor families should be offered more than traditional poor relief and social assistance.

Although the public lack of interest in children's educational needs did not change for a long time, some private pioneers fought for a better childhood policy. Between 1895 and 1917 the sisters Rosa and Carolina Agazzi instituted the *asilo* of Mompiano, near Brescia, with new pedagogical concepts for child care. At the National Congress for Pedagogy held in Turin in 1898, Rosa Agazzi presented the concepts on childhood education developed at Mompiano and called for a broad expansion of educational services with state participation. She emphasised the need for qualified teaching staff and for state involvement in didactical questions, to emphasise physical education and prohibit reading, writing, arithmetic and similar activities which might harm the child's harmonious development (Capaldo and Rondanini, 2004, pp. 12–14). Another pioneer in developing new didactical approaches was Maria Montessori, a paediatrician who became famous for the child-centred activities practised in the Casa dei Bambini she opened in Rome in 1906. Although this experiment was one of the few authentic Italian contributions to the evolution of childhood pedagogy with a vast international impact, it did not get much support in Italy (Novacco, 1977, pp. 57–58).

Subsequent reform debates relied mainly on the concepts developed by the Agazzi sisters, but Catholic groups succeeded in adapting these ideas to their own values and interests, especially after the Concordate of 1929 and again in 1947, when the conservative party Democrazia Cristiana (DC) came to power (Novacco, 1977, p. 55).

Public initiatives for institutional change at local or regional level

In the absence of a state regulatory framework for child care, these services continued to be offered by religious institutions without any formal link to the school system and mostly without any pedagogical aspirations. However, there were also some pioneering public child-care services at the local level, in particular in cities with a strong socialist or communist tradition like Reggio Emilia and Bologna in the region of Emilia Romagna.

Reggio Emilia was a pioneer among Italian cities, founding the first municipal child-care institutions (1910–1920). At the end of World War II postwar labour market conditions forced working mothers to migrate to other cities. To cope with the problem of unattended children Reggio Emilia established 24-hour child care, supported by the Italian women's organisation UDI (Unione Donne Italiane) and by the resistance movement (Göhlich, 1988, p. 136). Given this tradition of a strong public commitment to child care, Reggio Emilia was also a pioneer in opening the first municipal preschool in November 1963, after an arduous controversy with the provincial administrative council which tried to block it. Subsequently, the communist mayor Renzo Bonazzi established 19 municipal preschools (1963–1975), either by transforming existing preschools into public preschools or by founding new ones. The steady numerical expansion was accompanied by a strong commitment to innovative pedagogical concepts which made Reggio Emilia famous among scholars from other European countries.

Another example of a municipality engaged in expanding local preschool services ahead of national legislation is Bologna, where the number of classes grew from 132 to 222 and the number of children enrolled from 5,378 to 7,710 between 1960 and 1964. This growth continued during the next five years. Bologna also showed a strong commitment to improving the quality standards of preschools, under the influence of the pedagogical concepts of Bruno Ciari, a Marxist pedagogue who had played a key role in disseminating the idea of secular public preschools prior to national reform legislation.

Initiatives at state level after 1945

In the aftermath of World War II, the subcommittee for education set up by the Allied military government to reorganise the Italian school system also assumed responsibility for the preschool sector. Under the influence of its English and American members, the committee wanted to emphasise the primary role of the family and the mother in children's education, leaving a subsidiary role to preschool programmes. Maternal schools were to serve mostly social assistance functions. The same line prevailed in the Constitution adopted in 1948. Although the Constitution also traced the perspectives of the national education system providing, among other things, for explicit state intervention for all kinds of schools and all grades (Article 33 (2) of the Constitution), the state remained reluctant to become directly involved in maternal schools. At the national pedagogical congress in Rome in May 1948, Minister of Education Guido Gonnella stressed the fundamental social and educational objectives of maternal schools. At that time the number of places at maternal schools was completely insufficient to meet the real needs of the population: only a third of Italian children aged three to six could attend a maternal school. To improve the situation, Gonnella promised the institution of state maternal schools, but already two years later, in 1950, he retracted his earlier statements. Arguments against establishing state maternal schools were that (1) education of small children should not be unified; (2) state intervention would devaluate the work and merits of the non-state institutions which had until then borne the burden of existing preschool education, so a shift towards state institutions would lead to an unbearable burden on the state budget; (3) in a period of efforts to decentralise state powers it was politically inopportune to create a new sector of state centralism. According to Gonnella, the 'state, rather than spending directly on the institution of preschools, should support those who open schools in order to fulfil the duty of society – and the state – towards children's rights to education' (Catarsi, 1985, pp. 25, 27). The reform bill presented to the parliament in 1951 corresponded to these principles as it gave municipal authorities the power to set up maternal schools if no other institutions already existed which would receive funding from the municipal councils if the service was guaranteed. However, the bill was never debated because the parliament was dissolved prematurely. Again, educational services for the preschool sector were not seen as an imminent priority by legislators, and maternal schools remained unchanged.

In the meantime, a number of secular scholars started to request state intervention in preschool education, in particular in teacher training, which turned out to be one of the most controversial issues in the reform process. As early as January 1958, during a conference in Padua, a group of scholars argued that teachers' training schools and institutes (traditionally secondary schools) should be abolished and that university training would be more appropriate. This was strongly opposed by Catholic circles who wanted to maintain the existing structures. Another controversy between secular and Catholic scholars concerning the religious character of maternal schools emerged when the first curricula for maternal schools (*Orientamenti*) were adopted in 1958. At the least, these programmes focused on the right to education, thus giving educational objectives priority over care objectives and stressing the importance of competent educators (Capaldo and Rondanini, 2004, p. 14).[4]

During the reconstruction period of 1958–1963 new social needs regarding the provision of child care emerged due to significant migration from the rural areas in southern Italy to the industrial centres in the north. At the same time, the dominant conservative party Democrazia Cristiana started to lose the absolute majority it had held between 1947 and 1963. From after 1963 until the end of the 1980s, most Italian governments were formed by a centre-left coalition, with the participation of the socialists.

The political opening towards leftist parties in Italy helped foster more secular ideas and forces, including the idea of state responsibility for institutional child care and early education programmes. When the socialist party PSI proposed to the centre-left government the issue of maternal schools, the concept of childhood and the inalienable right of children to full education as early as possible did not yet have wide support among Italian pedagogical scholars. So it took several years of fierce struggle between different political forces until the traditional Church monopoly on institutional care for preschool-aged children could be broken and the legal framework for state preschools could finally be enacted in 1968.

3 The institution of state-run preschools under Act 444/1968 as a turning point in child-care policies

The question of state-run preschools in Italy was extremely controversial. The debates surrounding the adoption of Act 444 of 18 March 1968 on the institution of state maternal schools ended twice in a governmental crisis – the only ones ever linked to educational policies – and eventually forced the second government of Aldo Moro to resign.

After 1963/1964, various bills on state maternal schools were presented either by the opposition (socialists and communists) or by the government. The discussion of the government bill showed, however, that the proposal basically wanted to maintain pre-existing non-state institutions for child care, with only female teachers and assistants. This question became highly controversial and was extensively discussed and amended by the competent parliamentary commission.

In particular, Catholic groups feared that admitting men and those who had completed teacher college would put the many teacher training schools administered by Catholics at a disadvantage. Although the bill had already been approved by the parliamentary commission, it was rejected by secret ballot in the parliament with a vote of 250 to 221 on 1 December 1964. Opposition within his own party forced Aldo Moro and his government to resign. However, the reform project entailing a radical shift in child-care policy was only postponed. The political situation changed when the Socialist Party later became part of the third government headed by Aldo Moro. The new bill (No. 1869) on the institution of the state maternal school was approved by the senate and the parliament in 1968 as Act 444/1968. In 1969, the curriculum for (state) preschools was also reformed in view of the social changes going on in society and the family. The nonbinding curriculum emphasised the central pedagogical objective of meeting the real needs of the child. Because of its nonbinding character the curriculum was not intended to be applied by other than state-run preschools.

Critics may question whether Act 444/1968 on state maternal schools really constituted a point of no return in the evolution of institutional child care in Italy. At first glance, the changes introduced by the new law may seem less dramatic, especially because the new system did not attempt to radically replace previous patterns of care for preschool children but to supplement them. Existing structures could continue to operate, and the new state commitment concerned above all the southern areas which showed the greatest gaps in coverage. It is true that Act 444/1968 was a compromise and still contained a number of controversial aspects which limited its significance. Yet, despite a number of persistent shortcomings in the reform, especially the fact that Act 444/1968 did not immediately entail a corresponding state policy to develop preschools or the necessary institutional organisation, the law set a significant benchmark in the cultural battle fought by Catholic and familist circles that no future reform could ignore.

4   The contents of Act 444/1968

The law on state maternal schools explicitly recognised four functions: development, assistance, education and preparation for compulsory elementary school. Maternal schools were to integrate and complement – not replace – the functions of the family. Enrolment was voluntary, admission free, and opening hours were in principle to be no less than seven hours per day. According to certified local needs, shorter opening hours only in the morning or in the afternoon were permitted. This exception was a tribute to the dominant culture in the south and the islands where full-day coverage is still much less frequent than in the rest of Italy. The number of children per group was set at a minimum of 15 and a maximum of 30. The law provided for free transport to school. Medical and social security assistance were to be provided on the same terms as for primary schools. In this way, the maternal school was assigned an explicit educational dimension, as a pre-elementary grade intended to prepare pupils for elementary school. However, the educational functions were still combined with assistance and welfare functions. The staff, including custodians, was exclusively female, and there was still the figure of the 'assistant' serving the 'less noble needs of the children' (Catarsi, 1994, pp. 235–251).

Act 444/1968 also contained new provisions for funding maternal schools. The costs for the building, equipment and playing material were to be borne by the state. The municipalities had to cover the costs for building maintenance, heating, and running costs including costs for the (female) custodial staff. Funds were to be provided not only for state maternal schools or other public schools, but also for private schools and in particular private schools run by religious orders when they enrolled children from poor families. During the next decades following the adoption of Act 444/1968, it was thus possible for private maternal schools to receive public funding even if they enrolled only one child who fulfilled this condition.

Another critical aspect which indirectly helped support existing structures was the provision that state maternal schools could not be established if there was already a municipal or religious preschool with at least three sections able to guarantee such service.

According to Article 2 of the law, new guidelines for teachers in maternal schools were to be drawn up. The issue of religious teaching proved to be controversial. The Vatican pressed the minister of education to change the original text prepared by a commission of scholars. The recommendations issued in 1969 warned against avoiding harmful anticipation of school programmes and provided for voluntary enrolment.

All in all, Act 444 of 1968 was a turning point for child care in the form of preschool. It took almost three decades and subsequent legislative changes until the maternal school was completely integrated into the education system as the pre-primary and fundamental level of basic education. Defining this change as a major policy shift is based on two observations: the implementation of the new policy by further legislative evolution with respect to preschools and the outcomes in practice, especially related to the expansion in quantity, but also in quality of services.

5   Implementation of the public preschool system as a decisive element of change

The adoption of the law on state maternal schools is puzzling in many respects. It was not prompted by conventional factors such as pronatalist policies to support families in bringing up their children, nor by demands created by women's increased labour market participation. On the contrary, legislation was passed at a moment when women's labour market activity was actually declining (Della Sala, 2002, p. 176).[5] There was not even a strong pedagogical demand for preschool education. The driving forces were mainly the changes in the dynamics of political power within the centre-left government and the reform ideas that the Socialist Party had brought into the governing coalition. They corresponded to a growing consensus on the need to modernise the education system as part of a general process of modernising the Italian economy and society (Della Sala, 2002, p. 176). This perceived need for cultural change, especially in the area of institutional child care, may have been furthered by some scandals concerning child abuse and maltreatment within Church-run child-care institutions. These scandals probably helped to bring child-care options to the attention of a wider public, widening the window of opportunity for active state involvement in child-care institutions.[6]

The concept of public preschools can thus be seen as an educational reform designed to train future generations while preserving social policy objectives: children from poor families were guaranteed meals and healthcare in the maternal schools. Because of the compromise character of the law instituting state maternal schools, some highly controversial issues remained unresolved, including staff training and professional qualification.

The most obvious shortcomings of Act 444/1968 were resolved only by various subsequent laws. The first reform legislation with major influence on redesigning the maternal school was the *Legge Delega* (enabling law) 477 of 1973 and subsequent decrees which redefined and reduced the weekly working time of teaching staff from 42 to 36 hours and introduced two teachers per class. The legislative decrees also reformed the professional profile of the teachers at maternal schools. In 1974 a presidential decree provided for university training of professional teaching staff in maternal schools, transposed into law by reform legislation of 1991/1992. The equalisation of the preschool and elementary school level was a reform objective, but, again, it was not immediately implemented.

At the end of the 1970s the law on the integration of handicapped children had an important impact on the organisation of schools (Act 517 of 1977). Act No. 463 of 1978 finally abolished the anachronistic figure of the assistant and introduced two teachers per class while reducing the working time to 30 hours per week. The third important reform step was the introduction of equal treatment of men and women in the field of labour, which in 1983 ended the ban on male teachers at the pre-primary level (Capaldo and Rondanini, 2004, p. 15).[7]

Between the end of the 1960s and the early 1980s, the number of children covered by preschool education grew enormously. In the academic year of 1980/81, 76% of children aged three to six were enrolled in voluntary maternal schools. However, the attention to qualitative and didactical aspects and hence the necessary financial support provided to these schools depended rather on local and/or regional efforts than on state intervention. The state's proposal that teachers would have to prepare a general didactical programme was extended to preschools only in August 1982 (five years later than for compulsory schools).

The further evolution of maternal schools continued to stress the pedagogical and didactical approach over the more traditional child-care perspective, in particular via the new pedagogical programmes issued by decree of the Minister of Education on 3 June 1991. The programmes vigorously confirmed that preschools are an authentic educational institution with a proper educational mission of high quality, meant to be available all over the country without geographical inequalities (Piscopo and Fusaro, 2003, p. 47).

6 The outcomes of the policy shift in terms of quantity, institutional setting and quality

The outcomes of this new path in terms of expanded coverage and improved quality are legendary: almost all children – irrespective of their family situation – now attend preschools voluntarily. Although some typical regional disparities between the north and south still persist, they have considerably diminished under the new approach. In fact, qualitative shortcomings in the south are related most often to the lack of complementary social services such as transport or meals, which forces schools to operate only on a half-day basis.

This is a hint that deficiencies in the functioning of the preschool system are most often caused by the lack of social services provided by local welfare authorities. Child care left to social services has to compete with other needs at the local level and may not be given priority by the local welfare authorities as long as the state has not defined uniform (minimum) standards for such services to be guaranteed all over Italy. The scarcity of child care for the under-threes is symptomatic of this situation.[8] For this age group, responsibility lies with the regional and municipal departments of welfare. Although the state attempted to expand this service by legislative interventions providing for additional funding in 1971, the modest targets for expansion were achieved only three decades later, if at all. In Italy, child-care services left to the responsibility of local welfare authorities have never been able to develop as a universal public service available on demand.

Quantitative and institutional dimensions

The policy shift at the end of the 1960s concerned the expansion of *coverage* as well as the *providing institutions*. In the last school year before the reform legislation came into force (1968–1969), 50.8% of children were enrolled in preschool child care, while 95.2% of the places were provided by non-state maternal schools. Non-state providers included municipal preschools and private entities – mostly organised by religious orders, the Catholic Church or private individuals. Originally, the main providers were religious, accounting for 52.7% of all preschools in the early 1950s (di Pol, 2005, p. 260). The percentage of those providers gradually shrank to less than 20% in 2000/01. Already a decade after the initial reform legislation, in 1979–1980 enrolment in non-state maternal schools had fallen to 60%, partly due to the enormous expansion of state-run maternal schools, particularly in the south. Until the school year 1986/1987 state-run preschools remained in the minority as providers, but from then onwards state schools represented more than 50% because many municipal and also some private preschools were transformed into state schools for financial reasons.[9]

Today, there are three types of preschools: municipal, state and private preschools. State preschools are free, but charge fees for meals and school transport. The costs for municipal preschools may vary according to the local policy; about half of them are free, while for the remaining institutions parents have to pay according to their income, with the poorest families paying nothing. The same applies to private religious preschools depending on income and amount of state subsidy available.[10] The private, secular preschools are highly exclusive and very expensive. As to the plurality of providers, state-run preschools are predominant in the central and southern regions, while on average 30% of children attend a private autonomous (mostly religious) preschool;[11] municipal preschools are found mostly in the larger northern cities.

Although there are different providers of preschool services, it must be stressed that the quantitative expansion of preschools and their spread through Italy has been unprecedented. Persisting regional disparities are much smaller than in traditional social care services.

Qualitative dimensions of the policy shift

As to the qualitative dimensions of the shift towards a preschool system, in addition to the universality of the educational services resulting from the numerical expansion, further evidence of a substantial policy shift includes opening hours of preschools,[12] the improvement in quality indicators such as group size[13] and the ratio between children and teaching staff,[14] and improvements in staff working conditions. Preschool teachers are paid at the same rates as primary school teachers.

7 Conclusions and future prospects: link with social services?

Despite some small regional disparities in coverage between Northern and Southern Italy, preschools constitute an uncontested part of civil society. They are linked to the fundamental social right to education guaranteed democratically to all children. The recognition of such a fundamental social right of children – independent of the social and economic status of their family – is one of the major achievements that the Italian preschool legislation on state maternal schools can claim.

In view of the long-term quantitative and qualitative changes brought about by the shift to a preschool system under public responsibility, Act 444/1968 shows that there is no strict path-dependency in this policy sector but that a fundamental policy change is possible. The new path followed since the reform legislation of 1968 has been further developed and confirmed over the past four decades. The main reason for the policy shift was the desire to modernise in order to adapt to changing social and family structures. The separation from care services has been helpful in expanding educational services in the direction of a genuine universal service. However, persisting challenges are related to 'surrounding' social services that even well-organised preschools will have to face. Preschools will have to integrate with different other social services at local level, especially for after-school care and during summer vacation.

Annex 5.1 Table on preschools, classes, pupils and teachers

Year/Region	No. of preschools	No. of sections/ groups	No. of children	No. of educators/ teachers
1999–2000	25,208	68,168	1,582,527	125,745
2000–2001	25,044	68,110	1,576,562	128,972
2001–2002	25,041	69,605	1,596,431	133,034
2002–2003	25,097	70,543	1,630,784	137,177
2003–2004	25,016	73,503	1,643,713	137,177
2004–2005	**24,889**	**72,041**	**1,654,833**	**131,974**
North	*9,726*	*29,346*	*699,831*	*54,342*
Central	*4,383*	*12,779*	*297,359*	*24,032*
South	*10,780*	*29,916*	*657,643*	*53,600*
2005–2006	**24,886**	**72,624**	**1,662,139**	**140,687**

Source: Istat, *Annuario statistico italiano 2006*, p. 184, Table 7.1; Istat, *Annuario statistico italiano 2007*, p. 181, Table 7.1.

Notes

1. Legge 18 marzo 1968, n. 444: Ordinamento della scuola materna statale. The term *scuola materna* (maternal school) was officially replaced by the term *scuola dell'infanzia* (school of childhood) in 2003 in the comprehensive school reform of then Minister Moratti.
2. The implementation of this law made things even worse. Staff of the *asili* did not need any professional qualifications. Professional qualification requirements were also reduced for elementary schools.
3. *Regio decreto* (royal decree), 6.5.1923, No. 1024.
4. On the evolution of maternal schools in the political and cultural setting of Italy cf. also Soltendieck (1997) pp. 164–165.
5. The participation rate of women dropped from 31.2% in 1959 to 27.1% in 1968.

6. Cf. the 'Celestini' scandal as reported by Guidetti Serra and Santanera, 1973.
7. The Italian Constitutional Court also ruled that discrimination against male teachers was unconstitutional; cf. Corte cost. No. 173/1983, retrievable from the Court's official website at www.cortecostituzionale.it.
8. Care for children under three is highly exclusive; parents have to pay fees which vary according to income, on average 12% of disposable income.
9. Since 2000/2001, the coverage of state preschools has been close to 60% of children enrolled; cf. Ministero della Pubblica Istruzione, 2008, p. 39.
10. There are about 8,000 Catholic or Christian preschools around the country, organised by religious orders, churches, other organisations and parents' associations, covering about 550,000 children.
11. The highest incidence of private preschools is found in Veneto (60.2%), Lombardy (41.9%) and Emilia Romagna (36.4%) (as of 2000/01).
12. The opening hours may vary depending on the provider and local needs. Most preschools are open from 8:00 to 17:00, but half-day preschool groups are also possible (8:00 to 12:30).
13. The number of children per group has steadily fallen from 46.6 (1945/46) to about 23 today, which is slightly more than in primary school (18.3 students per class).
14. The child–teacher ratio was cut from 42.4:1 in 1945/1946 to 12.2:1 in 2000/01, due to the introduction of two teachers per group.

Bibliography

E. Becchi and M. Ferrari, 'Die Qualität von italienischen Erziehungseinrichtungen: Initiativen, Erfahrungen und Probleme in Krippe und Kindergarten', in W. Fthenakis and M. Textor (eds), *Qualität von Kinderbetreuung. Konzepte, Forschungsergebnisse, internationaler Vergleich* (Weinheim and Basel: Beltz Verlag, 1998), 182–190

F. Bimbi and V. Della Sala, 'Italy: policy without participation', in J. Jenson and M. Sineau (eds), *Who Cares? Women's Work, Childcare, and Welfare State Redesign* (Toronto: University of Toronto Press, 2001), 120–145

N. Capaldo and L. Rondanini, *La scuola dell'infanzia nella riforma. Tradizione e innovazione nell'educazione infantile* (Gardolo: Edizioni Erickson, 2004)

E. Catarsi, 'Italian preschool education (1946–1985)', in E. Catarsi (ed.), *Twentieth Century Preschool Education. Times, Ideas and Portraits* (Milan: Franco Angeli, 1985), 25–37

E. Catarsi, *L'asilo e la scuola dell'infanzia. Storia della scuola 'materna' e dei suoi programmi dall'Ottocento ai giorni nostri* (Florence: La nuova Italia editrice, 1994)

Centro Nazionale di documentazione e analisi per l'infanzia, *I servizi educativi per la prima infanzia*, No. 21 (Florence: 2002)

V. Della Sala, 'Modernization and welfare restructuring in Italy: the impact on child care', in S. Michel and R. Mahon (eds), *Child Care Policy at the Crossroads. Gender and Welfare State Restructuring* (New York/London: Routledge, 2002), 171–189

R. di Pol, *L'istruzione infantile in Italia. Dal Risorgimento alla Riforma Moratti* (Turin: Marco Valerio, 2005)

H. Göhlich, *Reggiopädagogik – Innovative Pädagogik heute. Zur Theorie und Praxis der kommunalen Kindertagesstätten von Reggio Emilia* (Frankfurt am Main: R.G. Fischer Verlag, 1988)

B. Guidetti Serra and F. Santanera (eds), *Il paese dei celestini. Istituti di Assistenza sotto processo* (Turin: Einaudi, 1973)

Istituto Nazionale di Statistica (Istat), *Annuario Statistico Italiano* (Rome: 2007)

M. Melino, *Scuola dell'Infanzia e progetto educativo. Gli Orientamenti del '9l. Lettura critica e commento analitico-sistematico* (Milan: Editrice Theorema Libri, 1999)

D. Novacco, *La scuola materna tra politica ed economia* (Rome: Editore Armando Armando, 1977)

A. Pinnelli, *La scuola materna negli anni '80. Riflessioni suggerite da un'analisi statistico demografico* (Rome: Università degli studi di Roma "La Sapienza", 1983)

C. Piscopo and F. Fusaro, *L'istruzione in Italia. Due percorsi di lettura* (Salerno: Edisud, 2003)

M. Soltendieck, 'Italien', in P. Oberhuemer and M. Ulich (eds), *Kinderbetreuung in Europa. Tageseinrichtungen und pädagogisches Personal. Eine Bestandsaufnahme in den Ländern der Europäischen Union* (Weinheim and Basel: Beltz Verlag, 1997), 163–181

R. Trifiletti, 'La politica della famiglia e la politica per l'infanzia oggi in Italia', in Comune di Firenze/ Gruppo Nazionale Nidi Infanzia (eds), *Percorsi educativi di qualità per le bambine e i bambini in Italia e in Europa* (Azzano San Paolo: Edizioni Junior, 2003), 117–136

6

Public and Private: the History of Early Education and Care Institutions in the United Kingdom*

Helen Penn

1 Introduction

The history of early education and care institutions in the United Kingdom reflects broader debates and trends in education and in society more generally. Social class has been, and continues to be, a powerful influence shaping provision.

A key question has concerned the values and function of education. Should the education system focus on delivering and regulating the transmission of reading, writing and arithmetic (the 3 'R's) to the poor; or should it be more ambitious, a universal service for all children based on concepts of self-development and mutual citizenship? In an editorial of 23 January 1926 the *Times Educational Supplement* remarked presciently that 'the national love of individual liberty responds to the appeal that children be allowed freedom for development, yet ingrained prudence prompts the demand that proof shall be forthcoming of money spent'. Alexander, writing 75 years later, argues little has changed. Education in England has always been parsimonious in outlook. Primary education, he claims, 'remains in some respects as it was a century ago deeply paternalistic, utilitarian and suspicious of change generated from within' (Alexander, 2000, p. 128). Since state education was grudgingly provided, and for much of its history has focused on keeping poor children off the streets and on delivering rudimentary literacy and numeracy skills, the middle and upper classes paid for an alternative system (confusingly called public schools) where more liberal traditions were followed (Cooter, 1992).

Social class also shaped views about the provision of childcare. The perception of the role of women and the nature of their obligations towards their children has always depended on income and class. If adequate arrangements – usually nannies or servants – could be made, it was entirely a private affair if a mother chose to work or otherwise occupy herself, and she was without blame. But if she were too poor to make such arrangements, she was regarded as feckless if she did not look after her children properly herself. Until relatively recently, day nurseries were regarded as places of last resort, used by poor working mothers or by inadequate mothers who could not care for their children themselves.

A third theme, especially in the first half of the twentieth century, was the empire. For example, The National League for Health, Maternity and Child Welfare made a film about the work of Infant Welfare centres with the title of *'Empire Builders'*.[1] Maintaining the glory of the empire and servicing its extremities shaped ideas about welfare and learning. 'Character-training', not to whine in the face of hardship, was a fundamental tenet for those in boys' public schools (Leinster-Mackay, 1984). The preoccupation with empire was also played out in innumerable discussions about race and eugenics. The Times newspaper published the annual reports of Sir George Newman, Chief Medical Officer to the Board of Education, who thundered that 'healthy motherhood, healthy infancy, and systematic medical supervision at school' were essential for the betterment of the nation (*Times Educational Supplement,* 5 January 1915). The empire has gone, but its aftermath remains; a preoccupation with physical robustness, immigration, diversity and religion which now pervades institutional provision for children of all ages.

It is within the framework of these debates, about the purpose of education, and the role of the family, especially that of mothers, and the existence and aftermath of empire, overlaid by the dominance of social class, that institutional development for young children has occurred. It is also the contention of this chapter that in the late twentieth and early twenty-first centuries in the United Kingdom a new imperative has been introduced; the development of institutions for young children now reflects above all the logic (or illogic) of the marketplace, and the neoliberal agenda.

2   Nursery education for the middle classes

In the absence of any English state interest in nursery education provision, the earliest initiatives in nursery education and nursery care were initiated by middle-class women who took up the ideas of well-known educationalists like Fröbel or Montessori.

Friedrich Fröbel, whose kindergarten movement was supported throughout Europe, was also influential in England. He believed that children should have freedom to play. His kindergartens were places where children's 'innate spiritual responsiveness' to nature could be developed, using a series of 'gifts' or play materials. In kindergarten children were unobtrusively guided by a 'mother made conscious', a professional, trained mother-figure. This concept drew on a sentimentalised view of motherhood (Steedman, 1988) but nevertheless offered women new career opportunities. The Girls' Public Day School Company, established in 1872, whose aim was to 'promote the establishment of good, cheap day schools for all classes', realised the potential career opening for women as kindergarten teachers. By 1878 all its 17 schools had kindergarten and infant classes based on Fröbelian ideas (Smart, 1982).

In 1884 a band of dedicated ladies formed the Froebel Society. By 1902, the Froebel Society offered a Froebel elementary certificate, and directly supported five kindergartens, and subsequently a network of training colleges. The aims of the society eventually broadened from the provision of Froebel kindergartens and training to endeavouring to 'educate the public on all matters concerning young children' and to 'bring together and promote better understanding between teachers (of all grades), parents, doctors, officials and all others interested in education' (Liebscher, 1991).

Maria Montessori is another well-known figure in the field of nursery education and her private nursery movement still exists under the title '*Montessori International*'. But in the 1920s and 1930s there were other, more radical experiments with nursery education in the private sector than those offered by Fröbel or Montessori. Bertrand Russell and his wife Dora set up an experimental school, Beacon Hill, inspired by the new 'science' of psychoanalysis, somewhat contradictorily mixed with behaviouristic ideas about regular training to inculcate good moral habits. The overriding idea was that repressing emotions and feelings in children would prove destructive in later life. Sexual repression was particularly deplored: 'education consists in the cultivation of the instincts, not in their suppression'. Russell spelt out his ideas in a book entitled *On Education – Especially in Early Childhood*, first published in 1926 and frequently reprinted over the next 30 years. He argued that the rich were at liberty – in fact had a duty – to pave the way for others in their experiments. He acknowledged his debt to Maria Montessori but argued that Montessori was too strict in forbidding children imaginative play and games (Russell, 1926).

Bertrand Russell was part of a wider group of similar radicals, many of whose experimental schools and teaching methods were chronicled in the journal, the *New Era*, coedited by the arch-radical, A. S. Neill of Summerhill, whose own school was run on ultra-democratic lines, children having an equal say to adults (Neill, 1990/1928). Beatrix Tudor-Hart, who had trained in Vienna and been on the staff of Beacon Hill, opened her cooperative nursery school at Fortis Green in the 1930s (after an eviction from her first premises, prompted by her irate neighbours in Hampstead complaining about the noise). Fortis Green was 'the first school in the country owned and controlled jointly by parents and teachers' (Tudor-Hart and Landau, 1938).

Perhaps the most famous of the radical nursery experiments was Malting House School in the 1930s, philanthropically supported, and run by Susan Isaacs, a leading psychologist (and later Kleinian psychoanalyst). This was also a school for the young children of professionals – mainly academics. One-third of the children were residential. The regime was inspired by the theories of the psychoanalyst, Melanie Klein, about childhood aggression and repression, and the need fully to express emotion. The job of the wise adult was to chronicle every nuanced step each child took on his or her emotional and intellectual journey. The school became legendary for the freedom it allowed to children, and reporters clustered on the doorstep for salacious copy. Susan Isaacs' own tone was more sober. She scrupulously observed the young children under her care, and subsequently wrote two highly regarded, and still cited, books about this experience (Isaacs, 1929; Isaacs, 1930). She became a highly influential lecturer on child development and nursery education at the Institute of Education, London and influenced many generations of teachers working in the state sector (Gardner, 1969).

3   Nursery education for the poor

Whilst Froebelian and Montessori-style kindergartens were becoming established for the middle classes, and the rich were at liberty to experiment, the poor were crammed into elementary schools. Schools in effect offered a free babysitting service to hard-pressed working-class parents. By the end of the nineteenth century, three- and four-year-olds had been admitted in considerable numbers to the cavernous Victorian primary schools. They sat alongside their elder brothers and sisters, in tiered rows, subject to the same rigid, didactic teaching. Katharine Bathurst, an Inspector for the Board of Education, in a famous report first published in 1905, castigated this system:

> Let us now follow the baby of three years through part of one day of school life. He is placed on a hard wooden seat with a desk in front of him ... he is told to fold his arms and keep quiet.... He is surrounded by a large number of babies all under similar alarming and incomprehensible conditions.... A certified teacher has 60 babies to instruct, many of whom are hungry, cold and dirty ... they are heavy eyed with unslept sleep ... what possible good is there in forcing a little child to master the names of letters and numbers at this age? The strain on teachers is terrific. (cited in Van der Eyken, 1973)

The result of this campaigning was at first simply to exclude young children from school. In 1907 funding was withdrawn for children under five in infant schools. The ineffectiveness of providing bulk education, without any attention to the physical conditions and social circumstances of the pupils, was raised by many social campaigners, including members of the Independent Labour Party, most notably Margaret McMillan, who argued forcefully for separate nursery schools (Steedman, 1990). In 1918 the Education Bill enabled LEAs (Local Education Authorities) to provide 'practical instruction suitable to the ages, capacities and circumstances of the children'. Section 19 of the Bill gave LEAs:

> the power to make arrangements as may be approved by the Board of Education for a) supplying or aiding the supply of nursery schools for children over two and under five years of age, whose home conditions are such that attendance at such a school is necessary or desirable for their healthy physical and mental development and b) attending to the health, nourishment and physical welfare of children attending nursery schools. (BAECE archives)

Activists like Margaret McMillan did their best to interpret the bill as a go-ahead for nursery education. But the wording of the bill did not voice the curricular concerns of the Froebel Society or other radicals; rather it reflected the decision, in 1907, to introduce systematic medical inspection in schools. As mentioned above, for 27 years the Chief Medical Officer, Sir George Newman, expressed his robust views in a series of annual reports to the Board of Education. Schools, especially those for young children, should promote good health. Children were stunted and unfit for service in the army, or for service in the colonies. Margaret McMillan helped draft the Labour Party response to the 1918 bill, echoing Newman's concerns. 'What young children require is fresh air, play and rest, and this is what the nursery school offers them. The development of nursery schools would tend greatly to raise the standard of physical health among the children' (BAECE archives).

Provision, however, was sparse and by 1939 even the radical London County Council had provided only five nursery schools and given financial assistance to 18 others maintained by voluntary organisations (Jackson, 1965). A few northern authorities made a splash. In February 1932, Accrington Road Nursery in Burnley was opened by George Newman himself. The building (which was still in use until very recently) was beautifully designed with spacious classrooms, large windows leading onto verandas where children could rest, a large walled garden and a smart kitchen.[2]

In 1923 the NSA (Nursery Schools Association) was formed to campaign for more nursery schools. It produced a series of pamphlets on nursery education, some of which sold more than 200,000 copies, such was the popular demand. In an authoritative policy statement of 1927 the NSA argued that children of nursery school age (2–7) 'should be put into the immediate care of fully qualified teachers specially trained for their work'. The essential of the curriculum was free activity:

> Underlying all mental and bodily development lies the need for free activity. Without it neither healthy growth of body and spirit, nor training in self-control is possible…. Free activity involves the provision of spontaneous and purposeful activity in spacious open-air conditions…as well as an atmosphere of love, joy and freedom…the daily routine must provide for the right alternation of rest and activity through the day…it is undesirable to accept the hours of the ordinary school day as the limit for nursery school (NSA, 1927)

Despite this vigorous campaigning, by 1933 there were still only 55 nursery schools, catering for some 4,500 children. Thirty of these were provided directly by LEAs and 25 by voluntary organisations which received some public financial support. The Hadow Committee on Infant and Nursery Schools, which reported to the Board of Education in 1933, also emphasised the importance of growth, nutrition, a proper balance of exercise and rest, and open air play. It concluded that: 'it seems highly desirable that (nursery education) should be developed separately (from school) and be left free to perfect its methods and to fulfil its special purpose' (Board of Education, 1933).

However, times were hard, and nursery schools were expensive, so the committee cautiously recommended expansion only for poor urban areas. This provoked an outcry from the NSA. Its members had long argued that nursery education should be for 'every child'; it should not be seen as a special remedial service for the poor (NSA, 1935). The numbers of nursery schools crept up. By 1939 there were 118 nursery schools; together with under-fives in infant schools they catered for 180,000 children.

4 Childcare for mothers

There was also a long-established tradition, in the upper and middle classes, of employing nannies for young children. These nannies were mainly working-class girls, for whom looking after children was a form of domestic service, although, as Gathorne-Hardy points out, nannies were entrusted with the upbringing and education of the young children in their care (Gathorne-Hardy, 1972). For those families serving abroad in the empire, who did not want their children to be brought up in what they saw as difficult or unhealthy parts of the world, there were a handful of 'Babies' Hotels', highly respected and respectable private children's homes that took children from babyhood to school age on a residential basis. They were used mainly by colonial and armed forces families, before children were sent on to preparatory and boarding schools. They also doubled up as training institutions for nannies. For example Miss Ethel Moon, the matron of a well-known Babies' Hotel, ran an advice column for several years in the 1920s in *Nursery World*, originally a magazine for mothers who used nannies (and still in print as a weekly magazine for all those concerned with early education and childcare). Miss Moon dispensed practical advice on looking after young children, and on the proper training of nannies.

However, for the poor, who could not afford nannies, or boarding schools, and whose relatives could not help out, day nurseries were the only solution. The NSDN (National Society of Day Nurseries) had been founded in 1906 to set standards and register day nurseries and crèches. It described itself as 'the only voluntary body specifically devoted to the problem of the care of young children whose mothers go out to work'. By 1914, 80 day nurseries were recognized, many of them mill nurseries. The Board of Education gave grants of four pence per child per week, but in 1919 the Ministry of Health assumed responsibility and gave 50 percent block grants. The officers of the Society met in the drawing rooms of Piccadilly, and held fund-raising balls at the Carlton Club, the bastion of the Establishment. Despite their fashionable charitable image, members of the NSDN made serious efforts to support the training of girls for nursery work, and to raise standards of private day nurseries and crèches. They felt seriously threatened by the NSA. In 1932 the Society realised that 'it was losing ground to the Nursery Schools Association... it was felt that the Ladies on the Committee, although deeply interested in Child Welfare work, could not be considered as expert authorities' (NSDN, 1932).

5 Wartime

World War II was a watershed in the history of early childhood institutions. The war brought those campaigning for nursery schools, those campaigning for day nurseries, and the voluntary movements like the Froebel society closer together, but also exacerbated their differences. At the beginning of the war, a joint statement by the Ministry of Health and the Board of Education urged the provision of nursery centres for billeted mothers and evacuee children – to be staffed if possible by voluntary workers. The Treasury, fearing demands for a massive expansion of nursery education, withheld funding. By 1941 it was obvious that more needed to be done to encourage women workers in industry. There was (familiar) confusion between the various ministries as to who should fund and supervise the expansion of provision. It was finally agreed that local authorities should make provision, while the Ministry of Health would fund and regulate the expansion. Once funds were agreed by the end of 1941, 194 nurseries were set up, and another 284 were in the pipeline. By the end of the war there were 1,450 wartime nurseries, each open for children from birth to five, from 7 am to 7 pm. Their cost was estimated at £10 million over the course of the war (Ferguson and Fitzgerald, 1954).

What should these nurseries be doing with children? 'Strong and divergent views were held on the scope of a nursery's work, its aims and its methods, and on the complementary question of how a nursery should be staffed' (Ferguson and Fitzgerald, 1954, p. 93). Both the NSA and the NSDN, which changed its name to NSCN (National Society of Children's Nurseries) to cover wartime residential nurseries, were asked to prepare expansion plans, and make suggestions about staffing and curriculum. The work of the NSCN in training nannies and nursery workers led to the establishment in 1945 of the NNEB (Nursery Nurse Examination Board) which still operates today as the main accreditation agency for non-teaching staff working with young children. The NSA, supported by the National Union of Teachers (NUT), resolutely demanded that trained teachers should be in charge of any nursery, whether it offered education or daycare. During the war the chairman of NSCN agreed to work with NSA providing they signed a joint memorandum of cooperation: 'Neither NSA nor NSCN will in public or in private attack the policy of the other'.[3] The respective chairmen, Major Nathan and Lady Allen, signed the memorandum, but the quarrels continued. The division between nursery nurses and nursery teachers, and their respective remits and remuneration, remains to this day.

6 The postwar consensus: nursery education and the ideas that informed it

Wartime disputes about nurseries had been as much about mothering and women at work as about children. The priority for social policy after the war was to re-establish and support traditional family life. A plethora of organisations, the National Council of Maternity and Child Welfare, the Socialist Medical Association, the National Union of Teachers (NUT), the Fabians, as well as NSA, argued that nursery schools would make a positive contribution to this family life. They could provide mothers with the break they needed from full-time housework, and offer young children an opportunity to work off their aggressive instincts (Riley, 1983).

The psychiatrist John Bowlby, based on his studies of refugee and displaced children for the World Health Organization, and heavily influenced by ethology and animal studies, had also put forward his theory of attachment – that children needed a warm continuous relationship with a mother figure and without it they would be emotionally damaged (Bowlby, 1952). This was widely (mis)interpreted to mean that it was wrong for mothers to work. Nursery schools, rather than day nurseries, were a better option for Government to pursue.

At the end of the war the Board of Education agreed that it would take responsibility for administering nurseries, although the Ministry of Health stipulated that some nurseries at least should be kept open for working mothers. Local authorities received some grant aid, but became directly responsible for their upkeep. By 1947, predictably, 700 nurseries had closed. Some of the remainder became nursery schools; others continued as social services day nurseries. Authorities which had heavy munitions industries, and had therefore provided many day nurseries, kept them as nursery schools; other local authorities simply closed them.

The pedagogical rationale for nursery education increasingly focused on providing outlets for emotion and instinctual expression in young children. Dorothy Gardner, an influential academic (and successor to Susan Isaacs, at the Institute of Education, London University) argued in 1956 that:

> we cannot educate a very unhappy child, or one who is even temporarily in the throes of jealousy, anger or mourning. We are also coming to realise that emotional satisfactions lie at the root of all intellectual interests and that feelings are the driving force between all intellectual effort. (Gardner, 1956, 11)

The influential child psychiatrist Winnicott tried to distinguish between the functions of day nurseries, which he saw as an aid to paediatric care, and the nursery school, whose function was to wean the child socially, and introduce him or her to company after the fundamental but claustrophobic relationship with the mother had been established. On 8 September 1951 he joined in avuncularly to a flurry of letters about nursery education in *The Times*, arguing that:

> Behind the day nursery is urgent need, so that the question of quality is secondary. Behind the nursery school on the other hand, is not so much need as value. Here the idea is to enrich the lives of children who have good homes of their own. The mothers have made a good start and they begin to make use of help...the nursery school justifies its existence only by being well-equipped and by having an enlightened staff trained to meet the individual needs, physical, emotional and educational, of growing small children. (Winnicott, 1951)

Winnicott also served on a UNESCO committee, which in 1951 published a report entitled *Mental Hygiene in the Nursery School*. This international committee of experts concluded that 'it is to such schools that we must look in future for the majority of theoretical and practical advances in nursery education as a whole' (UNESCO, 1953).

But by now there was a new theoretical giant on the scene – Jean Piaget – and rationales for nursery education again began to shift. At the 1960 NSA conference, W. D. Wall (previously working for UNESCO, then, successively, Director of National Foundation for Educational

Research, and Dean of the Institute of Education, University of London) gave a speech entitled 'The Enrichment of Childhood'. He argued that intellectual stimulation of young children was the proper role of nursery education: 'if we could raise by as little as five per cent the average operational intellectual effectiveness of our population, we would have no further immediate troubles in terms of shortage of highly skilled manpower' (NSA and Wall, 1960).

The Government, influenced by these views, and interested by the new approaches to education raised by Piaget, commissioned the Central Advisory Council for Education to produce a report on *Children and Their Primary Schools*. Bridget Plowden, the wife of a senior civil servant, was appointed chairperson. The Plowden Report, as it became known, included nursery education. It endorsed the theories of Jean Piaget about the child as an individual, self-propelled scientist experimenting with the world. It highlighted educational inequalities, except that working-class children were no longer characterised as physically stunted or unable to control their fierce emotional lives. They were now intellectually stunted, and the job of the nursery and primary school was to reawaken intellectual curiosity (Central Advisory Committee for Education, 1967). But Plowden was hostile to working mothers, and the report maintained that it was no business of the state to provide services for working parents. Nursery education, from then on (as it still is today) became a very part-time service, with the more limited objective of fostering children's intellectual development. The hours of nursery education became shorter than those of any other comparable European country – between 12 and 15 hours per week.

In 1972 Margaret Thatcher, Secretary of State for Education and Science, issued a white paper that firmly endorsed the educational approach and commitment to nursery education set out in the Plowden Report. In Circular 2/73, the Government committed itself to providing 250,000 new nursery places within 10 years, for 35 percent of three-year-olds and for 75 percent of four-year-olds and, surprisingly, an additional 15 per cent of full-time places. Urban aid would be used to fund the first tranche of nursery places, and some local authorities drew up plans for expansion (DES, 1973).

7 Too little too late

Whilst the Government had been deliberating about if and when it should provide nursery education, and who for, the shortage of nursery education places had prompted a mother, herself a teacher, called Belle Tutaev, to set up a campaign for more nursery education by encouraging mothers to start their own schools or playgroups on a voluntary or cooperative basis (*Guardian Woman's Page*, 25 August 1961). Various charitable organisations such as Save the Children already provided playgroups, that is, small local groups partly run by volunteers for two or three mornings a week for local children. The PPA (Pre-school Playgroups Association, now the Pre-school Learning Association), founded in 1961, is an example of an uncomfortable alliance between those pressing for better state provision and those advocating self-help, even if self-help meant accepting lower standards and operating outside the state sector. The relationship of the playgroup movement with nursery education was always difficult. In October 1970, an editorial in the PPA monthly *Contact* stated that 'it was once feared that PPA might weaken the case by providing nursery education on the cheap. In fact PPA may have helped shame the Government into its first activity for years.'

By the late 1970s, the PPA had commandeered the good and great to argue its case for being better than nursery education. Leading educationists, including Wall and Halsey (1978), and even Wall praised the contribution of playgroups to community life. Bridget Plowden was the most famous supporter of PPA, declaring that 'if I knew then what I know now' her report would have supported playgroups rather than nursery education (Plowden, 1983). Plowden portrayed 'parents' (meaning mothers) as lacking in confidence and in need of learning how to accept 'responsibility' for their children, a responsibility that they might otherwise cede to professionals. Playgroups, she argued, offered mothers an opportunity to contribute to the daily life of their children in a way that nursery schools could not (although Plowden herself had used nannies and boarding schools like any respectable upper-class parent). This assumption of maternal involvement through volunteering was implicitly – and sometimes explicitly – based on a traditional view of domesticity, in which women stayed at home to look after their children. Indeed, looking after children was their prime – if not always fulfilling – function. As one contributor to *Contact* reported in October 1965: 'I seem to be fighting a battle between the part of me that is determined not to be a domestic cabbage and the part that wants to do well the job of looking after husband, children and home'. For such middle-class, full-time housewives playgroups fitted the bill exactly. For the working classes, especially employed mothers, they were more problematic.

8 Outside the consensus: the status of day nurseries

Working mothers and their children were an unpopular cause. Simon Yudkin, a paediatrician, working closely with NSCN, tried to raise the issue, first in a book entitled *Working Mothers and Their Children* (1963) and secondly in a committee report for NSCN entitled *The Care of Pre-school Children* (1967), which was supported by some 30 organisations concerned with children. Yudkin detailed the large numbers of (mainly working-class) women who worked and the lack of childcare they faced. He said that there was no evidence for the common view, ascribed to Bowlby, that working mothers harmed their children. The report gave comparative statistics of different kinds of provision. In 1965 there were 448 LEA day nurseries offering 21,396 places; 2,245 private nurseries (mainly small factory and other workplace nurseries) offering 55,543 places; and 3,393 registered childminders offering an estimated 27,200 places. Only 30,000 places were available in nursery schools (although another 200,000 four-year-olds had started school early), and a further 4,500 children were in independent nursery schools – Montessori and other kinds of kindergartens. Only two percent of children aged three and four had access to state nursery education; and, out of a total population of 2,750,000 under-fives, only 11 percent of all children had any kind of out-of-home care. Yudkin and his committee recommended a proper government investigation into what they considered was an intolerable situation, which weighed heavily upon poor families, and in particular upon black children. The proportion of black working mothers, particularly from Afro-Caribbean backgrounds, was far higher than that of any other group.

But the prevailing ideology was too strong; mothers should stay at home with their children. The NSCN finally gave up its struggle for existence. In 1973, the executive of the NSCN sent a letter to all local authorities stating that:

> it is with mixed feelings that we report to you the passing of a great voluntary society which has led a continuous existence from 1906 to the present day...we have persistently endeavoured to publicize the value of nurseries to the public...we hope that day nurseries, whatever form they take, will be given due place in the future planning of provision for the pre-school child. (NSCN Letter to Directors of Social Services, September 1973, in BAECE Archives)

The economic crisis of 1973 led to widespread cutbacks in public expenditure. David Owen, the then Labour Minister for Health, advanced the view that nursery education – and any other form of childcare – could be achieved through 'low-cost daycare', that is reliance on playgroups. For those women who were obliged to work, childminders were the solution. At a notorious seminar in Sunningdale in 1976, he praised the 'non-professionals'. Playgroups and childminders were now portrayed, for the first time officially, as warm, homely and mothering, just the qualities a young child needed. Nursery education expansion was finished; day nurseries were an unnecessary expense on the public purse (DHSS, 1976).

There were protests. Jack Tizard, a paediatrician and professor at the Thomas Coram Research Unit and the University of London Institute of Education, and the distinguished team of researchers he gathered around him, produced a steady stream of research that argued that the Sunningdale approach was fundamentally wrong. 'Low-cost daycare' was no more than a euphemism for poor-quality provision, and an evasion of state responsibility for a necessary public service (DHSS, 1976). Tizard was a leading contributor to an OECD report, published in 1982, which carefully dismantled ideas about 'low-cost' and argued for sustained investment in coordinated education and care provision – a report which many contributing countries (but not the United Kingdom) took to heart (Tizard, 1982). The NUT and a few Labour LEAs continued arguing against the grain for nursery education (NUT, 1977).

The next Conservative Government in 1979 commissioned the distinguished psychologist Jerome Bruner to review the kinds of early years provision available. Bruner was critical of the relatively limited resourcing of playgroups and childminding, but added his weighty opinion to the position that support should be given to the voluntary sector rather than to a professionally delivered system of nursery education. 'No long term benefit could accrue by making early pre-school care seem like the domain of professionals. It would surely have a corrosive effect on the self-confidence of parents and reduce volunteer efforts' (Bruner, 1980).

The few local authority day nurseries that still existed, catering for about 1 percent of children, became places of last resort for dysfunctional families, and available only on a referral basis from social workers. In order to gain a place, mothers had to portray themselves as being inadequate and unable to cope with family responsibilities. These day nurseries, traditionally open for children aged 0–5 (5 being school starting age) also restricted the age and times at which children could attend. Babies were rarely allowed, and other children had limited access, because to allow otherwise was to undermine mothers' responsibilities.

9   Mothers at work again

In 1980 a group of feminists launched an organisation called the NCCC (National Childcare Campaign). Building on the work of local grass-roots campaigns, the NCCC argued that if women had the same access and entitlements to work as men, and the same income, then the problem of depressed and un-self-confident mothering would largely disappear. Men did not automatically become depressed and lacking in self-confidence by dint of being fathers. Gender inequalities (and racial inequalities) had been blurred or ignored; the problems of mothering, whilst real enough, had been mostly misdiagnosed and mistreated. Financially supported by the EOC (Equal Opportunities Commission), NCCC argued that the answer was a more comprehensive childcare system, funded, if not directly provided, by the state. In a closely argued discussion paper, *Childcare for All*, it outlined the case for a system which would benefit children – good nurseries, offering both education *and* care for the children of working parents, and staffed by well-trained women and men. Such nurseries would be flexible, community-run, and would involve volunteers or work-sharing if that seemed appropriate to the communities involved (NCCC, 1985). NCCC also worked with the CRE (Commission for Racial Equality) to draw attention to the racial inequalities that nursery provision would have to address in an increasingly diverse and multicultural society.

Community nurseries began to spring up, grant-aided by a few enterprising local authorities, most notably the GLC (Greater London Council). The DHSS (Department for Health and Social Security), which still held responsibility for all non-education provision for young children, had become interested in the community nursery idea, as a token towards the new gender agendas. As part of a wider voluntary sector programme, it financed a reluctant NCCC to establish a group of community nurseries (Department of Health, 1988). The NCCC felt its radical campaigning stance might be jeopardised by this offer, and set up a parallel organisation, the DCT (Daycare Trust), to run its DHSS programme. DCT, toned down from its NCCC days, has since become one of the most influential advocacy groups today for childcare and for a woman's agenda.

The Thatcher and Major governments were pursuing other changes in education. The Plowden Report was disgraced, because of its support for 'progressive teaching'.[4] A more formal curriculum was reintroduced and a new inspection regime, Ofsted (Office for Standards in Education), established. Education was marketised, and made internally competitive;

league tables were produced to compare schools' performance, and those schools that underperformed and did not attract pupils faced closure. Within this marketised framework, a voucher system was introduced entitling all four-year-olds to nursery education. Nursery education was defined minimally in terms of a set number of hours, a prescribed curriculum anticipating the 3Rs of formal schooling, and a satisfactory Ofsted inspection (School Curriculum and Assessment Authority, 1996). Nursery education did not have to be delivered within the state education system; private and voluntary bodies could equally well provide it. The voucher system resulted in primary schools rushing to admit four-year-olds to reception classes, in order to claim the voucher monies. The overwhelming majority of four-year-olds are now admitted directly to primary schools, a similar situation to the one to which Katharine Bathurst had so objected a hundred years earlier.

10   New wine in old bottles?

In 1997 the Labour government took power with what purported to be a radical agenda. The Government accepted the gender equality arguments. Women could and should work. Young children were important, the future of the nation; all children would be entitled to nursery education and poor children would have extra help. Race discrimination had no place in a civilized society. Much more money would be made available to support new developments. But essentially the institutional structures remained unchanged, and the division between very part-time nursery education and day nurseries remained. There were a plethora of short-term funded initiatives with catchy names grafted onto the existing systems. Sure Start, Centres of Early Excellence, Beacon Schools, Neighbourhood Nurseries, Early Years Development and Care Partnerships, New Opportunities Fund, and many others came, and after three years or so disappeared again, partly because they were less successful than anticipated, and partly because Government priorities rapidly shifted. At one point there were over 40 different funding streams for confused practitioners to try to tap (National Audit Commission, 2004, 2006).

But to step back and see this whirlwind activity in historical context, in many respects very little has changed. It is true that at a national level there have been some shifts. Regionalisation means that England, Scotland, Wales and Northern Ireland have been free to pursue somewhat different domestic agendas, and policies on early childhood are slightly different in each region. Within England, at a national administrative level, there have been several reorganisations of ministries, and all children's services are nominally under the new Department for Children, Schools and Families (previously the Department for Education and Skills). But the old divisions remain, and the same, unresolved debates are still taking place. Nursery education for children aged 3–4 is still very part-time, school-based, delivered by teachers, free at the point of use and is a supply-led system, although all children now have guaranteed access. In extending the system to three-year-olds, the Government has relied almost entirely on the private sector for places, much as the Tories did for four-year-olds in the 1990s. Most four-year-olds are now in schools, in regular primary classrooms, subject to a basic regime of literacy and numeracy. Childcare for the children aged 0–5 of working parents is provided in day nurseries outside the school system, delivered mainly by nursery nurses with basic vocational qualifications. It is still a parental responsibility to select and pay for the day nursery care, although a state subsidy child-care tax credit system helps them meet the costs. The pay, training, and conditions of employment of teachers and nursery nurses are controlled and regulated by different bodies. Children are still likely to experience many different kinds of provision before they start school, depending on their age, location and mothers' circumstances – sometimes four or five changes before starting school (Skinner, 2003).

In the absence of universal provision, class divisions and social stratification persist. There are separate targeted programmes for poor children, focusing on parental training, even although their effectiveness is in doubt (Rutter, 2006). Sure Start has now metamorphosed into Sure Start Children's Centres, but remains a programme aimed at the poor. Social mobility in the United Kingdom is lower now than it has been for many years, and schooling as well as early education and care tends to be socially and racially stratified (Vincent, 2006). Poverty levels, although falling slightly when the Labour Government first came to power, are still unacceptably high. One in six or seven of all children lives in poverty (Brewer, Muriel, Goodman and Sibieta, 2007). Ethnic minorities, especially refugee and asylum-seeking families, have less access to childcare (Bell, Bryan, Barnes and O'Shea, 2005).

However, in one sense at least there have been profound changes. The Government, following a neoliberal economic agenda, has retreated from public provision, in early education and care services, as for all public services (Ball, 2007). The Government takes the view that private services are invariably more efficient and more flexible than publicly provided services. In early education and childcare services it has increasingly relied on the private sector for expansion of provision, through a public subsidy system to private operators. In poorer areas, where private firms are less willing to invest, the Government has also provided capital, as well as revenue, subsidies. The Minister for Competitiveness announced in 2007 that, in all cases, private and voluntary operators should be given preference over local authority provision:

> Local authorities are "providers of last resort." It is a condition of Government funding that local authorities must consult, and consider using, PVI sector providers in their area when planning the development of new children's centres.
>
> We need a fair system for providers in the private, voluntary and independent sectors for funding the free entitlement for three and four year olds. It would make no sense to have one set of funding rules for PVI providers delivering the free entitlement, and another for those in the public sector – particularly when over 80 per cent of all childcare is delivered by PVI providers and a third of children access their free (nursery education) entitlement in PVI settings.[5]

The result of an economic policy which offers subsidies to the private sector has been to attract large corporations and private equity companies into the child-care and education market. Many child-care places are now provided by market chains, whose shares can be bought on the stock market (Penn, 2007). The Government has a regulatory system in place for early education and care which specifies a curriculum, staffing ratios and training, and minimum health and safety standards. But increasingly the format of nursery education and child-care is being determined from outside the United Kingdom, by multinational companies (*Forbes Magazine*, September 2007).

The European Union (1997) and the Organization for Economic Co-operation and Development (OECD, 2006) have both issued reports comparing the system of early education and childcare in the United Kingdom adversely with other European and economically advanced countries. The essence of these criticisms is that, in order to be equitable, the system has to be publicly funded (if not publicly provided) and deliver a separate and coherent system of education and care – neither watered-down schooling nor a commercial baby park. In the United Kingdom we have seen a century of intense but unsuccessful effort towards such goals, until, finally, they have been abandoned.

Notes

*Many organisations have changed their names over the period covered in this historical account. The Nursery Schools Association, NSA, changed its name to the British Association for Nursery Education (BAECE) and subsequently, in the 1990s, to Early Learning. The National Society for Day Nurseries changed its name to the National Society for Children's Nurseries. Their joint archives are stored in the BAECE collection at the British Library of Political and Economic Sciences, BLPES, London. The Board of Education became the Ministry of Education, then the Department for Education and Science (DES), then Department for Education and Employment (DfEE) and, most recently, Department for Children, Schools and Families (DfCSF). The nomenclature used in this article is the one which was valid at the time of publication of the cited sources.

1. BAECE Archives.
2. Source: Archives of the County Borough of Burnley, *Procedures for the Official Opening of Accrington Rd Nursery School*, 26 February 1932.
3. Letter from Major Nathan to Lady Allen, 30 June 1943 (BAECE Archives).
4. 'Plowden's Progress', *Economist*, 20 June 1998, pp. 31–35.
5. From a speech given by S. Timms at the International Centre for the Study of the Mixed Economy of Childcare (*www.uel.ac.uk/icmec*).

Bibliography

R. Alexander, *Culture and Pedagogy* (Oxford: Blackwell, 2000)

S. Ball, *Education plc: Understanding Private Sector Participation in Public Sector Education* (London: Routledge, 2007)

A. Bell, C. Bryan, M. Barnes and R. O'Shea, *Use of Childcare Amongst Families from Ethnic Minority Backgrounds* (London: DfEE, 2005)

Board of Education, *Report of the Consultative Committee on Infant and Nursery Schools* (London: HMSO, 1933)

J. Bowlby, *Maternal Care and Mental Health* (Geneva: WHO, 1952)

M. Brewer, A. Goodman, A. Muriel and L. Sibieta, *Poverty and Inequality in the UK: 2007* (London: Institute for Fiscal Studies, 2007)

J. Bruner, *Under Fives in Britain* (London: Grant McIntyre, 1980)

Central Advisory Committee for Education, *Children and Their Primary Schools: A Report of the Central Advisory Council for Education (England)* (London: HMSO, 1967)

R. Cooter (ed.), *In the Name of the Child: Health and Welfare 1880–1940* (London: Routledge, 1992)

Department of Education and Science, *Nursery Education, DES Circular 2/73, 31 January 1973* (London: DES, 1973)

Department for Health and Social Security, *Low Cost Day Provision for the Under Fives. Papers of a Conference held at the Civil Service College, Sunningdale Park, 9–10 January 1976* (London: DHSS, 1976)

Department of Health Under Fives Initiative, *Final Report* (London: DoH, 1988)

European Union, *Quality Indicators in Services for Young Children* (Brussels: EU, DV5, 1997)

S. Ferguson and H. Fitzgerald, *History of the Second World War: Studies in Social Services* (London: HMSO, 1954)

D. Gardner, *The Education of Young Children* (London: Methuen, 1956)

D. Gardner, *Susan Isaacs* (London: Methuen, 1969)

J. Gathorne-Hardy, *The Rise and Fall of the British Nanny* (London: Hodder and Stoughton, 1972)

S. Isaacs, *Intellectual Growth in Young Children* (London: Routledge, 1930)

S. Isaacs, *The Nursery Years: The Mind of the Child from Birth to Six Years* (London: Routledge, 1929)

E. Jackson, *Achievement: A Short History of the LCC* (London: Longmans, 1965)

Labour Party, *Nursery Schools. Memorandum prepared by the Advisory Committee on Education* (Labour Party, 1919)

D. Leinster-Mackay, *The Rise of the English Prep School* (London: Falmer, 1984)

J. Liebscher, *Foundations of Progressive Education: The History of the National Froebel Society* (Cambridge: Lutterworth Press, 1991)

National Audit Commission, *Early Years: Progress in Developing High Quality Childcare and Early Education Accessible to All* (London: HMSO, 2004)

National Audit Commission, *Sure Start Children's Centres* (London: HMSO, 2006)

National Childcare Campaign, *Childcare for All* (London: NCCC, 1985)

NCCC, *The Do-it-Yourself Nursery* (London: NCCC, 1980)

NSA, *Memorandum on the Educational Needs of Children Under Seven years of Age* (London: NSA, 1935)

NSA, *Nursery School Education. Statement of Policy* (London: NSA, 1927)

NSA and D. Wall, NSA Annual Conference Keynote speech 1960 (BAECE archives)

NSCN, *Minutes, Extraordinary General Meeting, 24 November 1932* (BAECE archives)

A. S. Neill, *Summerhill – A Radical Approach to Education* (London: Penguin, 1990, originally 1928)

NUT, *The Needs of the Under Fives* (London: NUT, 1977)

OECD, *Starting Strong: Thematic Review of Early Childhood Education and Care* (Paris: OECD, 2001)

H. Penn, 'Childcare Market Management: How the United Kingdom Government has Reshaped its Role in Developing Early Childhood Education and Care', *Contemporary Issues in Early Childhood*, 8 (2007) 192–207

B. Plowden, *Presidential Address* (London: PPA, 1983)

D. Riley, *War in the Nursery* (London: Virago, 1983)

B. Russell, *On Education, Especially in Early Childhood* (London: Allen and Unwin, 1926)

M. Rutter, 'Is Sure Start an Effective Preventative Intervention?', *Child and Adolescent Mental Health*, 11 (2006) 135–141

School Curriculum and Assessment Authority, *Desirable Learning Outcomes for Children's Learning on Entering Compulsory Education* (London: DfEE/SCAA, 1996)

C. Skinner, *Running Around in Circles: Co-ordinating Childcare, Education and Work* (Bristol: Joseph Rowntree Foundation/Policy Press, 2003)

R. Smart, *Bedford Training College: A History of a Froebel College and its Schools* (Bedford: Bedford Training College Publications Committee, 1982)

C. Steedman, *Childhood, Culture and Class in Britain: Margaret McMillan, 1860–1931* (London: Virago, 1990)

C. Steedman, '"Mother Made Conscious": The Historical Development of a Primary School Pedagogy', in M. Woodhead and A. McGrath (eds), *Family, School and Society* (London: Hodder and Stoughton, 1988), 82–95

J. Tizard, *Children and Society: Issues for Pre-school Reform* (Paris: CERI/OECD, 1982)

B. Tudor-Hart and E. Landau, *Play and Toys in the Nursery* (London: Country Life, 1938)

UNESCO, *Mental Hygiene in the Nursery, Report of a Joint WHO-UNESCO Expert Meeting* (Paris: UNESCO, 1953)

W. Van der Eyken (ed.), *Education, the Child and Society: A Documentary History 1900–1973* (London: Penguin, 1973); K. Bathurst, 'The Need for National Nurseries', *The Nineteenth Century and After*, (1905) 812–824

C. Vincent, *Childcare Choice and Class Practices: Middle Class Parents and their Children* (London: Routledge, 2006)

W. Wall and A. Halsey, *No Man is an Island: Two Speeches from the 17th Annual Conference of the Pre-school Playgroups Association* (Reading: Southern Region Pre-school Playgroups Association, 1978)

D. Winnicott, *Letter to the Times Newspaper, 8 September 1951*

S. Yudkin, *A Report on the Care of Pre-school Children* (London: NSDN, 1967)

S. Yudkin and A. Holme, *Working Mothers and Their Children* (London: Michael Joseph, 1963)

7
Danish Child-Care Policies within Path – Timing, Sequence, Actors and Opportunity Structures

Anette Borchorst

1 Introduction

The challenges from globalisation and ageing populations that all Western countries face have fostered increased interest in integrating women in employment. All over Europe, there is a clear trend towards dual-earner family models. Child care has long constituted a pressing problem, and feminist organisations, unions and particularly leftist political parties have argued for expanding child-care solutions, though with limited success in some countries. The new challenges have accentuated the issue, moving it up on the political agenda both nationally and within the European Union. There is, however, by no means agreement among the member state governments about *who should provide* and *who should pay* for the care of small children, and they have different traditions for *what kind of services* should be provided.

At the Lisbon summit in March 2000, where the European Council discussed how the challenges should be tackled, benchmarks were set for women's employment at 60% in 2010 (Lisbon European Council, 2000). An expert report from 2001 with recommendations for implementing the Lisbon strategy suggested Scandinavian solutions such as affordable child care, parental leave and provisions for work absence when children are ill. They characterised these as win-win solutions that could foster social inclusion and gender equality while improving economic competitiveness at the same time (Esping-Andersen et al., 2002, chapters 2, 3). At the Barcelona summit in March 2000, the heads of government agreed that their countries should remove disincentives for women's employment, and they decided that child care should be provided for at least 90% of children from age 3 to mandatory school age and for at least 33% of children under 3 by 2010 (Barcelona European Council, 2000). There are, however, considerable variations in the level of provision among the present member states (Bahle in this volume; Rostgaard, 2002). Some countries have to devote considerable efforts to meet them, whereas they do not represent appreciable challenges for others.

Denmark reached all the EU targets for women's employment and child care in the latter part of the 1970s, and today the gender gap in employment rates is below 10%. Furthermore, the country stands out with a comparatively high public commitment to child care, especially for the 0–2-year olds, of whom almost two-thirds are covered. More than 90% of the 3–6 age group are accommodated in child-care services, which are social, pedagogical and characterised by universalism.

In this chapter, the argument is that the three key characteristics – the high level of public commitment, the universalist principle underlying the policies and the social pedagogical objectives of the policies – have been generated by path-dependent processes, which were above all initiated by a political decision in 1964. I commence by describing the key characteristics of Danish child-care provision and explaining what the social pedagogical approach implies. Subsequently, I analyse the historical development from 1919 onwards and explore the significance of the 1964 reform when the Children and Young People's Act was passed and universalism became the guiding principle for child-care policies. I analyse the economic, political and discursive opportunity structures that characterised the decision, and I focus on the key actors and the role of timing and sequence as institutional factors. In the following section, I discuss what role women's employment has played in keeping the policy within the path, and I address the relation between child-care policies and women's employment. Finally, I deal with new concerns and dilemmas that have emerged, and I ask to what extent one may anticipate path-breaking developments in the near future.

2   Key characteristics of the Danish child-care system

There are three key characteristics of the Danish child-care model: (1) the relatively high public commitment to providing, organising and financing care for children below school age; (2) universalism as the central criterion of the policies; (3) social pedagogical objectives of the services. In this section, I describe these characteristics in more detail and briefly outline their historical background.

The level of provision and financing

Table 7.1 shows that coverage rates for public services have increased for all age groups since the 1980s. Throughout the period, there have been waiting lists, but today supply almost meets demand. Furthermore, it should be noted that the legislation on parental leave stipulates 52 weeks of parental leave, which entitles many parents (particularly mothers) to care for their new babies and return to their jobs afterwards.

Danish child care is predominantly full-day and year-round, but in recent years many municipalities have introduced so-called closing days due to the moratorium on tax increases issued by the government.

The national coverage rates hide considerable variations between the municipalities, which are responsible for running and organising the services. Parents pay on average 30% of the running costs, but there are great local variations in parents' fees. The facilities cover a range of different services, which are indicated in Table 7.2:

Some of these services focus on children with physical and mental disabilities, or they are forest or outdoor kindergartens. Local and private non-profit-making initiatives have historically played a vital role in establishing and running the services, and for many decades independently owned facilities made up one-third of them. They often had a special, for example, religious, profile or were based on Rudolf Steiner traditions. In recent years, the number of independently owned facilities has declined, and today they make up 23% of the services. Market and for-profit solutions play a very restricted role in Danish child care, apart from some private unlicensed childminders. There have been

Table 7.1 Number of children in publicly supported childcare services in percentage of all children. 1980–2006

Age	1980	1990	1995	2000	2006
0–2	34	47	48	56	63
3–5	50	76	83	92	96
6–9	13	73	63	79	82

Source: Danmarks Statistik. St. E. A 1981; Social Sikring og retsvæsen 1993:12, Sociale forhold, sundhed og retsvæsen 2001:13; Den Sociale Ressourceopgørelse 2006.

Table 7.2   Number of children in different types of services. 1980–2006

Type of Service	1980	1990	1995	2000	2006
Vuggestuer (crèches)	19,470	24,331	21,400	19,579	16,994
Dagpleje (family daycare)	61,418	65,879	68,437	81,327	65,666
Børnehaver (kindergartens)	105,167	89,774	105,234	126,906	106,087
Aldersintegrerede institutioner (age integrated institutions)	21,895	56,627	89,032	121,546	134,316
Fritidshjem (leisure time facilities)	33,311	36,009	32,096	37,356	33,253
SFO (school based leisure time facilities)		35,419	101,601	161,708	181,612
Total	241,261	308,039	417,800	548,422	562,800

Source: Danmarks Statistik. St. E. A 1981; Social Sikring og retsvæsen 1993:12, Sociale forhold, sundhed og retsvæsen 2001:13; Den Sociale Ressourceopgørelse 2006.

attempts to contract out child care, but the experience has so far been rather negative, and most facilities have been shut down.

Universalism

From 1919 to 1964, the guiding principle for child care was residualist, since subsidies were conditional on two-thirds of the children in care coming from low-income families. In the late 1940s, an element of universalism was introduced, and legislation opened the way for subsidies for facilities for children from all types of families. This was still the exception, and very few services were established in the 1950s.

From 1964, universalism became the key principle in the policy, and legislation kept a focus on children with special needs.

Social pedagogical measures and integration of care and education

As in Britain and other countries, a two-tier, class-based child-care model emerged in Denmark (Borchorst, 2002; Munck, 1981). One track focused on *care*. From 1828, philanthropists initially inspired by Robert Owen, among others, established asylums for working-class children. These facilities, which were financed by charity, typically enrolled 50 to 130 children with only a few adults to look after them. The momentum for establishing these facilities was the industrialisation process, and they accommodated a large number of children. They were poorly staffed and emphasised strict authoritarian values and discipline. A second track focused on *education*. Kindergartens financed by fees that only upper-class parents could afford provided part-time services for upper-class children. They were staffed by trained professionals. The first was established in 1870. The inspiration came from *Friedrich Fröbel*, a German pedagogue, and *Maria Montessori*, an Italian pedagogue.

The two tracks merged in early 1900, when *people's kindergartens* were introduced, inspired by German ideas. The main objective was to introduce Fröbelian ideas in services for working-class children. This idea never gained ground in Germany, but in Denmark the asylums, which were widely unpopular among the parents, were gradually replaced by people's kindergartens, and they became the backbone of public policies. It was mainly people's kindergartens, integrating care and education, that received public funding.

This development became influential for the introduction of what became a leading principle in Danish child-care policy, namely *social pedagogical ideas*. Since this tradition is not well-known outside the Nordic countries, it is important to specify what it implies. The term *pedagogic* has neither negative nor old-fashioned connotations as it has in the English language, and, when universalism was adopted in 1964, *social* no longer meant residual.

The social pedagogical tradition regarded early childhood and child care as part of lifelong learning, combining ideals of a good life with philosophical aspects and a focus on resources, values and the demands of individual children. It emphasises upbringing, cultural formation and empowerment, individually and collectively for children below school age. Today, most six-year-olds attend a year-long part-time kindergarten class, located in the schools, but staffed by trained social pedagogues rather than schoolteachers.

The social pedagogical ideas have been strengthened through the education of the staff. During the early decades, kindergarten staff were trained in Fröbelian pedagogy. During the 1950s, many staff members were nurses or had completed one year of training with a stress on health issues, because hygiene had become a critical issue. After the 1964 reform had institutionalised the social pedagogical tradition, it was decided to introduce a three-year education course based on social pedagogical ideas. This happened in 1969. Today the course lasts three and a half years, and there are good options for further training.

The integration of care and education has been strengthened administratively, since the child-care services have remained under the auspices of one ministry, the Ministry of Social Affairs (except for school-based extracurricular activities and kindergarten), and schooling objectives have not been predominant in the Danish child-care system.

3 Path-dependent policy

In this section, my ambition is to uncover some of the causal mechanisms for the path chosen in relation to the three distinctive features of the Danish child-care system: the level of provision, universalism and the social pedagogical services. Since the Danish state started subsidising child care relatively early, it seems obvious to reason that this in itself is the cause for the relatively high public commitment. As historical institutionalists have argued, the explanatory ability of the vague argument that 'history matters' is, however, not strong (Mahoney, 2000; Pierson, 2000). It simply implies that the past explains the future, but the point is that it explains policies as long as they are characterised by continuity. When this is no longer the case, it does not explain anything.

I focus on the interests of the dominant actors and the opportunity structures when the decisions were made and on the role of timing as an institutional factor. Mahoney (2000) distinguishes between different theoretical frameworks of historical institutionalism, one of them a *utilitarian framework* that pays attention to self-reinforcing economic dynamics and increasing returns generated by a chosen path. This makes it increasingly costly to change paths. A second framework is *political* in nature and focuses on power relations. According to this approach, institutions are reproduced because an elite group supports them. A third approach, the *legitimation approach*, implies that institutions are reproduced because actors believe they are appropriate and morally correct. I discuss whether some of these explanations are applicable to Danish child-care policy.[1]

I combine the historical–institutional approach with a focus on the different problem definitions that have been at play in the political debates and in the legislation. I follow Bacchi's argument (1999) that every policy proposal explicitly or implicitly contains a definition of the problem that causes the politicians to react, and the problem definition has implications for the policy solution that is chosen. Bacchi and

Fraser both demonstrate that there are competing problem definitions in relation to public child care, which carry distinct programmatic orientations in relation to funding, institutional siting and control, service design and eligibility (Bacchi, 1999, chapter 7; Fraser, 1989, p. 173). I argue that at least five different problem definitions may be identified in relation to child-care policies. Three of them relate to the children. The first is child care as preventive and residual welfare, targeted at poor and at-risk children; the second relates to social pedagogical objectives for child development; and the third is educational, focusing on improving reading and writing skills. Two objectives relate to women's employment: the first is economic in nature and is motivated by the wish to satisfy the demand of labour; the second is embedded in the wish to enhance gender equality.

The problem definitions are not mutually exclusive, and they may coexist. Thus, the three major types of child-care models that may be identified in the OECD area today (Bennett, 2005; OECD, 2006) are founded on a particular mix of problem definitions related to the situation of children and the employment of mothers.

In the following, I focus on the historical processes of Danish child-care policies.[2]

1919–1964

The key actors in the 1919 decision to subsidise child care were progressive pedagogues devoted to the cause of children of all classes. They formed strategic alliances with leading Social Democratic politicians in Copenhagen who became convinced that pedagogical ideas should be extended to working-class children. It was remarkable for the time that all the political parties in both chambers of the parliament voted for the proposal, and the minister of education noted that the support for the proposal exceeded any other proposal he had put forward. All the female politicians who had been represented in parliament for the first time the previous year participated in the debate, but they did not agree on the problem definition. The preventive issue was the major objective – hence the conceptualisation of the facilities as *preventive child care* – but the politicians referred to other policy frameworks during the debates, such as considering the children's development. The Social Democratic speaker voiced a concern for the preservation of the family. The decision signalled an emerging recognition among politicians that child care for the poor was a public responsibility. It was central that the problem definition related to social pedagogical and not to educational ideas. Hence, it was decisive that the key actors found the child-care solutions morally correct and appropriate, and that they convinced the politicians of this too.

During the following years, the subsidies were maintained and increased, and some services received subsidies from the municipalities. Still, there were only a limited number of child-care facilities in the bigger cities, and the need for child care was a recurrent issue in the public and political debate. The coming decades did not see any substantial increase in the number of services, even though there was much focus on the issue during the 1930s due to declining birth rates. In 1933, a major social reform was adopted. Child-care facilities became subject to regulation for the first time, and the residual practices were put into law. At this time, responsibility for child-care services was moved from the Ministry of Education and placed under the auspices of the newly established Ministry of Social Affairs.

During the following decades, there was much discussion about the need for child care. Policy recommendations for expanding and improving child-care facilities appeared in public reports in the 1950s, but the time was not ripe for these ideas. The economic crises and the Cold War buried the proposals. Hence, the 1919 decision became formative for Danish child-care policy by institutionalising the social pedagogical ideas.

The 1964 reform

The 1964 reform marks a path-breaking decision in terms of all three characteristics. The adoption of universalism and the social pedagogical objectives were highlighted in the change of vocabulary. Services were now referred to as *social pedagogical measures* targeted at all children, and the law stipulated that it was a public task to provide care for all children. During this process, progressive pedagogues also played an active role in influencing the legislation, as did civil servants in the Ministry of Social Affairs. Together they designed proposals which were enacted as law almost down to the exact wording. Like the 1919 decision, the 1964 decision was unanimous, but this was not unusual at the time. The Social Democratic party, which was quite influential during this period, was the main architect of the expansion of the welfare state, but consensual processes among the political parties characterised most decisions. However, there was one controversial issue during the negotiations on the reform. The law stipulated public support for family daycare, but, whereas the Social Democrats and the leftist parties saw this as an emergency solution, the conservative parties preferred family daycare to the child-care institutions.

The policy problem was above all framed in relation to children's needs, and the social pedagogical approach was regarded as the solution. Women's employment and gender considerations undoubtedly motivated the politicians, but did not play a central role in framing policy in the legislation or in the parliamentary debates.

The decision was facilitated by favourable opportunity structures during the early 1960s, when the economic opportunity structures had changed radically. There was a growing unmet demand for labour, and the welfare state was expanded in many areas. Feminist organisations also argued for securing women's economic autonomy. Hence, many different actors advocated expanding child-care facilities.

Timing was central for the 1964 reform. In 1965 a commission was established to deal with the changing situation of women, but here child care turned out to be a thorny issue. The major questions were whether mothers should care for children at home during the first three years, and whether child-care facilities were harmful to children or important for their development. The issue split the commission, which passed it on to medical and philosophical experts at the University of Copenhagen. At this time, the Child-Care Act had already been adopted.

Furthermore, it was crucial that the decision was taken before 1973, when economic, political and discursive opportunities changed dramatically. The Danish economy was hit by a severe economic crisis which caused massive unemployment and cutbacks in public expenditures. Politically, the so-called landslide election in 1973 drastically altered the political landscape. The strong tradition of political consensus among the four political parties that had occupied 90% of the seats in parliament was now undermined. Two new parties questioned the public commitment to child care; one of them was the newly formed Christian People's Party, which obtained 4% of the seats. During the first period, it advocated that small children should be cared for by 'one of the parents'. Another new party, the Progress Party, gained 16% of the seats. This party saw itself as an anti-tax party, and it was extremely critical of public expenditure in general. During the following years, it voiced radical criticism of public child care, in particular the pedagogues, whom it accused of indoctrinating the children with Marxist propaganda. This should be seen in light of the fact that the pedagogues had formed a proper union in 1974 that was rather leftist. The Progress Party did not gain much influence on practical politics, but it probably did influence the public and political debate, which was coloured by the recession, too.

The reform triggered a remarkable expansion of child-care services from 1966 on.[3] The number of available places in child-care facilities increased by 80%, compared with a 6% increase from 1960 to1965. This development may be regarded as an unintended consequence, since the calculations made for the parliamentary debates were based on a much more modest development. In spite of cutbacks in the 1970s, there were no radical changes during the next three decades in the Danish model, and the level of provision kept increasing.

Before turning to current developments in the last section, I would first like to conclude the discussion of path-dependent mechanisms so far.

4   Path-dependent mechanisms

I will argue that the processes shaping the key characteristics of Danish child-care policies have been highly path-dependent, with the 1964 reform as the critical juncture for institutionalising a high level of universal, social pedagogical child-care services. The 1919 decision was important for institutionalising the social pedagogical tradition, and in this way a path was chosen in relation to one of the key characteristics. Still, the policies were based on the residual principle for the next 45 years. The 1964 reform was path-breaking in stipulating the universalist principle, and it triggered a drastic expansion of the public commitment. The social pedagogical principles were considerably strengthened and nuanced, above all through the staff training. Timing constitutes a central institutional factor in itself for the 1964 reform. It was of central importance that the reform was adopted a few years before child care became highly politicised and nine years before the economic, political and discursive opportunity structure changed dramatically, and I will argue that it is not likely that the reform would have been adopted at this time.

The key actors for the decisions both in 1919 and in 1964 were progressive pedagogues who saw their jobs as a vocation. They did not represent a powerful elite that was maximising its own interests. In the early 1960s, they had gained an influential position within the state apparatus preparing the new legislation, and they were supported by the civil servants who were actively engaged in writing the proposal. The political decisions were unanimous, which also reflects the fact that the Danish political system during the formative years of the welfare state was responsive to political forces, movements and organisations in civil society. I will therefore argue that the legitimation approach to the historically dependent processes is the most likely explanation. The idea that child care should be considered a public good has obtained remarkable support, and the politicians are aware that parents who expect high-quality child care make up a large and visible part of the electorate.

Also noteworthy is a striking lack of opposition to the public commitment to public child care. The Progress Party and the Christian People's Party are exceptions, but their resistance was voiced during the latter part of the 1970s. Besides, the Danish Church has been on the sidelines politically, unlike religious organisations in many other European countries that have resisted the expansion of public child care.

I do not find much evidence that the economic approach is useful in explaining the processes. There is presumably an element of truth in the contention that it would have been costly to choose another path, but it is very complicated to calculate and weigh the cost and benefits for children, mothers and fathers, employers and society because they vary in nature and substance. Therefore, it is unlikely that this was a central issue during the political processes. The desire to increase women's employment and achieve gender equality in a broader sense was undoubtedly significant for the expansion of child-care services, so I now turn to the relation between these issues.

5   Women's employment

The expansion of child-care provision facilitated the mass entry of Danish women into the labour market, but the relation was not monocausal. It is more precise to conclude that the processes were simultaneous and mutually reinforcing, and the irreversibility of the two processes is intertwined. However, there may be a causal link between the fact that the expansion in child care involved full-day services and the comparatively low rate of part-time employment among Danish women, and that part-timers often work relatively long hours.

The integration of women into the labour force has accelerated and turned out to be irreversible. An important point here is that each new generation envisioned education and employment as a natural part of their identity. The male-breadwinner model, which was predominant only from the late 1940s until the early 1960s, crumbled within a relatively short time. In the late 1950s, 75% of all married women were housewives, and in 1970 half of them were active in the labour force. Hence, only one generation of women shaped their identity around full-time home-making. Mothers often supported their daughters seeking economic autonomy through education and work, and the new feminist movement, which emerged in the late 1960s, was influential in claiming new life perspectives and expectations for women. Finally, the radical changes in women's lives were nurtured by the widespread secularisation process during the 1960s and 1970s.

Nor did the changes in economic opportunity in the early 1970s send women back to the kitchen. More women than men became unemployed in the wake of the economic crisis, but the unemployment benefit system allowed both part-time and full-time workers to receive benefits and to remain in the work force. Furthermore, it was important that child-care services were regarded as entitlements of the children, and not related to the employment of the mother. As a rule, children of unemployed mothers could not be barred from attending child care once they had been accommodated. Furthermore, employment was seen as a means to achieve both social and gender equality, and, unlike in countries such as Norway, the Netherlands and Great Britain, single mothers were encouraged to work, and the child-care facilities allowed them to do so.

It is, however, important to note that the Danish case illustrates that a high level of child-care provision and women's participation in paid employment does not in itself foster gender equality. Although Danish women, and mothers in particular, have record high employment rates (OECD, 2005; European Commission, 2006), traditional problems with gender pay gaps have not been solved, and the labour market is highly gender-segregated. Furthermore, there is a child penalty on women: the more children they have, the lower their career chances, pension earnings and options for pay increases (Nielsen et al., 2003).

It is also a paradox that, although gender equality is often regarded as one of the outcomes of the high level of public child-care provision, neither women's employment nor gender equality has been a central aim of Danish policies during the parliamentary debates and in the legislation. Nor is child care considered part and parcel of the policies of gender equality or, for instance, part of the government's action plans for gender equality. This may be seen in relation to the rather weak significance of gender as a policy framework in Danish politics, compared for instance with Sweden and Norway (Borchorst, 2008).

6   Do recent developments represent path-breaking changes?

The Danish economy is faring well and the labour market is celebrated for its flexicurity, that is, the combination of a flexible labour market with a high level of security (European Commission, 2006). Contrary to conventional neoclassical wisdom, relatively high public expenditure has not harmed economic competitiveness. The flexicurity literature has largely ignored child care as part of the security dimension, but it is undoubtedly a key factor in understanding the fact that Danish women constitute a core group of the labour force, which is not marginal. Furthermore, the adaptation to a dual-breadwinner family model, among other things through child care, is part of the explanation for the relatively high Danish fertility rate. This also implies that population ageing is a less severe problem for the welfare system in Denmark than in many other countries.

Against this background, it is not surprising that child-care services have remained unquestioned in the recent debates about welfare reforms. Furthermore, a new problem definition that emphasises the need for child-care facilities has emerged during the past ten years. It is tied to a central issue of integrating ethnic minority groups that has become highly politicised in recent years. Child-care services are now portrayed as central for improving children's language skills and mothers' employment, since employment is considered to be the main integrative factor for minorities. This objective is stipulated in the legislation.

There are, however, some signs of changes in the child-care policies. Since the 1990s, meeting the demand for child care has had high priority, and the Social Democratic coalition government enacted a child-care guarantee. Today most municipalities have implemented a guarantee for children aged six months to five years. Furthermore, the present conservative government, which took office in 2001, has put strong economic pressure on municipalities in order to stop increasing taxes and reduce them in the longer run. Therefore, many municipalities have made cutbacks in child care, for instance by discontinuing free meals and introducing closing days and modular schemes that imply that the parents' payment is dependent on how long the children spend in care. Furthermore, services have become fewer and bigger, and leisure facilities have been replaced by services in schools, where the staff ratio is lower.

It is debated whether this development has caused a trade-off between quality and quantity, but since criteria for measuring quality are underdeveloped there are no clear conclusions. However, a study financed by the professional staff unions indicated that the time staff spend with children has been reduced considerably: more children have been accommodated, staff working hours have been shortened, and decentralisation has increased the burden of administrative tasks (Glavind et al., 2001). The formal staff ratio has decreased, especially for older children.

The social pedagogical ideas have been challenged by attempts to give priority to education in terms of teaching children to read and write. The OECD PISA studies have several times placed Danish children relatively low in reading and writing skills. This has triggered a broad debate of the PISA criteria, and on whether child care prepares children for today's qualification society. Since 2000, curricula for children in crèches and kindergartens are mandatory. It is explicitly stated that this should not relate to reading and writing skills, but it creates a tension between social pedagogical and educational ideas of the services. In addition, more children are starting school earlier. In recent years, the present government has improved the options for parents to look after their own children, and there is a focus on how the market may come to play a more important role in child-care provision. The bottom line is, however, that the key characteristics of the Danish child-care model remain unchallenged.

7 Conclusions and perspectives

In this chapter, I have argued that the 1919 decision instituted the social pedagogical objectives of Danish child-care policies and that the 1964 reform represented a path-breaking development. This reform represents a critical juncture that changed the path by instituting universalist and social pedagogical child care and triggering a dramatic expansion, which, however, was not anticipated when the decision was made. I have also stressed that timing was decisive for the 1964 reform, which according to historical institutionalism may represent a historical mechanism that may be significant for the irreversibility of the decision. The decision was passed a few years before the issue of child care became the subject of a heated debate about the changing situation of women, and about ten years before the economic, political and discursive opportunity structures drastically changed. The key actors during the formative processes of the Danish child-care model were the professional pedagogues, assisted by civil servants, and the politicians across the political spectrum were responsive to making public child care a public good. Equally important is the remarkable lack of prominent opponents.

A factor that has contributed to the path-dependent processes is that the increase in women's employment was largely irreversible and increased the pressure for child care.

In sum, path-breaking developments in the foreseeable future are not likely when it comes to the universal principles and the level of provision, but there are some indications of changes that relate to the social pedagogical content. There are indications of a trade-off between quantity and quality, and there is a tendency towards schoolification. Still, parents of small children, who represent a large and visible electorate that all political parties appeal to, expect high-quality care for their children. This was confirmed by a massive demonstration against cutbacks in child care announced by many municipalities in the autumn of 2006, which reminded the politicians that public child care is indeed regarded as a public good. There are many indications that processes shaping child-care models are path-dependent in most countries. This implies that the Danish (and Scandinavian) solutions are not easily exported to other EU countries, as the EU experts mentioned in the introduction have suggested. Besides, the heads of government have not given high priority to the agenda of social exclusion and gender equality recommended by the experts. The Barcelona targets were fostered by a relatively narrow economic focus on the level of employment that disregards the quality of services and the recognition of children as active subjects and citizens (Moss, 2005). Furthermore, the experience of Denmark (and other countries) has proven that integrating women in employment does not in itself generate gender equality. Thus, child-, woman- and family-friendly policies recommended by the experts require that the heads of government move beyond quantitative targets and start considering moral and political visions for the future.

Notes

1. I leave out a fourth framework that relates to a functional explanation.
2. The section is based on Borchorst (2002; 2005).
3. After a ban on public construction was abolished in 1966.

Bibliography

C. Bacchi, *Women, Policy and Politics: The Construction of Policy Problems* (London: Sage Publications, 1999)
Barcelona European Council, Presidency Conclusions, 15–16 March (2000)

J. Bennett, *Where Does Denmark Stand?* (OECD/BUPL/Paris, 2005)

A. Borchorst, 'Nøglen i de rigtige hænder. Lov om børne- og ungdomsforsorg 1964' [The key in the right hands. The Children and Young People's Act], in J. H. Petersen and K. Petersen (eds), *13 reformer af den danske velfærdsstat* (Odense: University of Southern Denmark Press, 2005), 133–146

A. Borchorst, 'Danish childcare policy: Continuity rather than radical change', in S. Michel and R. Mahon (eds), *Childcare Policy at the Crossroads: Gender and Welfare State Restructuring* (New York: Routledge, 2002), 267–285

A. Borchorst, 'Woman-friendly policy paradoxes? Childcare policies and gender equality visions in Scandinavia', in K. Melby, A-B. Ravn and C. Roman (eds), *Gender Equality and Welfare Politics in Scandinavia: The Limits of Political Ambition?* (Bristol: Policy Press, 2008) 27–42

G. Esping-Andersen with D. Gallie, A. Hemerijck and J.Myles, *Why We Need a New Welfare State* (Cornwall: Oxford University Press, 2002)

European Commission, *Employment in Europe 2006* (Brussels, 2006)

N. Fraser, *Unruly Practices, Power, Discourse and Gender in Contemporary Social Theory* (Cambridge: Policy Press, 1989)

N. Glavind, S. Pade and C. Pade, *Er der tid til børnene– når vi skal nå 'alt det andet'?: rapport om tidsanvendelse i daginstitutioner i København* (Bureau 2000, 2001)

J. Mahoney, 'Path dependence in historical sociology', *Theory and Society*, 29 (2000) 507–548

P. Moss, 'Getting beyond childcare and the Barcelona targets', Paper presented at the Wellchi Network Conference 1, St. Anne's College University of Oxford (2005)

A. Munck, 'Asyler, frøbelbørnehaver og folkebørnehaver i København 1828-ca. 1920, set fra en klassetilgangsvinkel', Master's thesis (Department of Political Science, University of Aarhus, 1981)

H. S. Nielsen, M. Simonsen and M. Verner, 'Does the gap in family-friendly policies drive the family gap?' *Working Paper No. 2000–01* (Aarhus: School of Economics and Management, University of Aarhus, 2003)

OECD, *Society at a Glance* (Paris: OECD Publishing, 2005)

OECD, *Starting Strong II* (Paris: OECD Publishing, 2006)

P. Pierson 'Increasing returns, path dependence, and the study of politics', *American Political Science Review*, 94 (2000) 251–267

T. Rostgaard, 'EU presidency conference on care services for children and other dependents – equal opportunities in the European employment strategy process', Conference paper, (The Danish National Institute of Social Research, Denmark, 2002)

8
Child Care as an Issue of Equality and Equity: The Example of the Nordic Countries

Pirkko-Liisa Rauhala

1 Introduction

The Nordic countries[1] have for some decades had children's daycare arrangements which differ from those of other Western societies. The pragmatic or functionalist explanation for public daycare is women's waged employment; rates of female employment are high in the Scandinavian societies, exceeded only by those in the former socialist countries. In a recent comparison of early childhood education and care services in 20 OECD countries, Denmark holds the top position in public expenditure on such services with a 2.0% share of GDP, followed by Sweden (1.7%), Norway (1.7%) and Finland (1.4%); France is in fifth place with 1%. Those spending 0.5% of GDP or less include the United States, the Netherlands, Germany and Italy (OECD, 2006, figure 5.3).

Children's daycare in Nordic countries is distinguished by public and private responsibilities and by the quantity of daycare supplied. In her comparative analysis of working parents and child care, Arnlaug Leira (2002) has studied the Nordic development in the context of parents' positions and roles as workers, carers and citizens. Leira (2002, p. 11) concludes: 'In the Nordic countries, social reproduction has, to a considerable degree, "gone public"'. As an outcome of a continuous development over decades, all children under school age in the Nordic countries are by law entitled to a place in public daycare, and local authorities must ensure that there are sufficient places available (NOSOSKO, 2004, pp. 59–60). Close to 90 % of all Nordic children aged three to six attend institutional or family daycare. Additionally, a variety of other care services (e.g. for families with chronically ill children), long parental leaves (approx. 12 months) for parents of newborns, universal benefits and allowances are available for children and their parents. In practice, all arrangements both outside and within the home are publicly subsidised and regulated by the government; nevertheless public, most often municipally organised, daycare is predominant (NOSOSKO, 2004).

This text raises the question of what kind of conclusions concerning equality and equity can be drawn while examining peculiarities of Nordic institutional daycare in the framework of its macro-level general development. The following discussion uses the endogenous comparison of the five Nordic countries as a generalised model based on identifying universals or similarities which have been reported in the extensive research literature. Comparison with the non-Nordic countries is conducted by specifying the unique features of the Nordic daycare model, which in this text is an ideal model in the sociological sense (Scheuch, 1990, p. 31). This text focuses on institutional daycare regulated by political decision-making in the form of laws and by public authorities in the form of concrete daycare arrangements outside the home.

Equality is understood in the classic sense which includes both the equal opportunities approach and the principle of compensating for inequalities. The phenomena interpreted as 'inequalities' in every society have been negotiated in time and space, usually within nation-states,[2] and as an outcome of more or less visible and hidden social contracts regulate the relations of social partners and stakeholders. Inequalities can concern social class/strata, education, gender, generation/age, region, ethnicity, and other social factors influencing the position of citizens and/or inhabitants.

Equity, in the sense of justice, overlaps with equality in the Nordic societies; an essential goal in the Nordic welfare states has been to ensure citizen participation with regard to both rights and obligations. All contribute something through taxation (high in international comparison) and loyalty as well, and all receive something in the form of social security as citizens, not first and foremost as employees. In this text, equity will be discussed in a pragmatic way: whether the Nordic daycare system effectively ensures justice for different stakeholders.

The following text is organised in four sections: first, general features of the Nordic daycare model are introduced; second, some specifically Nordic aspects of modern childhood are described; third, three scenarios based on women's studies are briefly discussed in order to consider and critique the Nordic model; and finally, some concluding remarks will be made.

2   The Nordic daycare model

Studies of children's daycare in the Nordic countries have been oriented on individual countries, have compared the Nordic countries to each other and have analysed them in international comparison. The variety of frameworks, designs and approaches taken by these studies is wide and overlapping: they have focused on macro-level social policy and social care policy (e.g. Kröger and Sipilä, 2005; Välimäki and Rauhala, 2000); on family changes and policies (e.g. Bradshaw and Hatland, 2006); on the relation of women and paid employment, including women employed as caregivers (e.g. Hobson, 2001); and on male-oriented gender policies as a new challenge for child care (Hobson, 2001; Holter, 2007), to mention only a few examples of the prolific activity in the field.

Much of this research has come to the clear conclusion that there is a Nordic model of taking care of children during their earliest years. This model includes the following elements: a high level of public – state and municipal – responsibility for both financing and organising daycare; the goal of gender equality in labour market participation as a guiding principle, even an ideology; the idea of addressing children's needs for both education and care in institutional daycare;[3] a long-term aim of reconciling work and family; and universalism as a principle in delivering and offering daycare services. Additionally, a distinctive architecture of daycare centres has been created in the Nordic countries.

Nordic daycare has its roots in the overall European development of modern childhood, which took shape in institutional systems and practices, including education and caregiving occupations. Starting at the end of the nineteenth century, child growth and development were interpreted as a distinct period in the human life-cycle. Children entered the stage of social policy and education at the same time as their numbers started to decrease as a share of the total population (Cohen and Hanagan, 1991).[4] Children's educational and care needs were institutionalised in the form of crèches, kindergartens, (nursery) schools, youth services, etc., and the development and education of children became the subject of scientific study.

The Nordic pioneers of child pedagogy were influenced by Heinrich Pestalozzi and Friedrich Fröbel, whose thoughts and methods were transferred and applied in daycare and school systems of the Nordic countries. An additional ingredient, unique to Nordic daycare since its very beginning, was the combining of pedagogical aims with social care needs of families. From the viewpoint of institutional development, children's daycare can be interpreted as a modern, universalistic social service offered to all families, not only to the poor on a selective basis (Kahn and Kamerman, 1975; Rauhala, 1996, pp. 164–176). Modern childhood as such was an egalitarian factor in the newly industrialised societies; kindergartens were the first forums where persons/children of all social classes could form an identity as citizens in the same spatial and social setting.

The structural background for the need for daycare outside the home is paid employment and women's entry into the labour market. The shift from an agrarian and preindustrial social order to that of waged employment meant the end of traditional care of children within the household. In the Nordic countries, there never were real preconditions for a housewife model; general poverty, scarce population resources and women's involvement in agrarian work meant that both genders were expected to join the labour market as employees or (small) entrepreneurs. The agrarian division of labour was transferred to and established in the labour market through the segmentation of male and female jobs and occupations; for example, women were employed in the textile and food industries, in cleaning, care and educational work. The change from the agrarian household into a dual-earner nuclear family is a generational issue, too: the two-generation family with parent(s) in paid labour, living in an urban environment, needed children's daycare. The separation between workplace and home no longer allowed small children to be cared for at home as part of traditional household work (Välimäki and Rauhala, 2000).

The privatisation of family, that is, establishing the nuclear family, was brought about through public intervention in child care – a kind of paradox of modernisation. Especially in the Nordic countries, children's daycare as such was not included in contracts between employers and employees, but was defined as a new social requirement to be regulated and organised by the state/public authorities. Parents had to entrust their children to care outside the home, separate from household tasks. The (nation-)state as a mediator between social partners had to establish and facilitate the new industrial order of production which led to the need for care systems including daycare.

The interest in nation-building was a shared European development, and it was played out also in daycare – in the kindergarten movement at the end of the nineteenth century. Population policies and family

policies evolved and were conducted on the basis of national(istic) interests; Alva Myrdal (1941) has described the early Swedish experiment
of adjusting nation and family. The modern family was viewed as the
smallest unit of a nation, and thus the formation of heterosexual families was a convenient model to be implemented by population and
family policies.

The two-generation and dual-earner family has been cultivated
since the 1930s in the Nordic countries, especially in Sweden with
its 'people's home' (*folkhemmet* in Swedish) model, which consists of
nuclear families protected and supported by the state (Hirdman, 1989).
According to the 'people's home' model, equality is a legitimating
factor. On the other hand, a strict demand for conformity leads to a lack
of equity while regulating individual lifestyle choices. Analysts outside
Scandinavia often focus on the equality/equity dilemma mentioned
above. In the case of daycare, US sociologist Alan Wolfe has criticised
the Scandinavian model, concluding that it is possible 'to have two
full-time employed parents, state-financed daycare institutions, and
well-functioning families, but not all three at once' (Wolfe, 1989, p. 153).

3   Modern childhood as a locus of equality and equity

The educational-pedagogical orientation in the form of kindergarten was
a modern innovation launched by Swiss–German pedagogical thinking. It has been argued that kindergarten was the most important
qualitative change in the social organisation of modern childhood.
Kindergarten ideology and care arrangements defined (small) children
as persons who had to have an opportunity – even a right – to spend
their active daytime, usually four hours per day, with their peers under
the supervision of scientifically educated adults. In the Nordic context,
this goal took shape in the ideology of equality: children of different
social classes were all important for the nation's future, and therefore it
was reasonable to open kindergartens to all families. In this idea, equality
and equity are intertwined.

Before long, it was obvious that kindergarten as such was not enough
to meet family demands caused by waged employment. Children had
to be looked after, too, and that was an important argument for extending kindergarten in the direction of daycare, a special institution with
material and immaterial resources available to care for small children
while their parents – especially their mothers – were at work. *The social
care of small children* in the form of modern social services was launched

and organised. In this process, it also became apparent that workers in the public care sector would be women; men showed no interest in working as carers, kindergarten teachers or other staff in the field of social (and health) care services. While considering gender equality, one might argue that fordist production was established on the basis of a male-dominated gender order which appeared in the division between 'productive' and 'reproductive' labour.[5]

While conceptualising pre-primary education in a framework of social care services, daycare focused not only on educational needs but also on working families who needed services in order to manage their daily routines. Social services were not a residual solution but a new way of organising modern urban life; the original idea of social services is not to manage poverty but to facilitate everyday life (Hall, 1952; Rauhala, 1996). Daycare institutions built on the shared reponsibility of state and municipalities provided a solution in which educational, pedagogical and care needs were combined and all seen as part of taking care of children under school age.

In the Nordic societies, a speciality of societal dynamics is the close relation of *Gesellschaft* and *Gemeinschaft* – state and civil society (e.g. Sipilä, 1997). The Nordic nations with their small numbers of inhabitants living at great geographic distances from each other have altered the relation of centre and periphery in a context where mutual dependency and regional or local autonomy have developed into a special form of adhesive loyalty. It is embodied in a peculiar mutual trust: citizens of the Nordic countries trust in the state, politicians and public authorities. And vice versa: politicians/decision-makers have to keep their promises made during election campaigns, and the public authorities are not corrupt. These dynamics can be found in daycare, too; parents have favoured public daycare over private care.

Children's institutional daycare in the Nordic countries developed in a process of politicising and defamilisation (Leira, 2002, pp. 15–44); daycare was defined as a public issue in societies where both men and women were urgently needed to work in industrial production and in the public sector. Nordic daycare results from a coincidence of four dimensions or goals: facilitating the daily lives of modern nuclear dual-earner families; building nations with well-educated and competent citizens; encouraging women to enter the labour market, including public-sector occupations such as child care, with the consequence that there was no room for any 'grey' child-care market; preventing or buffering the effects of poverty through dual-earner families.

Strictly speaking, the Scandinavian model is one ideal way to manage the dilemma of production and reproduction: the latter was thought to be subordinate to the former, or, stated in a neutral way, industrialised societies need an infrastructure which guarantees flexible processes of production. In this sense, the Nordic countries have been very industry-friendly in launching well-functioning public sectors with a high level of political consensus. Additionally, the Nordic model can be seen as the first and quite successful model for reconciling family and work by defamilising daycare.

4   Other side of the coin: what was not taken into consideration in Scandinavian daycare

In choosing public institutional daycare the Nordic countries have obviously ignored some interests. Alternative choices were not focused on but were left to the private sphere. First, the division of the labour market was taken 'for granted'; women entered industrial and clerical occupations like men, but men did not take up employment in the reproductive sector. Women were educated and recruited into fields of care and education. Additionally, the traditional division of work within the private family did not change: women took the main responsibility for domestic work. The nuclear family model continued to feed the old labour division, and probably even increased it because of new hygiene, nutrition and other norms. In the light of contemporary discussions, men lost the historical opportunity to participate in family work, especially care of children. Families were understood as units of two earners, not a unit of parents who could negotiate family obligations. Since the 1970s, parental leave has provided a context to correct the former lack of opportunities for negotiation.

The public organisation of daycare gave priority to institutional care: the domestic sphere was seen as inadequate to respond to the needs of children and families (Hirdman, 1989). Individual differences, preferences and choices were not respected; instead, paid employment was declared to be the standard for every individual, including women. Especially in Sweden there were many who supported this approach (Myrdal and Klein, 1956), although the ideal was best realised in Finland, which ultimately reached the highest rate of female full-time employment.

In the Nordic societies, women could reach full citizenship and equality with men through similar participation in the labour market, and at the same time women had the right or opportunity to demand professional and occupational help and advice for intimate issues and problems, child care and education included. A critical Foucaultian comment might be that human needs were institutionalised in the process of developing the welfare state; in general, individuals making free choices were not ideal citizens in the first stages of capitalism. Notwithstanding the modern citizen norms, in their everyday lives people had the freedom to make individual choices without repression in democratic societies. In practice, working parents were even forced to make their own choices due to a shortage of public daycare; the supply of daycare has been sufficient only since the 1980s.

The third critical remark concerns the understanding of modern childhood. Children are no longer regarded as miniature adults, but there is still no concrete and coherent understanding of a child as a person who could have a voice in solutions concerning him/herself or be a stakeholder in his/her own life. Childhood became an object of expert study which scientifically educated kindergarten teachers, teachers, psychologists, care workers and other staff involved with children were entitled to carry out. Parents were left with the role of laypersons in issues concerning their children's development and care (Hirdman, 1989). Mass care and professional care standards were launched and legitimised, and adult-centred (professional) practices emerged.[6]

From the viewpoint of equity, the aspects discussed in this section can be interpreted as deficits and weaknesses of the Nordic daycare model. Nevertheless, the dimensions have never occurred in any 'pure' form but are more conceptual criticisms of institutional daycare as currently implemented. On the other hand, equity is a qualitative dimension which in the case of social services appears on the agenda only after enough arrangements and practices in quantity have been established.

5   Revisiting the three classic conceptualisations

Women's studies-oriented research on the Nordic welfare states distinguishes between three classic scenarios of the state as an authority regulating the gender order: woman-friendly welfare state; state patriarchy; and the welfare state as machinery to amalgamate production and reproduction (Rauhala et al., 1997). It is possible to apply these scenarios to the discussion of daycare. The following is based on the results of a welfare research programme conducted by the Nordic Council of Ministers (2006).[7]

In the scenario *Nordic welfare state as a woman-friendly state*, women and the state are seen as partners of mutual change: by organising education and care, usually by municipalities, the state has enabled women to participate in the labour market, through which women have gained an independent position as paid employees and are not primarily dependent on their husbands for financial support. Women have had an opportunity to participate in (occupational) education, and the public educational systems have through their equal opportunity programmes advanced women's chances to develop their potential. In the Nordic context, there is strong evidence that women have benefited and continue to benefit from the opportunities which the welfare state has offered women: both gender equality and equity in the sense of equal opportunities have been carried out in order to advance women's education and labour market participation.

However, problems remain. Rigid gender-biased segregation of the labour market is a fact in the Nordic countries: there are men's jobs and women's jobs. It seems that the equal opportunity policies enable women to enter traditionally masculine fields but not vice versa. In the field of social care, the great majority of workers and professionals are women, as in all industrialised countries; daycare centres are prominent evidence of this, and no change is to be expected in the near future. The second problem is that women still shoulder the main responsibility of domestic work, though no longer only in the form of 'women must do housework'. In research on new masculinities, there are debates on women's dominance which excludes men from caring for children. A challenge is to develop a men-friendly welfare state, which has already been initiated by quotas for paternal leave and by consolidating men's rights as fathers, especially in the situation of divorce.

The woman-friendly welfare state is based on the dual-earner family as an ideal, and for this reason the welfare state has been woman-friendly for single mothers by compensating for the second salary. At the same time, the role of men as fathers and carers has not been made visible. Additionally, the woman-friendly welfare state has not shown enough sensitivity towards step-families as an increasing family model, not to mention the diversity which is emerging through multi-ethnic and transnational family formation. The future challenges of the Nordic daycare model involve organising work, family and time in a child-centred way in postmodern society (Honig, 2006). The equal right of men and women to both work and family, and children as stakeholders, are the main challenges for the Nordic 'women-friendly' model.

Foucaultian theory views the Nordic welfare state as a *reorganised state patriarchy* in which male dominance is established in public institutions instead of or in addition to that within marriage; men control female sexuality, reproductive capacity and labour force through the state machinery, and women are involved as 'partners' in the form of public (low-paid) care and educational occupations where they deliver services for other women in paid employment and their children (Holter, 1984). Hirdman (1989) has analysed how paid employment became the norm for both genders, and how, in the same process, women's household competence was undermined and women were made undervalued amateurs as domestic workers. Because of the strong two-breadwinner model, salaries have generally remained low in the Nordic countries (and high taxation has an impact on disposable household income, too), which means that women do not have the opportunity to escape the labour market by moving into the private sphere. In parallel, men cannot afford a stay-at-home wife.

Although this notion of a state patriarchy is exaggerated, it does have a certain analytical power to explain the gender division of labour. Additionally, men's position and role in the private sphere have come under consideration and have had an impact on reorganising the care of newborns at home. Leira (2002, pp. 75–105) has used the term 'refamilising' to describe current trends in Scandinavian child care: more and more children under age three are cared for by their own parent at home with public support in the form of cash benefits and time off. This shift can be considered also as a shift away from mothers' worker–carer obligations towards reorganising care on the basis of parental choices.

The *division of production and reproduction* has already been criticised above. Today, this distinction is mostly discussed in the context of reconciling work and family. The Nordic countries with their history of daycare can be interpreted as a vanguard in giving equal value to productive and reproductive work; when organising institutional daycare, the care as such was defined as an important social and public issue. Women were thought to need economic independence, which care within the private family could not provide. On the other hand, daycare solutions were made under the dominance of waged employment and the labour market. In the case of Scandinavia, it is clear that there is no returning to a situation in which women are not in the labour market. It seems evident that innovative efforts are needed to solve the dualism of production and reproduction, also in the field of conceptualisations.

6 Concluding remarks

In this review, the Nordic daycare model has been discussed at a general macro-level against the background of the similarities between the systems (rather than the differences, which also exist). It is argued that the ideology of equality, especially gender equality understood as balancing the roles in work and family, has been the most shared idea in all countries. The issues challenging equality as a goal concern choices which people can and should be entitled to make at different phases in their lives. The uniform framework of waged employment has not been very sensitive in a life-cycle perspective. The same is true of the concept 'family' in the increasingly multicultural atmosphere of the Scandinavian societies; newcomers to these countries may have a different understanding of family obligations, gender and relations between the generations, etc.

In the Nordic context, weak pronatalism can be mentioned as a sign of equity. Although most of the allowances and benefits are related to the number of children, no special obligations are expected of couples having more or fewer children. The position of single parents has been favoured by some additional benefits and access to services but that has not been enough to prevent the risk of poverty among single parents.

The Scandinavian countries are regarded as the first to organise gender relations along the waged employment order. Recently, there have been some signs that the gender division of child care is changing in Scandinavia; men have become more conscious of their rights as fathers and as carers of (their own) children, and there are already clear indications that new masculinities are evolving in the Scandinavian societies (Holter, 2007). It is too early to say how this trend will be reflected in daycare policies in the long run. Quotas for men taking paternity leave to care for children during their early years have been introduced. Care work in public institutions continues to be female work – or the work of immigrant men in lower-level positions, especially in healthcare.

The European societies have chosen different solutions to deal with the changes in women's and children's positions. The Nordic countries are prominent with their public institutional daycare, which in the European discussions is often interpreted as a benchmark or 'best practice'. The European Union has declared the goal of increasing the labour force, and, in fact, there are three sources of labour to fulfil this goal: immigrants, older workers remaining in the labour force longer, and women (mothers of small children). The Nordic countries have a relatively long experience of the last mentioned.

Equality has been advanced by universalism, which has been the dominant ideology of Nordic social policy, including social care services. Equality, especially gender equality, in Scandinavia is an ideology which all political partners share to a certain degree. Besides ideology, the increased public responsibility of citizens' wellbeing in the form of social services has been realised in the goal of general equality which the Scandinavians view as ensuring justice. Leira (2002, pp. 7–10) has stated that the Nordic idea has been to combine the roles of adults with small children as workers, carers and citizens, and the rights and obligations have been developed in line with this trinity. There is a strong path-dependency in trying to reconcile work and family. The neoliberalistic atmosphere has put forward the discussion of labour division and responsibilities between private and public in general; however, there is still a consensus concerning the importance of several daycare opportunities. The current generations with small children seem to demand more opportunities to maximise their own wishes for daycare.

Notes

1. The five Nordic or Scandinavian countries – Denmark, Finland, Iceland, Norway and Sweden – and the three autonomous regions Aland, Faroe Islands and Kalaalit Nunaat (Greenland) make up a region with approx. 25 million inhabitants. According to the UN's Human Development Index and by GNP, the Nordic countries are among the richest and most developed societies on the globe; all the Nordic countries are among the ten least corrupt states in the world. Since the early 1950s the Nordic countries have coordinated several policy sectors through the Nordic Council; in fact, since the 1960s the Nordic countries have had an internal market with market freedoms similar to those of the European Union today. In social policy, the Nordic countries have without any special regulations applied the Open Method of Coordination while imitating each other's arrangements, changing ideas oriented on best practices, through regular reciprocal visits of experts and administrators. The large number of comparative welfare sociological and social policy analyses have confirmed that, since the 1970s, one can arguably speak of a special Nordic welfare (state) model (e.g. Esping-Andersen, 1990; Kuhnle, 1978; Nordic Council of Ministers, 2006; Sipilä, 1997). An important dimension of the welfare model is the citizen identity the Scandinavians share: social democracy (in a wider sense than that of a political party), equality and social citizenship are the

ingredients for a common identity; citizens' equality is valued highly in all these countries, which can be described as 'hard-core' work societies. The Lutheran religion has unified the Scandinavian societies for centuries, as has the democratic orientation of Nordic monarchs. Nordic social policy is a mix of Bismarckian and Beveridgean ideas, with the latter predominating. In spite of similarities in establishing and conducting social policy, the Nordic countries have been autonomous in developing their international affiliations; Denmark and Norway are members of NATO; Denmark, Finland and Sweden are members of the EU, though Sweden and Denmark are not in the EMU; Norway and Iceland do not belong to the EU.

2. In the European Union, where a growing labour force is seen as an important factor for advancing competitiveness, and reconciling work and family is thus emphasised as a common goal, gender inequalities in labour market participation are already being negotiated at the supranational level.

3. The OECD has classified institutional daycare in the Nordic countries as an EduCare model (OECD, 2006).

4. The decrease in fertility continues to be a catalyst for family policy; small children are the focus of social policies even in countries such as Estonia, where social policy as such does not have a high priority on the political agenda (von Maydell et al., 2006, pp. 223–246). It should be mentioned that the elderly have become a more visible focus of social policy as their number has increased.

5. The division between production and reproduction is all too simplistic and bipolar to explain the complexity of the gender order which welfare capitalism has developed. The two-dimensional understanding of the fordist production-order has neglected both women's and men's needs as human beings; waged employment meant less work compared to the agrarian order. At the same time, all spheres of everyday living were organised on a new basis. However, the agrarian division of gender subordination remained and materialised in the segregation of the labour market. Today, the service-based production order challenges the (conceptual) division of reproduction and production as distinct spheres.

6. In the Central European countries, where institutional daycare developed later, there are also more opportunities to focus on sociological childhood research and new interpretations of daycare in a child-centred framework (e.g. Honig, 2006). Perhaps only ageing and the urgent demand for more workers are factors which will finally make childhood a serious issue concerning the time and space of and for children and parents.

7. The Welfare Research Programme of the Nordic Council of Ministers (2001–2006). The author was a member of the programme's steering committee. Retrieved 26 September 2008 at www.program.forskningsradet.no/nmr/.

Bibliography

J. Bradshaw and A. Hatland (eds), *Social Policy, Employment and Family Change in Comparative Perspective* (Cheltenham: Edward Elgar, 2006)

M. Cohen and M. Hanagan, 'The politics of gender and the making of welfare state, 1900–1940: A comparative perspective', *Journal of Social History* 24 (1991) 469–484

G. Esping-Andersen, *The Three Worlds of Welfare Capitalism* (Cambridge: Polity Press, 1990)

P. Hall, *The Social Services of Modern England* (London: Routledge & Kegan Paul Ltd, 1952)

Y. Hirdman, *Att lägga livet till rätta – studier i svensk folkhemspolitik* (Stockholm: Carlssons, 1989)

B. Hobson (ed.), *Making Men into Fathers: Men, Masculinities and Social Politics of Fatherhood* (Cambridge: Cambridge University Press, 2001)

H. Holter (ed.) *Patriarchy in a Welfare Society* (Oslo: Scandinavian University Press, 1984)

Ö. Holter, *Män i rörelse. Jämställdhet, förändring och social innovation i Norden* (Riga: Gidlunds förlag, 2007)

M. Honig, 'An den Grenzen der Individualisierung. Die Vereinbarkeit von Familie und Beruf als sozialpädagogisches Thema', *neue praxis – Zeitschrift für Sozialarbeit, Sozialpädagogik und Sozialpolitik* 36 (2006) 25–36

A. Kahn and S. Kamerman, *Not for the Poor Alone* (Philadelphia: Temple University Press, 1975)

T. Kröger and J. Sipilä (eds), *Overstretched: European Families Up Against the Demands of Work and Care* (Oxford: Blackwell, 2005)

S. Kuhnle, 'The beginnings of the Nordic welfare states: similarities and differences', *Acta Sociologica*, 21, Supplement (1978) 9–35

A. Leira, *Working Parents and the Welfare State. Family Change and Policy Reform in Scandinavia* (Cambridge: Cambridge University Press, 2002)

B. v. Maydell, K. Borchardt, K. Henke, R. Leitner, R. Muffels, M. Quante, P. Rauhala, G. Verschraegen and M. Żukowski, *Enabling Social Europe* (Berlin: Springer, 2006)

A. Myrdal, *Nation and Family. The Swedish Experiment in Democratic Family and Population Policy* (London: Harper & Brothers, 1941)

A. Myrdal and V. Klein, *Women's Two Roles* (London: Routledge and Kegan Paul, 1956)

The Nordic Council of Ministers, Nordisk Ministerråds Velferdsforskningsprogram. Programkomitéens sluttrapport. TemaNord 2006:521 (Copenhagen: Nordisk Ministerråd, 2006)

NOSOSKO (Nordic Social-Statistical Committee), *Social Protection in the Nordic Countries 2004* (Copenhagen: NOSOSKO, 2004)

OECD (Organisation for Economic Cooperation and Development), *Starting Strong II: Early Childhood Education and Care* (Paris: OECD, 2006)

P. Rauhala, Miten sosiaalipalvelut tulivat suomalaiseen sosiaaliturvaan? In Finnish; Habil. Diss.; Acta Universitatis Tamperensis ser A vol 447 (Tampere: University of Tampere, 1996)

P. Rauhala with M. Andersson, G. Eydal, O. Ketola, and H. Warming Nielsen, 'Why are social care services a gender issue?', in J. Sipilä (ed.), *Social Care Services: The Key to the Scandinavian Welfare Model* (Aldershot: Avebury, 1997), 131–155

E. Scheuch, 'The development of comparative research: towards causal explanations', in E. Öyen (ed.), *Comparative Methodology. Theory and Practice in International Social Research* (London: SAGE, 1990), 19–37

J. Sipilä (ed.), *Social Care Services: The Key to the Scandinavian Welfare Model* (Aldershot: Avebury, 1997)

A. Välimäki and P. Rauhala, 'Lasten päivähoidon taipuminen yhteiskunnallisiin muutoksiin Suomessa', *Yhteiskuntapolitiikka* 65 (2000) 387–405

A. Wolfe, *Whose Keeper? Social Science and Moral Obligation* (Berkeley: University of California Press, 1989)

9
The Politics of (De)centralisation: Early Care and Education in France and Sweden

Michelle J. Neuman

1 Introduction

Since the 1980s, many European countries have shifted significant responsibilities for education and social policy – including early care and education (ECE) – from the central state to lower levels of government. This chapter explores the origins and consequences of decentralisation of early care and education in France and Sweden between 1980 and 2005.[1] *Decentralisation* refers to the extent to which the authority (e.g., administration, staffing, regulation, quality assurance, provision) has been delegated to subnational levels of government, and, sometimes, to the school or programme level. First, I discuss the process of decentralisation of ECE in France and Sweden since the 1980s, with special attention to the actors and institutions involved. Second, I compare the implications of these governance changes in both countries for ECE policy and politics.

Why France and Sweden? These two countries have similar economic contexts and high female labour force participation rates, as well as a long tradition of publicly supported child care and preschool for children from birth to six. The vast majority of the costs of ECE are covered by the public sector in both countries. Yet, they have taken somewhat different approaches to governing their early childhood systems. I argue that a comparison of France and Sweden can shed light on the role of both institutions and ideology on the policies and services available to young children.

2   Trends in (de)centralisation of early care and education

As with other areas of public policy, governments justify increasing decentralisation of ECE to promote local democracy, bring decision-making closer to those who are being served, reduce bureaucracy, and encourage more client-oriented services (De Vries, 2000; Karlsen, 2000; Oberhuemer and Ulich, 1997). Advocates for decentralisation often urge the use of more business-oriented management tools to improve performance in the public sector. The next sections provide a closer look at the origins and consequences of ECE centralisation and decentralisation in France and Sweden. Figure 9.1 provides an overview of the (de)centralisation that occurred over the period 1980 to 2005. In

	1980	1985	1990	1995	2000
France: 0–2	Centralised	Decentralisation			
France: 2–5	Centralised throughout				
Sweden: 1–6	Centralised		Decentralisation		Recentralisation

Figure 9.1   France and Sweden: Summary of decentralisation trends

Table 9.1   France and Sweden: Early care and education policy functions decentralised

	Administration	Employment of lead staff	Staff-child ratios	Group size	Curriculum	Evaluation	Parent Fees	Financing
France: 2–5	No	No	Yes	Yes	No	No	n/a	No
France: 0–3	Yes	Yes	No	No	Yes	Yes	No	Yes
Sweden: 0–6	Yes	Yes	Yes	Yes	No	Yes	Yes (until 2003)	Yes

Note: Yes: function is decentralised; No: function is not decentralised; N/A: not applicable.

France, decentralisation has mainly concerned the child-care sector for children under three. In Sweden, a period of decentralisation in the 1990s was followed by recentralisation.

Table 9.1 summarises the functions that have been decentralised in the two countries.

2.1 France

Preschool: a national responsibility with a local role

The French education system was built on Republican ideals supporting centralisation and uniformity. Unlike other levels of schooling in France, which were state-run, the central government and the municipalities have shared responsibility for the *écoles maternelles* and the elementary schools since 1883. Specifically, the state is responsible for teacher salaries, the national curriculum (including 2–5-year-olds) and evaluation, and the municipality takes care of the facilities and support staff. Given this division of responsibilities, the preschools have been largely unaffected by administrative and financial decentralisation of education to the regional and local levels since the 1980s (Cole, 2001). The Education Law of 1989 created an *entitlement* to free preschool for children from the age of three. The law also encouraged greater school-based management, which included the preschools, but, in general, there is a great deal of central control and uniform pedagogy across the country (OECD, 2004).

The national preschool system was well-institutionalised within the education bureaucracy and offered almost universal provision by the late 1970s, when an economic crisis hit France. Preschool's institutional position within education has protected it from budget cuts. There is a strong constituency of parents who support preschool as the first stage of education and view it as a national public responsibility. The unionised teachers also lobby the central government to preserve the budget and resist any decentralisation efforts. However, the fact that the *école maternelle* is quite centralised makes it more challenging to coordinate with other forms of early childhood provision.

Variation in access and quality primarily affects the provision for two-year-olds. Access to preschool for two-year-olds is not an entitlement, and is an official priority only in disadvantaged areas. Coverage ranges from 4 to 66 percent and depends on local initiative, demographics, and school facilities. In my interviews, the teachers' unions expressed concern that some municipalities have developed innovative practices for welcoming two-year-olds in the *maternelles*, whereas others do not serve them at all, or do so under unsatisfactory pedagogical conditions, which 'does not allow for reducing the educational inequalities that can be observed already in preschool'.

Infant-toddler care: tension between decentralisation and diversification

Alongside the centralised universal preschool system, a diverse and decentralised child-care system has developed for children from birth to three. Traditionally, the state has played a role in regulating quality and stimulating the expansion of services. Between 1981 and 1983, Mitterand's socialist government funded a rapid expansion of the number of *crèche* places. However, this initiative was interrupted by decentralisation. The Socialist government argued that decentralisation would improve local democracy and participation. The economic slowdown and budget constraints also fostered efforts to promote efficiency and to shed responsibilities from the state to subnational units of government (Morgan, 2002a).

The Decentralisation Law of 1982 transferred administrative and funding responsibility for social affairs, including child care services for 0–3-year olds, from the state to lower levels of government. In 1989, the *Conseils Généraux* became responsible for child and maternal health services (*Protection Maternelle et Infantile* – PMI), which were formerly attached to the state, including the authorisation and monitoring of individual (e.g., family daycare providers known as *assistantes maternelles*) and group child-care services (e.g., *crèches*). The central government now focuses on legislating, training, and planning. Even after decentralisation, however, national rules and regulations governing the *crèches* remain for child–staff ratios, group sizes, and staff qualifications.

What is peculiar about France is that no agency or level of government has the legal obligation to create new infant and toddler programmes. Instead, this responsibility is carried out in partnership and negotiation across agencies and with private, non-profit-making providers (David, 1999). A more cynical view expressed by respondents is that the government wanted to avoid the difficult political decision of mandating the expensive responsibility for providing child care. According to a local policy official in Nantes, '[t]he State does not have direct competence, and the decentralisation laws ... did not say anything about the legal responsibility for child care in France'.

Whatever the reason for the governance change, decentralisation has attracted new local political actors from the public and non-profit-making sectors into the policy-making arena (Morgan, 2001). First, decentralisation in the 1980s gave more options to lower levels of government to develop local solutions adapted to the needs of their residents. Although the *Conseils Généraux* are required to provide child and maternal health and child protection services, the law is ambiguous with regard to child care. If the *Conseils* choose to make it a priority, they can also fund, provide technical assistance, and coordinate services. In general, their role has been rather limited (Eme and Fraisse, 2002), but the situation is diverse nationwide.

Since the 1980s, some local politicians, especially mayors, have taken responsibility for 0–5-year olds, recognising that ECE is important for local families and economic development. It is not uncommon for parents to go the town hall with their child-care troubles, which has created political incentives for local officials to invest in ECE. This pressure from local voters has made child care popular with most political parties, though the focus of policies differs. Conservative politicians generally favour subsidies for individual forms of care (e.g., *assistantes maternelles*), whereas Socialists tend to support public *crèches*. Not surprisingly, there are strong regional disparities in funding and access, with urban areas providing the most extensive and diverse range of services.

Another major player is the National Family Benefits Fund (CNAF), which oversees the management of family policy funds into which workers and employers pay contributions. Directed by representatives from business, labour, and family associations, the CNAF sets national priorities and guidelines which are carried out by the 125 local family allowance funds (CAF) (Morgan, 2002b). In the early 1980s, the CNAF's Board of Directors decided to focus on the expansion and improvement of early childhood services (David, 1999). Morgan (2002a) argues that without the family allowance funds the child-care sector would not have developed much after the decentralisation law.

As local authorities received more responsibility for child care, the local CAFs also obtained greater autonomy over resource allocation and policy development. The CAFs are quite autonomous in defining policies to meet local economic and social contexts, such as the distribution of centre-based or family daycare options. In recent years, conservative family associations have dominated governing boards of many CAFs. Working with local conservative politicians who share their beliefs, these policy networks have focused more resources to individual, less formal child care rather than to the *crèches* (Morgan, 2002a).

To provide financial incentives for the municipalities to develop a diverse supply of ECE and increase the quality of existing services, the CNAF created 'contracts' (*contrats-enfance*) between local CAFs and local authorities in 1988 (OECD, 2004). In addition to subsidising 50–70 percent of new expenses for *crèches* and other services, through the contracts, the CAFs support coordination, provide information to families, train professionals, offer technical assistance, and financially support capital investment and operating costs. As an indication of the programme's success, 3,500 contracts were signed in 2001, covering 68 percent of children under six. These contracts facilitated the expansion of services in semi-urban and rural areas, which had lagged behind more urban areas (OECD, 2004). Despite these accomplishments, the CNAF incentives have not overcome local disparities in access and funding at the local level, and funding requirements to sign a contract are often too burdensome on financially strapped rural communities (David, 1999).

2.2   Sweden

Early care and education: local freedom and deregulation

The provision of ECE has always been a municipal responsibility in Sweden; there have never been 'state preschools'. During the 1970s and 1980s, a period of great expansion, child care was part of the centralised government funding and costs were divided as follows: 45 percent state; 45 percent municipality, 10 percent parent fees (Bergqvist and Nyberg, 2002). The state set detailed rules, from staff-to-child ratios to the number of windows in the centre. In the middle of the 1980s, the government realised that the expansion of childcare was not meeting demand – there were long waiting lists – and the municipalities argued that overregulation was limiting the possibilities for more rapid development. In response, the central government removed the guidelines, allowing local authorities more freedom.

In the early 1990s, the government changed its administrative approach further to reflect the views of the centre-right parties in power. As part of the Local Government Act of 1991, national goals replaced central rules for ECE. To support municipal self-government, local authorities gained the freedom to organise themselves and address the needs of their citizens as they saw fit. One change many municipalities made with this additional freedom was to integrate child care and primary education together into one local administrative unit to foster improved efficiency and coherence.

During this process of decentralisation, targeted funding to meet specific goals replaced the earlier steering-by-regulations approach. The central government now defines goals and provides funding, and localities monitor services in centres and family daycare homes. Local authorities may decide to further decentralise responsibilities by allowing individual preschools to determine group size, measures for children in need of special support, and measures for professional development (Gunnarsson, Korpi, and Nordenstam, 1999). A second major change was that, in 1991, the government rolled earmarked funds for child care into general block grants to give municipalities more flexibility in allocating resources and organising ECE provision. According to a senior Ministry of Education official, municipalities pressed the central government for these changes to help them better meet local needs of children and families:

> [The] municipalities said ... stop with the guidelines. We can manage. We know now what quality is and we have to have more manoeuvre. The second step was give us all the money in one bag. We can make it much better if we can get the money and make our own priorities.

Municipalities supported this change in funding, but the trade unions preferred earmarking to ensure that child care would be adequately funded. Unions argued that, by using block grants, the national government could reduce overall funding to the municipalities without being politically responsible for which programmes would be cut.

Economic pressures and local disparities

Although municipalities acquired more flexibility in allocating resources and organising ECE, the 1995 Act on Child Care tightened and clarified municipal obligations to provide full-day child care to all children from age one with parents who work or study. The Act required the municipalities to meet family requests 'without unreasonable delay' of three to four months (Gunnarsson et al., 1999). By creating a national entitlement, but allowing local government autonomy, the Swedish welfare state could promote its equality objectives.

At the beginning of the 1990s, however, an economic crisis hit Sweden. Required to meet the 1995 law, municipalities expanded access, without investing in quality. Structural conditions (e.g., group size, child–staff ratios) of ECE worsened, as did geographic disparities. Despite these economic challenges, 95 percent of municipalities could offer a place to families within three or four months of their application. Initially, to meet the demand for public child care, municipalities relied on family daycare, which was less costly and faster to expand than centre-based provision (Morgan, 2006). To keep costs down, while meeting the national requirements, municipalities also raised parent fees and instituted time- and income-related scales. Public investment per child decreased by 4 percent, and parents' share of the costs increased to about 18 percent, rather than the government fee guideline of 10 percent (Bergqvist and Nyberg, 2002).

As in France, local politics have influenced ECE policy and have led to differences between and within municipalities. During the 1990s, local governments led by Social Democrats tended to levy higher local taxes, charge lower parental fees (until the maximum fee reform discussed below), and require lower child–staff ratios than conservative-led ones. A recent evaluation found that financial resources and political priorities are more likely to determine group size, a measure of quality, than other local conditions (Skolverket, 2004).

The distribution of family daycare and preschools also varies by region. Family daycare is more common in rural areas and much less common in larger cities, because of the challenges of providing centre-based arrangements in sparsely populated areas, as well as political considerations and parental preferences. The Centre party, which is very popular with more politically conservative residents of rural areas, is a proponent of family daycare as less institutional and more 'family like'. In Northern Sweden, however, which is also sparsely populated, there is little family daycare, and Social Democratic and the Left parties in power have invested heavily in preschools in this region. Political as well as practical considerations play a role in the distribution of centre- and home-based arrangements.

Lifelong learning and recentralisation?

The last ten years have brought another series of governance reforms under the leadership of Prime Minister Göran Persson's coalition government. After moving all early childhood services from the Ministry of Social Affairs to the Ministry of Education in 1996, Sweden introduced free, part-day sessions for four- and five-year-olds. Children with an unemployed parent or a parent on parental leave – two groups originally excluded – obtained a *right* to attend preschool activities for up to three hours a day or 15 hours a week (Lenz, Taguchi and Munkammar, 2003). By placing more requirements on local authorities to ensure access, these reforms are a form of *recentralisation*.

Another form of recentralisation is the preschool curriculum created in 1998. The curriculum is more specific about the goals and pedagogical tasks of the preschool when compared to the earlier steering document, known as the 'pedagogical program'. Although some experts argue that the curriculum is an example of greater national steering of the content and methods of the preschools, others point out that the curriculum provides only a broad framework and is thus consistent with the overall decentralised approach to Swedish education. For example, municipalities develop the aims and working methods of local (pre) schools, and the professionals have great flexibility to do the work with the children.

National evaluations have identified that the conditions for children in preschool vary from community to community, and overall fewer resources and more children in preschools have affected the quality of the learning environments for children. According to the 2004 evaluation conducted by the National Agency for Education:

> Variation in ways of interpreting and carrying out the task is a natural consequence of a large and complex system, built on local freedom and professional responsibility... On the other hand, variations may be a source of problems if they are caused by municipalities and preschools facing different conditions for carrying out their task and adapting preschooling to the different needs and preconditions of children. (p. 32)

Although the new curriculum aimed to support preschools of equivalent quality, the evaluation found that variables such as community resources and parents' socioeconomic background play a role in influencing preschool quality (Skolverket, 2004).

In response to access and quality disparities which threaten the guiding principle of equity, the national government has asserted a stronger role in policy development for ECE. Now the budget situation is healthier, the government has reintroduced earmarked money to steer the system. To reduce the geographic variation in parental fees, for example, the state introduced the maximum fee (*maxtaxa*) and compensates localities for revenue loss. The government also introduced a plan to allocate 2 billion Swedish crowns for hiring more staff to reduce group sizes and improve staff–child ratios, which will help sparsely populated areas and low resource areas in cities struggling to recruit qualified staff (Skolverket, 2004). The Union of Municipalities opposes these new grants as a form of earmarking which restricts local freedom (though the funds will eventually become part of the municipal block grant).

Table 9.2 France and Sweden: Consequences of decentralisation changes

	France (0–2)	France (2–5)	Sweden (1–6)
Access	–	=	+
Quality	=	=	–
Coherence	+	=	+

Notes: +: positive change; −: negative change; =: no change.

3   Comparative analysis: (de)centralisation

In the next section, I discuss several cross-national findings of decentralisation for ECE policy and politics. First, I find that decentralisation has had different consequences for quality, access, and coherence in France and in Sweden (see Table 9.2 for a summary). Specifically, decentralisation has increased geographical disparities in access in France (for under-threes), but quality has become more uneven in Sweden. Coherence is more of a challenge in France, because the 'care' and 'education' sectors are governed at local and national levels respectively.

Second, I discuss four main consequences of decentralisation for ECE politics. Challenging economic contexts have mediated the impact of decentralisation on ECE. As the venues for education and social policy decisions shift to the local level, new actors and institutions have emerged as decision-makers. Although both France and Sweden justify decentralisation with the need for promoting local autonomy and democracy, the realisation of these objectives depends on local capacity. Finally, decentralisation fosters the diversification of providers, which can help meet the needs of children and families but also raises serious equity concerns.

4   Consequences of decentralisation for access, quality, and coherence

4.1   Access

Decentralisation has been very limited in the French education system, in particular in the early childhood years. State–local divisions of responsibility for preschools were established early on, and the strong role of the state has changed little since the nineteenth century. It was important that the *école maternelle* was institutionalised within the bureaucracy of the education system and garnered the support of a strong middle-class constituency and the teachers' unions by the 1970s. These factors helped achieve universal, free access of 3–5-year-olds in both legislation and practice. The integration of preschools within the education system may also have prevented the more radical decentralisation that occurred in the social services, including early child care. Preschool staff have no interest in decentralisation, especially if it might mean 'escaping from national education system' that has protected it, as one interviewee explained.

In terms of access, the variation in enrolment of two-year-olds across France remains an issue that generates much discussion and debate, even though the proportion of two-year-olds in school has remained relatively stable since the 1980s. Without a national entitlement, policy for the two-year-olds is largely decentralised. The lack of political (and professional) consensus around the merits of having two-year-olds in school leads to policy ambiguity. In practice, two-year-olds are used as an 'adjustment factor'. When enrolments in primary schools are low, schools encourage two-year-olds to attend (to prevent closures), but when enrolments increase there is less effort to accommodate them. This strategy does not reflect the rights-based approach that exists for children from the age of three, nor does it meet the needs of families who cannot afford other quality ECE arrangements. The exception is that there is political and legal consensus that children from poor, immigrant backgrounds living in priority education zones receive priority access.

In contrast to the preschools, the lack of clear responsibility for child care in France has had serious consequences for access. Given that there is no obligation for the municipalities to provide infant–toddler services (i.e., aside from the *écoles maternelles*), the development of services varies based on the local political priorities and resources, as well as by demographic situations, parental preferences and cultural attitudes (David, 1999). Decentralisation has also placed limits on the role of the state in France in expanding access. For example, the state can create framework laws but the local authorities are responsible for implementing them (or not). The state cannot mandate additional financial responsibilities to the municipalities, but rather is dependent on a system of incentives and guiding policies.

Unlike in Sweden, decentralisation of child care in France has been associated with geographical disparities in funding, supply, and access.

On average, there are 6.1 *crèche* places for 100 children under three, but up to 10.8 for cities with more than 30,000 residents (Clément and Nicolas, 2003). While nationally 11 percent of children under three are in *crèches*, the coverage rate in *départements* varies from 2 percent to 41 percent. Most *crèches* are concentrated in large urban areas with greater financial resources (OECD, 2004).

While Sweden has created a mandate for municipalities to provide access to child care, the main strategy for increasing supply in France within the decentralised system is through financial incentives rather than obligations, which has failed to ensure equitable access across the country. The intervention of the CAFs though the *contrats-enfance* have stimulated growth in areas where local officials are amenable to investing in this policy area. Negotiation between the CAFs and local authorities is a political process. Where the political will does not exist, there is no safeguard to ensure that services will be provided.

In Sweden, access for one- to five-year-olds has expanded continuously over the past 25 years – from about 20 percent in 1980 to almost 80 percent in 2003 (see Figure 9.2). Unlike France, the entire system in Sweden was decentralised in terms of regulations and funding in the 1990s. At the same time, legal requirements that municipalities provide preschool fuelled expansion within this decentralised delivery system.

Although the pressures of the 1995 Act on Child Care combined with decentralisation and economic difficulties initially led to variation and increases in the average level of parental fees in the 1990s, the maximum fee has capped these disparities, making ECE more affordable

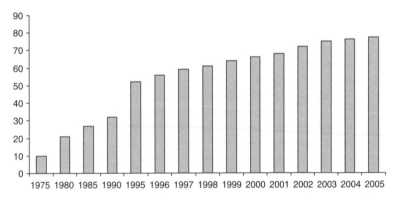

Figure 9.2   Sweden: Proportion of children aged 1–5 in preschool, 1975–2005
Source: Swedish National Agency for Education, 2006.

Table 9.3 Sweden: Proportion of 1–5-year-olds enrolled in preschool by municipality type, 1997–2005

	Big cities	Suburban municipalities	Industrial municipalities	Rural municipalities	Sparsely-populated municipalities
1997	68	61	52	43	55
1999	72	66	57	50	60
2001	74	70	63	55	61
2003	78	76	72	68	72
2005	79	78	74	71	73

Source: Swedish National Agency for Education, 2006.

and accessible for all families. (The maximum fee is voluntary, but all municipalities have agreed to participate, because the reform is so popular with parents.) Enrolment rates do vary depending on the size of the municipalities, but these differences have decreased over time (see Table 9.3). In the vast majority of cases, municipalities can provide a place 'without unreasonable delay'.

Decentralisation also affects access in terms of the distribution of different types of ECE provision. In both countries, there is some regional variation in the distribution of family daycare and centres. In general, more conservative local politicians and more rural areas tend to favour more individual arrangements. It is difficult to disentangle the extent to which these local decisions to support certain forms of ECE reflect parental preferences or the financial and practical constraints of municipalities, however.

Overall, France and Sweden diverge when it comes to trends in family daycare. In Sweden, there has been a decline in family daycare (Figure 9.3), whereas in France this form of ECE is increasing (Figure 9.4). Today, the vast majority of children in Sweden are in centre-based preschool (fewer than 10 percent are in family daycare), including one- and two-year-olds. In sharp contrast, 18 percent of children under three are in registered family daycare in France.

Although decentralisation plays a role in determining the distribution of provision, the trends also reflect different understandings of the

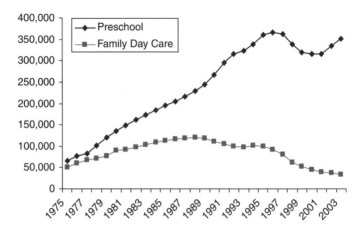

Figure 9.3   Sweden: Number of children in preschool and family day care, 1975–2003

Source: Swedish National Agency for Education, 2003.

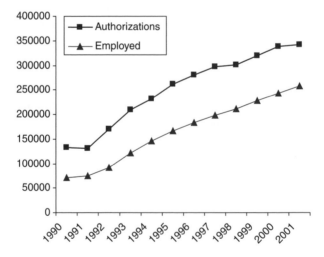

Figure 9.4   France: Increasing numbers of assistantes maternelles, 1990–2001

Source: Algava and Ruault, 2003.

purposes of ECE for young children. In Sweden, local governments and parents favour preschools for their emphasis on pedagogical quality. The educational role of services for under-threes has received less attention in France.

4.2 Quality

One interesting cross-national contrast is that there are central regulations for ratios and group size for French *crèches*, but not for preschools in France or Sweden. The degree of regulation is associated with policy outcomes related to quality. For example, although the average number of children per class in France has decreased since the early days of expansion (see Table 9.4), this also varies across regions. Class sizes can be quite large (over 30 children) by Swedish and international standards. In ZEPs (*zones d'éducation prioritaire*), schools receive additional funds to reduce ratios.

The quality of learning environments (e.g., class size, age-appropriate materials and facilities, organisation of activities) for two-year-olds varies depending on the initiative and interest of local education inspectors and policy-makers. For older children, quality is more uniform, in part because teachers have more experience working with this age group.

Unlike France, Sweden deregulated the ECE sector in the early 1990s to give local authorities and programmes more flexibility in some aspects of programme quality. There is much discussion in the Swedish press about the larger group sizes and child–staff ratios that ensued. Average group size increased from 13 in 1980, peaked at 17.5 in 2000, and dropped slightly to 17.2 in 2003. Child–staff ratios rose from 4.2:1 in 1980 to 5.7:1 in the late 1990s, and then dropped to 5.4:1 (see Table 9.5 and Figure 9.5). As a comparison, the required staff–child ratio in the French *crèches* is one adult for five children who do not walk, and one adult for eight children who walk.

Table 9.4 France: Decreasing average group Size in École maternelle, 1960–2001

Year	Number of Children per Group
1960	42.9
1970	40.3
1980	30.0
1990	27.9
2001	25.5

Source: Ministry of Education data, 2004.

Table 9.5 Sweden: Increasing average number of children per group and child-to-staff ratio in preschool, 1980–2003

Year	Number of children per group	Child : staff ratio in preschool
1980	13.0	4.2
1985	14.3	4.3
1990	14.4	4.4
1995	16.7	5.5
2000	17.5	5.4
2003	17.2	5.4

Source: National Agency for Education, 2005.

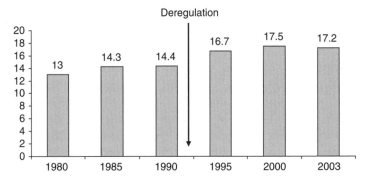

Figure 9.5 Sweden: Deregulation in the 1990s is associated with larger groups
Source: Swedish National Agency for Education, 2005.

Accordion staffing is common in Sweden, meaning that the number of staff working with children will fluctuate during the day according to the age of the child and the activity. Although compared with France, especially in the *écoles maternelles*, the group sizes and ratios are quite low, the Swedish government has responded to the concerns of parents and child development experts with new financial incentives for localities to hire staff. At the same time that these ratios and group sizes have increased, preschool staff are required to complete more training which may help them with these challenges.

In the French child-care sector, one consequence of decentralisation is that there are now greater diversity and flexible forms of provision to meet family needs. However, national regulations for child care only apply to centres. Although these regulations ensure an even level of quality variation in these settings across geographical areas, quality standards for other forms of child care are much weaker. Depending on local policies, some children will have access to *crèches* staffed by professionals whereas others will be in family daycare with a provider with little formal education and only 60 hours of in-service training.[2] From a child wellbeing perspective, it does not make sense for staff requirements, ratios, and pedagogical approaches to differ so greatly from one form of provision to another.

4.3 Coherence

The consequences of decentralisation for coherence are more problematic in France than in Sweden, mostly due to the French bifurcated system. Given that the child-care sector in France is more decentralised than the education sector, the Ministry of Education – which has the clear overarching leadership role for the education sector – does not have a main contact with which to consult and collaborate. In some cases, it is the Ministry of Health, whereas in others it is the Inter-Ministerial Delegation on the Family. Creating linkages to promote coherence across different forms of ECE services can be challenging when the systems are governed at two different levels: the central government continues to direct the education system, but the *Conseils Généraux* and localities oversee the child-care system.

When an entire system is decentralised (e.g., for one- to six-year-olds in Sweden and for under-threes in France), however, the increased flexibility in local administration and service delivery create opportunities for creating linkages across programmes. For example, decentralisation in Sweden allowed local authorities to administratively integrate child care and primary education into one department. In France, despite the significant institutional barriers, several respondents cited examples of *local* coordination. For example, the early childhood coordinators can foster coherence across the different forms of centre and home-based child care and sometimes with schools too.

Another aspect of coherence relates to the distribution of quality and access across geographical areas. As shown above, decentralisation in Sweden has brought some variation in access and quality across municipalities, but much less than in France. This variation can meet the diverse needs of families, if children have equal access to the different forms of provision, which is not currently the case. In Sweden, there is not much evidence that any existing geographical variation is a concern or undermines equality objectives. The Swedish government's legal entitlement to ECE and national curriculum to guide services across the country mitigates some of the potential inequities of decentralisation. Neither of these safeguards exists for child care in France.

5 Consequences of decentralisation for early care and education politics

5.1 Decentralisation effects are magnified by economic context

Several of the decentralisation efforts in both France and Sweden occurred during a time of great fiscal and economic pressure to limit public spending. This can be viewed as a deliberate effort by the state to shift the financial burden of public services to lower levels of government and, in some cases, to the private sector, thereby making the budgetary cuts less visible to voters. Given that some of the decentralisation efforts began *before* the economic crisis, cost-shifting was not the only rationale for these governance changes. Perhaps equally important was the declining confidence in the state as a welfare institution (Bergqvist and Nyberg, 2002). The economic crunch may have accelerated this emerging trend. Regardless of the rationale, it is clear that children are especially vulnerable during economic difficulties.

Historical institutionalists (e.g., Pierson, 2000) highlight the importance of timing and sequencing of events for determining future outcomes. For example, Morgan (2002) argues that one reason that the French preschools became institutionalised as universal whereas child care did not was that the *écoles maternelles* expanded before the economic crisis. The fact that the economic situation in France has improved, but spending for child care is still insufficient to meet the demand, suggests that other factors are at work, such as views about what is best for the child and political ideologies with regard to responsibility for the care and education of young children. As noted earlier, arrangements for children under three are not viewed as a right for the child but more as a support for working parents.

In Sweden, the preschool reforms were introduced at a time when changes in structural conditions and decentralisation meant that schools were facing new demands and challenges without the benefit of new resources (Skolverket, 2004). According to a social democrat Member of Parliament involved in education for many years, '... I think that the economic difficulties that we had in the 90s would have been worse if we hadn't done this decentralisation'. Indeed, removing some of the regulatory constraints on municipalities may have allowed them to allocate limited resources more efficiently during that crisis. Nonetheless, serious disparities in fees, access, and quality standards were consequences of decentralisation during the economic crisis.

Now that the Swedish economy is healthier, the government has increased investments in social welfare programmes, which suggests that changes in the 1990s were temporary rather than significant welfare retrenchments (Bergqvist and Nyberg, 2002). The government introduced other requirements such as the legal right to services and 'voluntary' instruments such as the maximum fee and incentives for raising quality. With safeguards, including targeted funding by the state, these inequities were reduced to address the disparities in quality and access that developed after decentralisation.

5.2 Decentralisation privileges new actors and institutions in policy-making

As a result of decentralisation, new actors and institutions have emerged in the policy-making arena. The main venue for advocacy, political debate, and decision-making has shifted from the national to the local level. Consequently, perhaps the most important new players are the local elected officials who now hold greater discretion in setting ECE policy. Although this means that local policies are more subject to shifting political winds, decentralised governance also provides an opportunity for mayors and other local officials to respond to the preferences of voters.

In both countries, families with young children are a strong lobby, with more influence locally than at the national level. Parents have successfully pressured reluctant local politicians to invest in ECE in both countries. National organisations representing local actors (e.g., Association of Local Authorities) have gained power, as traditional actors (Minister of Education, Parliament) have weakened. In France, the CAFs, which are uniquely situated between families, local officials, and the state, have become very influential in shaping and expanding ECE policy. The role of the CAF is to incentivise partnerships to expand and improve child care through the *contrats-enfance* rather than to create a legal entitlement as in Sweden. The challenge is that not all localities have the political will or resources to form strong partnerships with CAF to expand ECE. The negotiation process is most smooth when local authorities and the CAF share political views about child care.

The expanded role of the school system in ECE has strengthened the support of a powerful and established interest group of teachers in both countries. In the French preschool sector, in the Republican tradition, the role of the state in the *école maternelle* is considered essential to protecting children's rights to an equal education. In Sweden, governance changes – the shift from governance by rules to objectives – have increased professional responsibilities of teachers and school leaders at the local level (Lundahl, 2002). Swedish teachers welcomed the opportunity to compete for jobs and negotiate salaries locally; the neocorporatist relationship between French teachers' unions and the state remains strong.

5.3   Decentralisation increases freedom, democracy, and the need for local capacity

In both countries, interviewees evoked the discourses of freedom and democracy. Decentralisation creates new responsibilities in municipalities and in the preschools. One Swedish national politician (Green Party) described decentralisation as giving teachers, staff, and parents the opportunity to take their own initiative. Perhaps one reason that decentralisation was so smooth in Sweden is the political consensus, as an early childhood researcher described:

> There are many different parties and many different ideas in Sweden, how it should be run. But in a way there's an agreement that there has to be a lot of freedom, because it's part of the democratic way of thinking. But you must also guarantee each child's right to get a good education.

In a system with so much local freedom and autonomy, it is important for there to be local capacity to assess and meet local needs. As described by an education researcher:

> So that is part of decentralisation, what I talked about, that this reform needs very competent teachers. And very competent local authority people to make good judgments and take responsibility. So it's a huge reform, even sometimes I feel it's too much burden on the teacher, if you take this reform seriously...

The high level of teacher training in Sweden facilitates the acceptance of increased responsibility for local decision-making in the preschools.

In France, with more rural areas with less of a tradition of dual-parent employment, local politicians seem to have less information and understanding of the potential value of child care and early education for children and their parents. The CAFs have helped to provide technical know-how to local officials and administrators wishing to develop early childhood policies and programmes and overcome barriers of information and political will.

5.4   Decentralisation and diversity raise equity concerns

Based on the two cases, decentralisation leads to a greater diversification of services that can cater to a wider set of interests, but raises serious equity concerns. Differences in provision within and across localities can be positive if it means that policies are adapting to local needs and circumstances, a primary objective of decentralisation. The diversification of early childhood provision to include non-profit-making, and in some cases for-profit, alternatives to state and municipal services has offered flexibility to meet the diverse needs of parents and children in both countries. In particular, the non-profit-making sector in France is recognised for stimulating innovative practices.

Decentralisation may also help empower local actors to more efficiently allocate the available resources. Given that policy decisions are influenced by local politics and economic circumstances, parents' choices are often limited. In Sweden, there is renewed state involvement to steer with resources rather than with detailed rules or mandates. The maximum fee, for instance, helped the state to retain power and promote more uniformity of parental fees. This can be characterised as a form of recentralisation. In France, diversification raises equity concerns because the different forms of ECE do not offer the same level of quality. Decentralisation may also have accelerated the trend toward more individual arrangements such as family daycare and nannies, which many local officials favour for both philosophical and financial reasons. They are less expensive for local governments and more flexible for some parents (e.g., opening hours) than the *crèches*.

6   Summary

This chapter has explored the origins and consequences of decentralisation of ECE since 1980. In both countries, the central government's methods have changed, but its importance has not diminished. Public financing, regulation, and monitoring are still prominent in ECE systems, but states now focus more on steering and incentive-based policies, consistent with governance trends, than prescriptions and mandates. The comparative analysis suggests that the consequences of decentralisation have been distinct in France and Sweden. The two countries seem to be on similar paths for the three- to five-year-olds. For the younger children, France is moving toward a more decentralised and private approach, which leads to more geographical variation, whereas Sweden stresses universalism and balances local freedom on the one hand with goals-led steering on the other. Decentralisation obviously involves trade-offs between fostering local control and ensuring national goals. There are equity concerns, particularly when where a family lives determines what services are available, but it is possible to provide safeguards through some national steering and targeted funding.

Notes

1. This paper is part of a study of governance of early care and education in France and Sweden (Neuman, 2007). During fieldwork, I assembled key *public documents* and conducted 80 *semi-structured interviews* with: (a) national, regional, and local elected officials and civil servants; (b) representatives of key interest groups (e.g., teachers' unions, associations of local authorities, child advocates, professional associations, parent groups); and (c) researchers and scholars. I selected interviewees for their significant role in creating, implementing, or studying early childhood policy. The research was funded by the German Marshall Fund of the United States, American–Scandinavian Foundation, Council for European Studies/Florence Gould Foundation, Teachers College Office for Policy Research, and Columbia University Public Policy Consortium.
2. The Decree of 2000 requires at least of half of the staff in centres to hold a child nurse, early childhood educator, or nurse auxiliary degree. A quarter of the staff need to have a health, social work, or related degree (OECD, 2004).

Bibliography

C. Bergqvist and A. Nyberg, 'Welfare state restructuring and child care in Sweden', in S. Michel and R. Mahon (eds), *Child care policy at the crossroads: Gender and welfare state restructuring* (London: Routledge, 2002), 287–308

D. Clément and M. Nicolas, *Les disparités territoriales de l'accueil des jeunes enfants* (L'essentiel No. 12) (Paris: CNAF, 2003)

A. Cole, 'The new governance of French education?' *Public Administration*, 79 (2001) 707–724

O. David, 'L'accueil des jeunes enfants: Concentration des équipements et inégalités d'accès aux services', *Espace, Populations, Sociétés*, 3 (1999) 483–494

M. S. De Vries, 'The rise and fall of decentralization: A comparative analysis of arguments and practices in European countries', *European Journal of Political Research*, 38 (2000) 193–224

B. Eme and L. Fraisse, *La transformation des structures familiales et des politiques sociales et les modes d'accueil des jeunes enfants: Rapport national France* (Paris: TSFEPS Project, 2002)

L. Gunnarsson, B. Martin Korpi and U. Nordenstam, *Early childhood education and care policy in Sweden* (Background Report prepared for the OECD Thematic Review of Early Childhood Education and Care Policy) (Stockholm, Sweden: Ministry of Education and Science in Sweden, 1999)

G. E. Karlsen, 'Decentralized centralism: Framework for a better understanding of governance in the field of education', *Journal of Education Policy*, 15 (2000) 525–538

H. Lenz Taguchi and I. Munkammar, *Consolidating governmental early childhood education and care services under the ministry of education and sciences: A Swedish case study* (Paris: UNESCO, 2003)

L. Lundahl, 'From centralization to decentralization: Governance of education in Sweden', *European Educational Research Journal*, 1 (2002) 625–636

K. J. Morgan, *'Conservative parties and working women in France'* Paper presented at the Annual Meeting of the American Political Science Association, San Francisco, CA, 2001

K. J. Morgan, 'Does anyone have a "libre choix"? Subversive liberalism and the politics of French child care policy', in S. Michel and R. Mahon (eds), *Child care policy at the crossroads: Gender and welfare state restructuring* (New York: Routledge, 2002a) 143–170

K. J. Morgan, 'Forging the frontiers between state, church, and family: Religious cleavages and the origins of early childhood education and care policies in France, Sweden, and Germany', *Politics & Society*, 30 (2002b) 113–148

K. J. Morgan, 'Les politiques du temps de l'enfant en Europe occidentale: tendances et implications', *Recherches et Prévisions*, 83 (2006) 29–43

M. J. Neuman, *Governance of early care and education: Politics and policy in France and Sweden*, unpublished PhD dissertation (New York: Columbia University, 2007)

P. Oberhuemer and M. Ulich, *Working with young children in Europe: Provision and staff training* (London: Paul Chapman, 1997)

OECD, *Early childhood education and care policy in France: OECD Country Note* (Paris: OECD, 2004)

P. Pierson, 'Increasing returns, path dependence, and the study of politics', *American Political Science Review*, 94 (2000) 251–267

Skolverket, *Pre-school in transition: A national evaluation of the Swedish pre-school.* (A summary of Report No. 239) (Stockholm: Skolverket, 2004)

10

Slow Motion – Institutional Factors as Obstacles to the Expansion of Early Childhood Education in the FRG

Kirsten Scheiwe

1 Introduction

The development and expansion of early childhood education in the Federal Republic of Germany (FRG) – at least in the western part – has lagged somewhat behind that of other European countries. Although the number of children aged three years to school age attending kindergarten has increased considerably since 1991, when a right to a kindergarten place was introduced by law, and now ranges between 90.5 percent in Western Germany and 100 percent in the East,[1] there are other indicators of slow development. All-day places offering lunch are rare in many parts of the country and accounted for only 23.6 percent of all places for children aged three to school age in the western *Länder* (but for 98.1 percent in the east). Kindergarten frequently ends around 12 pm without providing a meal. The situation for under-threes is particularly poor: places are provided for 2.4 percent of this age group in the western *Länder* (but for 37 percent in eastern Germany). Therefore Germany has to work hard to comply with the EU benchmarks to provide places for 33 percent of all young children by 2010 (the 'Barcelona targets').

Although this issue has gained considerable public attention in recent months and was pushed onto the political agenda of the governing CDU/SPD grand coalition by a Christian-Democrat minister, Ursula von der Leyen, it is very difficult to reach political agreement between the different political actors involved. This is due not only to some more outmoded voices of clerical hardliners like Bishop Mixa of Augsburg, who declared that women would be reduced to 'childbearing machines' if such plans for public child-care provision were pursued further; in fact, his statement represents a rather isolated opinion.

Major obstacles to the further enhancement of early childhood education result from institutional features of the organisation of the German welfare state and the federal political system. Basic institutional decisions date back to the 1920s, even to the second half of the nineteenth century. Child-care institutions were politically controversial as early as 1851, when the Prussian government prohibited the Fröbel kindergarten. It is argued that particular institutional configurations shaped this path already rather early and are still difficult to overcome today, especially due to the fact that early childhood education has been assigned to the realm of welfare rather than integrated into the educational sector, to the particularities of German federalism and to the special role of the Federal Constitutional Court, which can overrule parliamentary legislation when it is found to be in breach of constitutional principles.

Characteristic of the FRG is a rigid separation between kindergarten and daycare facilities for children below school age on the one hand, and schools and formal education on the other hand. Kindergarten is still widely conceptualised as care, not as education (or *Bildung*), despite the normative regulation that child care should follow an integrated pedagogical approach that encompasses education and care, according to para. 22 sec. 3 of the Child and Youth Welfare Act. Child care is integrated into the social welfare sector and organised under the authority of the youth welfare office as part of local municipal responsibility for administration and financing. Seen in international comparison, this is not only a German *Sonderweg*; quite a number of countries developed the same organisational principles. The Scandinavian countries and Austria and Switzerland are also part of the group which followed a 'welfare model' or a 'care model' for young children and separated early childhood education from formal education in schools. In contrast, some countries followed a 'preschool model' (France, Belgium, Luxembourg, Italy, today also Spain) and included facilities for children aged two or two and a half (in Spain from birth on) in the educational sector under the aegis of school authorities. The international trend points towards stronger emphasis on the educational aspects of early childhood education, which is more than care and supervision for children. What is unique to the FRG is the fact that this rigid institutional separation – which was institutionalised under particular historical conditions and power relations in the 1920s – is still reinforced and upheld by institutional constraints and strong interest groups today.

This reinforces path-dependencies and works as an obstacle to a more dynamic expansion of early childhood education.

2 Public welfare or education? Split legislative competences under German federalism

While the Länder alone are responsible for regulating schooling and education, the Federation (government at federal level) has a prerogative to regulate child care as part of public welfare. There is no centralised federal power to regulate school education (as in France or in Belgium until 1971). This has political consequences: if kindergarten and early childhood education are assigned to the educational sector, the 16 Länder, not the Federation, have exclusive authority to regulate it.

Basically, the Federation has exclusive legislative power (Article 73 of Germany's constitution, the Basic Law) in the fields of foreign affairs and defence, citizenship, passports, migration, unity of the customs and trading area, etc. Next comes the concurrent legislative power of the Federation (Articles 72 and 74 of the Basic Law): the Federation has a prior right to legislate if necessary in the national interest (subject to further specification that was amended in 1994 and 2006), and the Länder have power to legislate so long as and to the extent that the Federation has not exercised its legislative power. One subject of this concurrent legislation is public welfare (Art. 74 (1) no. 7 Basic Law) – this is actually the competence for regulating youth welfare and child-care institutions. And finally the Länder have exclusive legislative power (Art. 70 (1) Basic Law) to regulate matters where the Federation has no explicit competences, such as education, schooling and culture.

The *Länder* have the right and the duty to provide school education, to supervise the school system and to oblige children to attend school once they reach compulsory school age. Thus the state has the mission to provide education (*Bildungsauftrag*) in its own right,[2] which limits parental rights. Basic legal guidance is provided in Art. 7 of the Basic Law, but more detailed provisions are found in the *Länder* constitutions and statutory school law.

Financing obligations are connected to this division of competences. The administrative and financing competences for youth welfare lie with the local municipalities, which receive only some funding from the Länder and no federal funding. Direct federal funding to the Länder in this area is even forbidden on the constitutional principle that the financing competence has to follow the administrative competence (Art. 104a Basic Law), and therefore financial burdens can be shifted only indirectly between the Federation and the Länder in package arrangements. The municipalities are overburdened by this task. Many of the political struggles between the Federation and the Länder in different political fields are due to these financial issues deriving from constitutional principles.

3   The historical roots: exclusion of child care from the educational system and its integration into the welfare system in the 1920s

The development of public institutions for young children in Germany since the nineteenth century had, as elsewhere, different roots; institutions for otherwise unsupervised children (*Kleinkindbewahranstalt*) were established partly in reaction to industrialisation and pauperism, but there was also a pedagogical impetus and movement based on the ideas of Pestalozzi and Fröbel, who pursued particular educational goals. However, Fröbel's more pantheistic and republican pedagogical ideas not only attracted the enthusiasm of bourgeois middle classes who wanted to educate their children and the support of Jewish families who did not want to send their children to church-run institutions, they also provoked intervention by the Prussian state authorities, who prohibited the Fröbel kindergartens in 1851. Fröbel himself moved to the more liberal Switzerland. Pestalozzi's ideas met with less political opposition than Fröbel's in Germany, while Fröbel had much more success in other countries than in Germany until the end of the German empire in 1919.

Child-care institutions were institutionalised in the nineteenth century initially along class lines, with *Bürgerkindergarten* for middle-class children and *Volkskindergarten* for the lower classes as two separate fields of socialisation (Reyer, 1981). These institutions were considered to be part of education and were supervised and controlled by school authorities. For example, a Prussian decree of 1839 defined 'waiting schools' (*Warteschulen*) as educational institutions under the control of school authorities. This changed in the early twentieth century, when the privatisation and idealisation of the patriarchal bourgeois family, of the mother as housewife and of the intimate mother–child relationship, had become very influential. At this stage, public education and care for young children were considered to be only a makeshift (*Nothbehelf*) in an emergency situation with a lower quality of socialisation than maternal love and care in the private home. Daycare was conceptualised as part of youth welfare for the first time in the Prussian Statute on Youth Welfare

Education of 2 July 1890. Local municipalities developed services for needy children and families in the following decades. In 1920, following World War I and the end of the monarchy, the proclamation of the Weimar Republic and the election of the first Social-Democratic government, a national 'school conference' took place which had the task of discussing the restructuring of the educational system, encompassing schools as well as child-care institutions. Dismantling the old privileges of the *Ständegesellschaft* was at stake. The parties on the political left wanted an integrated, uniform school system (*Einheitsschule*) that included preschools, encompassing the period 'from kindergarten to university'. They took up this old slogan of the liberal democratic reformers of 1848, but it was only a minority position in the 'imperial school conference' of 1920. Churches wanted kindergartens to be private, charitable welfare institutions; the Social Democrats argued for nonconfessional, public kindergartens run by the municipalities and the state as a first step of the envisaged integrated school, and the representatives of the Fröbel association pleaded for a compromise to maintain the prerogatives of private associations to run the kindergarten and a secondary role for the state. Ultimately, the majority voted to keep child-care institutions in the welfare sector and out of the educational domain. Private associations (mainly the churches) were to be the primary providers, while the municipalities were obliged and allowed to step in only if private provision was insufficient. Known as the subsidiarity principle, this arrangement was enshrined in the Imperial Youth Welfare Act of 1922 and is still the basic organisational principle in the FRG. In 1922 the Imperial Youth Welfare Act defined the provision of daycare as a responsibility of local municipalities and as a task of youth welfare authorities. After World War II, this did not change in the new Federal Republic, while the German Democratic Republic (GDR) took a different path, integrating kindergarten and after-school care into the school system under the Ministry of Education. However, after German reunification in 1990, this was revised: early childhood education was returned to the field of welfare and confirmed in the Children and Youth Welfare Act of 1990/1991.

4   From the 1970s to the present: path-dependency and contradictory approaches within the set path

Again in the 1970s, the assignment of early childhood education to the field of social welfare was contested, and the demand to integrate daycare institutions for young children into the educational system returned to the agenda. During the school and university reforms of the 1970s, important actors such as the joint federal–*Länder* commission for educational planning (*Bund-Länder-Kommission für Bildungsplanung*) asked in 1973 for a different approach: to regard daycare as elementary education and as the first step in the educational system. In 1972, the *Land* of Bavaria enacted a new statute concerning kindergarten based explicitly on the legislative competence to regulate education and schooling under Art. 70 of the Basic Law, not on the concurrent competence to regulate public welfare. This legal opinion of the *Land* was backed up by the Bavarian Constitutional Court in a decision of 4 November 1976, which argued that giving up the old legislative competence of public welfare and shifting it to the legislative competence of the *Land* based on education reflected a modern understanding of kindergarten as an educational institution (*Bildungseinrichtung*).[3] Bavaria's position here plainly contradicted the Federation's legal competence for regulating public welfare. The new national Children and Youth Welfare Act (*Kinder- und Jugendhilfegesetz*), which entered into force in 1990/1991, acknowledges the Bavarian position, stating in para. 26 that *Land* legislation which integrates child daycare into the educational sector remains unaffected. Although various lawyers pointed out that this approach was in itself contradictory, and that it should decide for one or the other – the competence of a *Land* to regulate the educational system, or the competence of the Federation to regulate public welfare – it has remained in place, since no-one has an interest in challenging this inconsistent compromise before the Federal Constitutional Court.

The 1991 Children and Youth Welfare Act brought about one important change: each child aged three and over was granted a subjective right to a kindergarten place. Although this does not mean a right to a full-day place, this was an important instrument for expanding kindergarten provision in the western *Länder* in subsequent years. This right was partly an effect of Federal Constitutional Court rulings. The court had overruled the statute on abortion law which the national parliament had enacted after German reunification. The court had turned down a more liberal approach to abortion rights and asked for measures to protect not only 'unborn life', but also those already living. The compromise package decided by the parliament after the court's decision introduced the child's right to a kindergarten place. This meant a definite shift from a targeted approach for children in need towards a universal right of all children aged three and over. This change weakened the argument that early childhood education should be part of social welfare, since it is not only directed at those in need, but grants a universal right. The ongoing debate about kindergarten as part of welfare or of the educational system came up again in 2002 in response to Germany's shock at its low ranking in an international study of educational achievement (PISA). As a result, the conference of the ministers of the 16 *Länder* responsible for youth declared that education (*Bildung*) had priority in early childhood education, while care came second (Youth Ministers of the *Länder*, 2002).

5   Is early childhood education social welfare? What is school, what is not school? Interpretations by courts and legal literature

The Federal Constitutional Court had to rule on the legislative competence to regulate early childhood education in a case decided on 10 March 1998.[4] The court had stated in a 1967 ruling that youth welfare implied not only those measures related to youth or families at risk (*Jugendfürsorge*), but also those youth services and programmes directed at young persons in general (*Jugendpflege*), and, since these two tasks are very much intertwined in practice due to their substance, they should be based on the same legislative competence, thus on the competence to regulate public welfare (Art. 74 (1) no. 7 Basic Law).[5] The Federal Constitutional Court relied on this basic argument again in 1998 and said that the concurring legislative competence for public welfare also encompassed preventive measures for children and youth, since youth welfare should counteract developmental problems of young people and prevent risks. Further, the court said that the main emphasis of kindergarten activities lies on care-giving, with the purpose of promoting social behaviour and thus preventing conflicts,[6] and that the task of daycare institutions to promote preschool education is secondary to this preventive goal which is inherent to public welfare.

Although the Federal Constitutional Court's argument that preventing conflict and promoting social behaviour comes first and preschool education comes second is not entirely convincing, there are some plausible arguments to back up this position. The court's reasoning may also be based on political restraint and the idea of leaving it up to the politicians to potentially shift early childhood education from the sphere of public welfare to education – which implies shifting it from the prerogative of the Federation to regulate the matter within its concurring legislative competence to the exclusive legislative competence of the *Länder*.

If one looks at the other side of the coin and asks 'What is school?', it turns out that lawyers cannot provide exact answers. Definitions in the legal literature are somewhat tautological: schools are all institutions which act to provide knowledge through lessons and which are organised as schools, where teaching is provided by specialised staff according to methodological standards and curricula. It is said that kindergarten is non-school, since no teaching takes place.[7] This sounds a bit crude: school is what is organised like school. But if compulsory attendance is not a decisive criterion, as the Federal Constitutional Court said,[8] nor is the age of pupils, why should a kindergarten not be a school? It is more convincing that a kindergarten or after-school care (*Hort*) could be school, and that it depends on the organisation and activities of these institutions (Schmitt-Kammler, 2007 , Rn. 9). This is a political decision to be taken by legislators – and international comparison shows the diversity of approaches in assigning it either to social welfare or to the educational sector.

6   Consequences of the institutional assignment of early childhood education to welfare

The assignment of early childhood education to social welfare provision, rather than to the educational sector, has definite consequences due to the logic of the system. In the field of early childhood education, parental rights are primary, while the state has only limited authority to support and supplement education. Therefore the state cannot oblige children to attend kindergarten (this is considered an infringement of parental rights), while the state can regulate compulsory schooling or even lower the age when children have to go to school, since the state has the power to regulate school education in its own right (based on Art. 7 Basic Law and the constitutions of the *Länder*, since school education falls within the exclusive legislative competence of the *Länder*). Therefore parents have a right to choose the daycare institution according to their pedagogical, religious or other preferences.

In the field of social welfare services, churches, NGOs and private associations have a prerogative to provide daycare institutions (for which they receive public funding from local municipalities); local municipalities may provide child-care services only if demand is not met by charities and NGOs (so-called subsidiarity principle). In the school sector, by contrast, this relation is reversed: the provision of public schools has priority, while private schools are allowed only if they can prove a special demand not met by public schools.

Parents have to pay fees for children to attend kindergarten or crèches, while school education is free of charge for parents and considered to be a public good.

The idea that child daycare only supplements parental education and that the mother at home should be available to care for the child reinforces what the 2005 OECD report calls the 'maternalist assumption' of the (western) German daycare system (see the contribution of Rabe-Kleberg), which imposes serious obstacles to labour market participation by mothers and increases the risk of poverty.

The professional training of staff qualified for early childhood education, their status and pay are considerably lower than those of school teachers and lag behind the standards of various other European countries (Oberhuemer and Ulich, 1997); this situation urgently needs improvement.

Daycare provision is very decentralised, since local municipalities are responsible for providing, administering and funding child-care institutions (with only some financial support from the *Länder*, subject to different legislation in Germany's 16 *Länder*). No federal funding is even permitted, due to constraints resulting from constitutional rules on principles of financing. Caused by the serious financial crisis of the municipalities, early childhood education is notoriously underfunded: municipalities are overwhelmed by these expenses, set different priorities and hesitate to expand child care.

7   The political culture of constitutionalism in the FRG and the Federal Constitutional Court as a political actor

The prominent role of the Federal Constitutional Court (*Bundesverfassungsgericht*), with its far-reaching authority to overturn and annul statutory law which violates constitutional law and to overrule parliamentary decisions, works as an incentive to shift political struggles from the political arena of parliamentary decision-making towards the judicial arena, especially for actors who were voted down when the parliament enacted statutory law (Vanberg, 2005). Federal law that is in breach of human rights enshrined in Germany's Basic Law can be declared null and void. Not only individuals can bring a claim before the Federal Constitutional Court, relying on human rights; the *Länder* may do so as well if principles of the Basic Law are at stake concerning the division of competences between the Federation and the *Länder*. The court has the power to resolve differences of opinion or doubts on the formal and material compatibility of federal or *Länder* law with the Basic Law.[9] This procedure, known as abstract judicial review, can be initiated by the Federal Government or the government of one of the *Länder*, or by a vote of one-third of the members of the Bundestag. No concrete litigation involving parties in judicial proceedings before a regular court is required; a complaint by one of the 16 *Länder* is enough to start this review procedure before the Federal Constitutional Court. This can be an important weapon in political struggles: since the Federal Constitutional Court can overrule the parliament, political opponents who could not find a majority for their position often use the legal forum and court procedure to challenge on constitutional grounds a statute voted on by the parliament. The political culture in the FRG is therefore very much shaped by 'constitutionalism' and continuous arguments about draft law being or not being in breach of the Basic Law, with different actors threatening to initiate a review by the Federal Constitutional Court.

The court has used this power to overrule the parliament on highly contested subjects (such as abortion law). But since the constitutional reform of 1994 the court has rejected the priority of federal legal authority in a number of cases on different legislative matters,[10] stating that the Federation's legislative competence took priority over that of the *Länder* only if growing divergence between standards of living in the FRG might harm the social order of the nation, or if concrete indications of such a development were apparent. This was a restricted and narrow interpretation of Art. 72 (2) of the Basic Law, which was amended in 1994.

During the revision of the constitution in 1994 following German reunification, the conditions under which the Federation's use of concurring legislative competences takes priority over the *Länder*[11] have been restricted.[12] The Federation can take the regulatory lead in an area prior to the *Länder* only if federal legislation is necessary to reach the goal of creating equivalent living standards throughout the FRG and if this goal cannot be reached without federal intervention, or if necessary to secure legal or economic unity in the national interest which cannot otherwise be maintained without federal legislative intervention. Reforms of federalism in 1994 after German reunification and in 2006 under the grand coalition of Social Democrats and Christian Democrats have further restricted federal leeway for regulating child daycare. Moreover, since the federalism reforms in 1994 the Federal Constitutional Court has interpreted the wording of the Constitution in a very narrow way, which sets further incentives for the *Länder* or groups of members of parliament to initiate proceedings before the court. The legislative competence of the Federation to regulate child and youth welfare under the legislative competence for social welfare (Art. 74 (1) no. 7 Basic Law) (which was controversial in former debates) remains unaffected, but it was explicitly formulated that federal law cannot impose new tasks or duties upon local municipalities (Art. 84 (1) Basic Law) in areas such as youth welfare. This area traditionally lies within the self-government of local municipalities under their administrative and financing competences, while the Federation has no administrative and financing authority in this area. Thus federal law cannot extend rights to a kindergarten place beyond the existing level without the consent of the Länder since this would impose new obligations upon local municipalities responsible for provision and financing. However, the federation can modify already existing rights. But it is contested whether the introduction of a right to a kindergarten place for a child under the age of three, or the right to a full-day place instead of a part-time place is a modification of a former provision or a new right.

8   Self-restraint by political actors in the wake of Federal Constitutional Court rulings: the example of the federal Day-Care Development Act 2005

In order to improve the supply of child daycare (particularly in Germany's western *Länder*) and to strive for compliance with the EU benchmarks to provide places for 33 percent of all young children by 2010, in 2004 a national draft statute was brought into parliamentary debate under the governing Social Democrat/Green coalition. The statute in force since 1 January 2005 brought about only modest reforms. The main point was the explicitly formulated obligation of municipalities to provide a sufficient number of places for children under three and of all-day places (which existed already in former legislation), but the legislation did not introduce any further subjective rights of the child or parent. The following graph 10.1 shows the current situation.

The current law specifies that municipalities are required to plan and provide the necessary number of places to fulfil these needs: places should be provided at least for children of two employed parents or a lone parent in employment and for parents in vocational training or full-time education.[13] The law does not explicitly address the lack of full-time places (the number of hours of daily care is to be defined according to individual need). The reform also resulted in some regulation of

Graph 10.1 Legal entitlement to public child care

	Half-day places	All-day places
Children under three years	No subjective right of the child; obligation of municipalities to provide a sufficient number of places for under-threes Reform envisaged in 2013: subjective right of a child aged 1 year to a place	No subjective right of the child to a place; obligation of municipalities to plan and provide for a sufficient number of all-day places
Children from three years up to school age	Subjective right to a kindergarten place half-day	No subjective right; obligation of municipalities to provide a sufficient number of all-day places
Children or families at risk	A parent may have a right to a place as 'educational aid' under youth welfare law if necessary to prevent endangering the child's welfare[a]	
Lone parent	No special right; but priority when scarce places are distributed; income support and employment agencies shall help them to find a place in cooperation with the local youth office	

Note: [a] Para. 27 Social Law Book VIII.

quality management[14] and in further regulation of registered private childminders,[15] but has been criticised because the required qualifications and training for registered childminders are defined very vaguely and at a low level.

Once again, the whole parliamentary procedure was dominated by quarrels over financing and the division of authority between the federal, *Länder* and municipal levels. The Bundesrat, the second chamber of the national parliament, voted against the draft law based on these arguments. Different actors threatened a review procedure before the Federal Constitutional Court. However, the Bundesrat's veto was overruled by a majority vote in the Bundestag and the legislation entered into force on 1 January 2005. But the Social Democrat–Green majority governing at the time refrained from any more far-reaching reforms (such as giving children under age three the right to a place in kindergarten or daycare) in view of the Federal Constitutional Court restrictions of federal legislative competences under the Basic Law.

9   Conceptualising the problem: the 'federal policy entanglement trap' (Scharpf)

The political scientist Scharpf has described the particular institutional features causing these problems and blocking reform as the 'federal policy entanglement trap' or the 'joint decision trap' (Scharpf, 1985; 1988), referring to a decision-making structure which produces systematically inefficient and inadequate solutions due to its institutional logic; at the same time, this structure is unable to change the institutional framework of its decision-making logic. This situation is the result of a complex system of legislative, administrative and financing authority split between the Federation and the Länder. Taken together, the interconnectedness of these issues, the need for the first and second chambers of parliament, the Bundestag and Bundesrat,[16] to cooperate in the legislative process, the Bundesrat's type of veto power in those legislative matters which require its consent, and the complexities of the financing system[17] all favour strategic behaviour and can block reform, since fiscal aspects and power games overrule arguments related to the subject matter.

10   Path-dependency and change – future prospects

A path-setting institutional decision – assigning kindergarten and early childhood education to the welfare sector – dates back to the early 1920s. The segmentation of child-care institutions developed in the second half of the nineteenth century and has not been overcome for a long period (in contrast to Denmark; see Borchorst in this volume). A shift towards a universal right to a kindergarten place for each child aged three and over occurred only under exceptional circumstances after German reunification in 1991, when this right was part of a political compromise package following a decision of the Federal Constitutional Court which overruled parliamentary legislation on abortion. However, under 'normal' political circumstances, federal initiatives to expand early childhood education, to introduce new rights (e.g., for under-threes or to full-day places) meet with political resistance and institutional obstacles, mainly due to certain features of federalism, the distribution of legal competences to regulate early childhood education and administrative and financing powers. To step out of the 'federal policy entanglement trap' at the national level looks fairly difficult. This not only reinforces path-dependency, but also acts as a stumbling block in the German case.

Change might be easier at the level of the Länder, the main actors to develop further initiatives. Here considerable differences between the 16 Länder are already noticeable – not only between Eastern and Western Germany, which are already a split culture, but also within these groups. The Länder can shift early childhood education more under the auspices of education or extend subjective rights beyond the existing level in national law, as a few Länder have already done.[18] This leads to uneven development at Länder level, with provision being far from sufficient, especially for the under-threes in the western part and with regard to full-day places for all age groups. Meeting the Lisbon targets by 2010 will be a challenge under these conditions.

However, at present there is a certain 'window of opportunity' due to the fact that Germany is governed by a grand coalition of Christian Democrats and Social Democrats. This is one prerequisite for a political majority on such a controversial issue, because the Länder (represented in the Bundesrat, the second chamber in the parliamentary system) also have to agree. There is also a Christian-Democrat minister of family affairs who is trying to push the issue; the government seems willing to introduce a right to a child-care place for children aged one year starting in 2013, to create 750,000 new places in kindergarten and daycare for under-threes (to cover 35 percent of the age group) and to put some of the federal budget surplus resulting from the strong economy into a national fund for child-care vouchers. However, these cabinet plans got through parliamentary voting in September 2008 and have to find the consensus of a majority of the Länder.[19] Even if by some good fortune all this were to happen, a Land might still call on the Federal Constitutional Court to oppose such a solution on constitutional grounds. Thus, future prospects for growth and expansion of early childhood education at the national level look somewhat promising at the moment, but they are fragile and depend on the political good behaviour of different actors. If one of them (e.g., local communities or one of the Länder) challenges the intended reforms before the Federal Constitutional Court, it might well be that the whole reform packages collapse again. What is needed is a broader reform that overcomes some of the institutional traps resulting from particular principles of federalism in Germany – but, as it stands, no such path-breaking development is in sight. This makes the envisaged reforms – a late modernisation of early childhood education in (West) Germany – particularly vulnerable to blockages.

Notes

1. Figures relate to the situation on 31 December 2002 (as a percentage of all children of the age group) and are drawn from Deutsches Jugendinstitut (2005).

2. *Bundesverfassungsgerichtsentscheidungen* vol. 34, p. 165/182f.; vol. 47, p. 46/71ff.; vol. 96, p. 288/304; vol. 98, p. 218/244f.
3. *Entscheidungen des Bayerischen Verfassungsgerichtshofs* (BayVerfGHE) vol. 29, p. 191.
4. *Bundesverfassungsgerichtsentscheidungen* vol. 97, p. 332.
5. *Bundesverfassungsgerichtsentscheidungen* vol. 22, p. 180/212.
6. *Bundesverfassungsgerichtsentscheidungen* vol. 97, p. 332/341f.
7. Hemmrich, 2000, Rn. 5; Constitutional Court of Sachsen-Anhalt, *Landesverfassungsgerichtsentscheidungen* vol. 9, p. 361/367.
8. *Bundesverfassungsgerichtsentscheidungen* vol. 75, p. 40/77.
9. Art. 93 (1) no. 2 Basic Law.
10. At stake was federal legislation related to the training and qualifications needed by persons providing care to the elderly; opening hours for shops; restrictions on keeping attack dogs; regulation of university matters (junior professorships, fees for university students, introduction of student representatives and commissions).
11. The subjects of *konkurrierende Gesetzgebung* are listed in Art. 74 Basic Law and include civil law, penal law, migration law, labour law, economic law, and the abovementioned competence to enact legislation in the field of welfare law and social law.
12. Art. 72 (2) Basic Law, amended in 1994.
13. Para. 24 sec. 3 Social Law Book VIII, as amended from 1 January 2005 onwards.
14. The providers of institutional childcare shall ensure quality through adequate planning and evaluation measures, para. 22a sec. 1 Social Law Book VIII.
15. Smaller improvements are definitions of fees for registered private childminders, including the costs of work accident insurance and a part of pension insurance costs, para. 23 Social Law Book VIII.
16. The Bundestag is the elected national parliament, while the Bundesrat – the second chamber – represents the *Länder*. Throughout most of the history of the FRG, the political parties not represented in the federal government have had a majority in the Bundesrat, which results in a certain political stalemate. Therefore important political reforms have been achieved only in a compromise between the Federal Government and the *Länder*, in an official coalition between Social Democrats and Christian Democrats or as a political compromise between them.
17. There is a large body of economic literature related to the political economy of fiscal federalism, its risks and (in)efficiencies, and problems of public finance within federal multilevel government systems.
18. The *Länder* Brandenburg, Mecklenburg-Western Pomerania, Rhineland-Palatinate and Saarland grant the right to a kindergarten place for six hours a day; Hamburg, North Rhine-Westphalia and Saxony-Anhalt grant the right to a place for five hours a day. Some have extended the right to a kindergarten place to younger children (from two years on in Brandenburg, two and half years in Thuringia, and under-threes in Saxony-Anhalt).
19. A federal statute on financing issues that created a federal fund to subsidise investments in buildings for crèches has already been enacted

on 31 December 2007, but the reform of the Federal Children and Youth Welfare Act of 1990/1991 and the introduction of a right to a place in child care for under-threes in 2013 is still under debate. The first chamber of parliament has decided to introduce this right, but as of September 2008 the approval of the second chamber still stands out.

Bibliography

Deutsches Jugendinstitut, *Zahlenspiegel 2005 – Kindertagesbetreuung im Spiegel der Statistik* (Munich: dji, 2005)

U. Hemmrich, 'Artikel 7 Grundgesetz', in I. v. Münch and B.-O. Bryde, *Grundgesetz-Kommentar*, vol. 1, 5th ed. (Munich: Beck, 2000)

P. Oberhuemer and M. Ulich, *Working with young children in Europe: Provision and staff training* (London: Paul Chapman, 1997)

OECD, *Die Politik der frühkindlichen Betreuung, Bildung, Erziehung in der Bundesrepublik Deutschland: Ein Länderbericht der Organisation für wirtschaftliche Zusammenarbeit und Entwicklung* (Berlin, 2005)

J. Reyer, 'Familie, Kindheit und öffentliche Kleinkinderziehung: Die Entstehung geteilter Sozialisationsfelder im 19. Jahrhundert in Deutschland', in C. Sachße and F. Tennstedt (eds), *Jahrbuch der Sozialarbeit 4. Geschichte und Geschichten* (Reinbek: Rohwolt Verlag, 1981) 299–343

F. Scharpf, 'Die Politikverflechtungs-Falle: Europäische Integration und deutscher Föderalismus im Vergleich', *Politische Vierteljahresschrift* 26 (1985) 323–356

F. Scharpf, 'The Joint Decision Trap: Lessons from German Federalism and European Integration', *Public Administration* 66 (1988) 239–278

K. Scheiwe, 'Rechtliche Rahmenbedingungen der Kindertageseinrichtungen für Kinder ab drei Jahren bis zum Schuleintritt – das deutsche Modell aus vergleichender Perspektive', in K. Scheiwe and M. Schuler-Harms, *Aktuelle Rechtsfragen der Familienpolitik aus vergleichender Sicht* (Baden-Baden: Nomos, 2008) 78–153.

A. Schmitt-Kammler, 'Artikel 7 Grundgesetz', in M. Sachs and U. Battis, *Grundgesetz: Kommentar*, 4th ed. (Munich: Beck, 2007)

G. Vanberg, *The politics of constitutional review in Germany* (New York: Cambridge University Press, 2005)

Youth Ministers of the Länder, 'Bildung fängt im frühen Kindesalter an', *Forum Jugendhilfe* 3 (2002) 19–21

11
Private Family and Institutionalised Public Care for Young Children in Germany and the United States, 1857–1933: An Analysis of Pedagogical Discourses

Meike Sophia Baader

1 Introduction

This chapter looks at the relationship between family and institutionalised care for young children in Germany and the United States in the second half of the nineteenth and early twentieth century as portrayed in German and American 'histories of education'. I have searched these 'histories of education' for references to Fröbel, kindergarten, primary schools and primary education. In the process, it became clear that there are major differences between the German and American 'histories of education'; each has its own heroes and cult figures, each favours and rejects different institutions.[1] 'Histories of education' are obviously strongly rooted in, or create, national constructs and frameworks for interpreting the history of education and its various semantics. A comparative approach can reveal these national semantics and constructs, so that we can learn something about various national interpretations, their backgrounds and how they have been handed down. In the words of the American historian Hayden White, these can be described as 'narratives'. That is, they interpret history – in our case, the history of education – in narrative form, using certain narrative structures, which may include the production of myths and heroes (White, 1996, p. 69).

In methodological terms, my analysis will follow White's thesis that every act of writing history relies on narrative forms, and I seek to uncover the different narratives German and American histories of education have produced on these themes.

Comparing the 'histories of education', one finds something rather surprising: one of the key figures in the American 'histories of education'is the German pedagogue Friedrich Fröbel (1782–1852), founder of kindergartens in Germany in the 1840s.

A 1901 American work on the history of education calls Fröbel a 'sun', saying that 'all future education must be built upon the foundation laid by Fröbel' (Davidson, 1901, p. 239). In 1911, the American pedagogue and developmental psychologist Stanley Hall also associated Fröbel with a heavenly body, calling him the 'morning star' of the 'child study movement' devoted to the empirical study of childhood (Hall, 1911, vol. 1, p. 16 f.; Allen, 2000a, p. 179). These quotes and this view of the German pedagogue's fundamental significance for modern pedagogy are representative of how Fröbel was regarded in American histories of education during the period under review. With good reason, therefore, we can describe Fröbel as a 'cult figure' or hero in the American construction of the history of education.

However, if we look at German 'histories of education' from the same period, we note that Fröbel is either not mentioned at all or at best plays only a marginal role. He seems rather to be an anti-hero, indirectly accused of destroying the family, as in the 1857 edition of Karl von Raumer's *Geschichte der Pädagogik* (first published 1843/44).

On the US side, then, Fröbel is a cult figure or hero; on the German side, he is a persona non grata, and we have a different hero: Pestalozzi. These differing, indeed opposing, views of Fröbel's pedagogical ideas constitute an interesting case study and point to the different ways of constructing pedagogy in different countries.

In this chapter, I will first describe the German construction of the Fröbel case as reflected in histories of education. In a second step, the American interpretation will be recreated. The third section analyses the reasons for the different assessments, which are largely based on differing notions of the relationship between public and private education as well as different views of the family. The fourth and last section formulates conclusions and finds parallels to the current situation. Fröbel's sceptical reception in German 'histories of education' can be seen as part of a long tradition of reservations against the public education of young children which continues to have an influence today and is currently the subject of public debate.

2   The case of Fröbel in German historiography

Fröbel's marginal presence in German histories of education up to the 1930s is clearly a reaction to the ban on kindergartens in Prussia as a result of the 1848/49 revolutions. First issued in Prussia in 1851, the kindergarten ban was not lifted until 1860. In the reaction against the revolutions, kindergartens were thought by the Prussian rulers to instil 'socialism and atheism' in children. In fact, a number of prominent democrats had organised around the Fröbel kindergarten associations, supported kindergartens, and, when they emigrated, helped introduce kindergartens abroad, especially in Switzerland, England and the United States. Often it was the wives of leading figures of the revolution who headed the kindergartens. There are many examples to illustrate this constellation; for instance, in the years 1849/50, the *Frauenzeitung* put out by Louise Otto repeatedly called on readers to support kindergartens, saying that educating children according to Fröbel's teachings was women's specific contribution to the revolution (Baader, 1998, p. 214). Indeed, it was mainly women who helped spread Fröbel's notion of kindergarten, as Ann T. Allen has shown for the United States in particular (Allen, 1989). As we know, the job of kindergarten teacher was one of the first occupations for women in the field of social services (Göschel and Sachße, 1981; Mayer, 1996).

Democrats and revolutionaries supported kindergartens above all because they were not run by churches and were based on the assumption that all children – regardless of their social class or religious affiliation – were equal; this applied in particular to Jewish children. Kindergartens accepted boys and girls and offered women the opportunity for occupational training. And, lastly, kindergarten was a public institution for educating young children; Fröbel intended it especially for working-class children, but in practice it was attended by children from the middle classes, whose parents believed in the institution. These characteristics, which inspired the democrats' support, were listed in the files of the Prussian ministry of education as reasons for banning kindergartens. The chief accusation was that kindergarten was un-Christian and taught children that all people were equal.[2]

Against this background, it is easier to understand Fröbel's virtual absence from German 'histories of education', as well as the subtle, indirect references to him. In von Raumer's *Geschichte der Pädagogik* of 1857, Fröbel appears solely in an appendix listing persons who once spent time with Pestalozzi. The chapter on the education of young children states that schools for young children are appropriate only in case of absolute need.

> If it is not possible to demonstrate such need in the case of schools for young children which have recently been founded (!), this is cause for concern. The bands of affection which unite family members are growing looser in our day; father, mother, child – each thinks only of himself, each goes his own way. Anything that encourages this loveless dissolution and dispersal of the family should be avoided at all costs. Pestalozzi felt this deeply. The family home was so sacred to him that he spoke out against school attendance for young children and left initial schooling up to the mothers. It seems as if children's place is not to be at home, but only at school! (von Raumer, 1857, vol. II, part 3, p. 11)

This is a hidden reference to Fröbel and his kindergartens and an indirect accusation that he advocated sending children to school too early, destroyed family ties and encouraged the individualisation of family members. By contrast, von Raumer devotes a total of 110 pages of his history of pedagogy to Pestalozzi, whom he describes as leaving children where they belong: in the family home. Von Raumer goes on to say that unfortunately 'in our day the exceptions to the rule are on the rise. This is why ours is an age of surrogates. Thus a surrogate is also needed for some mothers – mainly those who neglect their children' (ibid., p. 12 and vol. I, part 1, p. V). This stance is clearly opposed to Fröbel's kindergartens and public education for young children. Mothers who send their children to kindergarten are regarded as 'neglecting their children'; the accusation and the term for such mothers – *Rabenmütter* (literally: 'raven mothers') – has a long tradition. In his section on 'girls' schools', von Raumer also argues that girls should be educated entirely at home (ibid., vol. II, part 3, pp. 450–537). His ideal model of family life is the one Pestalozzi developed in 1771–1775 in his novel *Lienhard und Gertrud*, and he states that no one knew better than Luther that the state order was grounded in an orderly family life (Ibid).

A similar view can be found in Schmid's *Geschichte der Erziehung* (History of education) of 1901, which calls for 'Christian education'and agrees with Friedrich Wilhelm IV that Germany's revolution, among other things, was the fault of the *Gymnasien* (secondary schools preparing pupils for university) because they were too removed from religion. This reflects the specific relationship between church/crown and education policy before and after the founding of the German Empire in 1871. For Schmid, 'being brought up to fear God' is the decisive criterion for all education and child-raising (Schmid, 1901, vol. V, part 1, p. 330 ff).

The basic positions of von Raumer and Schmid are clear: Young children should be raised and educated within the family; this is the responsibility of mothers, whose place is in the private sphere. The education of girls is also the responsibility of the family, which – also according to Luther – is the foundation for the state. Further 'histories of pedagogy' follow the same pattern as von Raumer's and Schmid's; once established, the pattern repeats itself. Apart from a single exception (Regener, 1912, p. 436), Fröbel does not receive fuller treatment until Hermann Nohl's history of pedagogy and his construct of the 'pedagogical movement' of 1933 (Nohl and Pallat, 1933). Nohl emphasises Fröbel's roots in the Romantic movement, considers him a pioneer of the 'new pedagogy' of the youth movement, *Landerziehungsheime* and reform pedagogy, sees him entirely 'within the context of the dynamic, creative will of the German Movement'and calls him the founder 'of a modern pedagogy as an academic discipline based on life, expression and comprehension'. Following Fichte, action (*That-Handlung*) takes the place of Pestalozzi's passive observation.[3] Adding the element of nationalism to his history of pedagogy and constructing a 'German pedagogical movement', Nohl provides a surprising reassessment of Fröbel and Pestalozzi: Fröbel is now declared a hero, though the institution of kindergarten receives no special mention. The German Fröbel fits better than the Swiss Pestalozzi into the notion of a pedagogy of the 'German Movement' with roots in German culture.[4] Nohl makes Fröbel into one of the founders of the 'pedagogy of the German Movement', thus generating a founding myth for this movement.

3   The American reception and the creation of a cult figure

The American accounts note that Fröbel's kindergartens were banned in Prussia in connection with the revolutions of 1848/49; in 1920, Cubberly, for example, comments that the spirit of kindergarten 'does not harmonise with autocratic government'(Cubberly, 1920, pp. 765–766).

They also mention that Fröbel considered emigrating to the United States, the country which he regarded as being the best suited to benefit from his teachings.[5]

'In no country in the world has the kindergarten taken so strong a hold and made so great progress as in America', Seely wrote in 1899; Vandewalker notes that 'In the United States the kindergarten has found a cordial reception and its doctrines exerted a great influence' (Seely, 1899, p. 272; Vandewalker, 1918, p. 603).

Among the pioneers in disseminating kindergarten in the United States were the Bonn revolutionary Carl Schurz and his wife Margarethe, who founded the first kindergarten in Watertown, Wisconsin.[6] Schurz, a well-known and respected politician and reformer in the United States, leader of the Liberal Republican Party, senator from Missouri and Secretary of the Interior, figures in American 'histories of pedagogy' as a 'student of Friedrich Fröbel'.[7]

Fröbel is thus explicitly linked here with politics, democracy and a nonautocratic system of government. This also applies to kindergarten, the institution he founded.

The 'histories of education' by Painter (1896), Seely (1899), Davidson (1901), Monroe (1908, 1915) and Cubberly (1920) largely agree in their view of kindergarten as a microcosm of society; they saw education in kindergartens as democratic and spoke in this connection of a children's republic, drawing on the title of a well-known book on kindergarten, *The Republic of Childhood* (Wiggin and Smith, 1896).

The idea of the Fröbelian kindergarten as a microcosm or 'epitome' of society, which is found again and again in these histories, interprets the kindergartens from the perspective – one could say through the eyes – of the American pragmatist and school reformer John Dewey. Dewey regarded school as one of the central institutions of the modern age and the most important organisation for producing an autonomous 'modern self' capable of action and for making children into future citizens. Dewey developed this connection in his famous, internationally received book, *The School and Society* (1899). In his view, school is a 'society within society' where democracy is practised as a way of life and where the 'modern self' and future citizens are formed.[8]

In the American reception of Fröbel, Dewey's view of school as a 'society within society' or an 'embryonic society' is then transferred to the institution of kindergarten. Kindergarten too appears as a microcosm of society. In this view, Fröbel is also Dewey's predecessor, and Dewey is seen as continuing and refining Fröbel's work, which is centred on the 'self-activity' of the child. Dewey reorganised 'the work of the kindergarten along different and larger lines' (Cubberly, 1920, pp. 780–782).

In *The School and Society*, Dewey himself refers to Fröbel and stresses his influence on Dewey's own system of education (Dewey, 1899, p. 131). At the same time, he says that authoritarian German structures had deformed kindergarten. Democratic America thus becomes the ideal place for Fröbelian pedagogy to realise its possibilities. Here too, we are dealing with a kind of founding myth: modern pedagogy begins with Fröbel, whose potential could only be achieved in the United States.

Fröbel is seen not only as Dewey's predecessor, however; from a Darwinist perspective influenced by evolutionary theory, he is regarded as having recognised that education was the most advanced phase in the process of evolution (Monroe, 1908, p. 335). But this reading ignores the fact that Fröbel's most important writings were published between 1820 and 1840, well before Darwin's groundbreaking work on natural selection, which appeared in 1852.

The above-mentioned 'histories of education' value Fröbel more highly than Rousseau, Pestalozzi and Herbart, giving reasons in each case. Compared with Pestalozzi, we read of Fröbel that '[t]he work was far more substantial than the similar work of Pestalozzi'. Pestalozzi concentrated exclusively on the individual, they write, but the challenges of the Industrial Revolution would have required a shift of focus from the individual to the society, which Herbart and Fröbel then undertook. Fröbel is described as having moved more at the level of contemporary philosophy, psychology and scientific thought (ibid., pp. 331–349).

Fröbel is thus seen as the founder of a modern school of pedagogy focused on the child's activity and development and in harmony with Darwin's theory of evolution and with contemporary psychological and scientific approaches. In this view, Fröbel's greatest legacy, which was further developed by others, includes the educational institution he founded, the pedagogical significance of 'self-activity' regarded as an important basis for the modern self, the awareness of the need for contact with the child's environment and the importance of manual activity.

4 Home education versus making citizens

The reason why Fröbel was rejected by the Germans up to 1933 and why his kindergarten was so highly regarded by the Americans is a fundamental difference in the relation between public and private education, closely linked to differing views of the family.

In America's immigrant society, it was important to integrate children of highly diverse cultural and linguistic backgrounds within American society. The family alone was unable to achieve this task, so public kindergarten was relied on to help.

'The parents are unable to give the child within the house all the education that he needs at this period. He needs association with other children and with teachers from beyond the family circle,' we read in the foreword to the American translation of Fröbel's *The Education of Man* (Fröbel, 1888, p. viii).

The fundamental difference between the American and German reception lies in the perspective on the family. Whereas in Germany the institution of kindergarten was seen as an 'attack' on 'family ties', in the immigrant society of the United States kindergarten proved useful in integrating children from widely differing family and linguistic backgrounds. This also explains why Pestalozzi was so highly regarded in Germany and less so in the United States: Pestalozzi 'made home education central; Froebel aimed at the adaptation of the life of the child to all his institutional relationships, especially for example, to his duties as a citizen' (Cole, 1918, p. 720).

The 'education of citizens' is thus necessarily tied to a public institution and cannot be carried out by the family alone. A century later in 1987, developmental psychologist Lawrence Kohlberg uses almost the same words in a similar explanation of the need for moral and democratic education at school: the family is unable to produce democratic citizens, because it is only a small group, a primary group (Kohlberg, 1987).

The challenges of an immigrant society and the need for integration also explain why the Americans placed so much emphasis on the kindergarten as a 'society of children' where 'social cooperation' in particular is taught. For them, kindergarten was a miniature society 'in which the laws underlying social coordination and control are learned by practice' (Vandewalker, 1918, pp. 598–599, 605).

Integration into society was supposed to start already before school age, and the kindergartens were to serve as miniature models of the desired integration and social cooperation and practise democracy as a way of life.

Kindergarten was regarded in the United States as a means for making citizens – especially out of immigrants. This also explains why, starting in 1890, kindergartens were integrated into the public school system. The American histories of education note with surprise that kindergartens were not part of the educational system in Germany (ibid., p. 601). In fact, committed teachers' associations tried by addressing the National Assembly in 1848 to make kindergartens the first step in a national system of education (Heiland, 1982, p. 115).

The American reception of kindergarten was similar to the situation in England, which however had its own tradition of infant schools. In his 1902 book *The Making of Citizens*, R. E. Hughes writes:

> In the best English Infant Schools a profound revolution has taken place during recent years. Formal lessons ... have disappeared and the whole of the training of the little ones has been based on the principles of the kindergarten as enunciated by Froebel. (Vandewalker, p. 602)

The national construct and national narrative used to make Fröbel into a cult figure in the United States can be summarised as follows: Fröbel's persecution in connection with the democratic revolution of 1848 is contrasted with his acceptance and further development in the United States. His idea of public education for young children is useful for the immigrant society. Fröbel ultimately becomes a founder of modern education in America when he is linked with Darwin and Dewey; a direct line is seen between Fröbel and Dewey in that kindergarten, just like school, is regarded as a microcosm of society and its goal is citizenship education. This education should be provided mainly through public institutions such as kindergarten and school and cannot be achieved by the family alone.

In Germany, by contrast, it was believed that – as Luther said – only the family and a well-ordered 'family regime' could produce a good and conscientious citizen. If the 'family regime' was in order, then the state would also be in order, because family life was supposedly the 'source of blessing for all peoples' (von Raumer, 1857, vol. II, part 3, p. 450), as we read in von Raumer. The fundamentally different views on how to make citizens point to the different types of modern societies and the difference between 'the state' in Germany and 'society' in the United States.

In Germany, kindergarten was generally seen as a threat to the family, and public child-care institutions were justified only for children of 'needy' families, as von Raumer expressed it. The fact that kindergarten in the Federal Republic of Germany today remains separate from the educational system, which the Americans found odd already in 1900, and is instead part of the system of child and youth welfare, is one of the long-term effects of the constellations sketched out here. The imperial youth welfare act (Reichsjugendwohlfahrtsgesetz) of 1922 made kindergarten part of child and youth welfare, and this structure was retained in West Germany after World War II.

A look at other countries makes clear that we are likely dealing with a German 'Sonderweg' in this field. Since 1881, France has had the institution of *ecole maternelle*, voluntary preschools for three- to six-year-olds that belong to the system of public education and are free of charge. As in Belgium, 70 percent of all children attended such preschools already in the 1920s (Scheiwe, 2006, p. 51). In Germany, only 33 percent of three- to five-year-olds attended kindergarten in 1960 (Zeiher, 1989, p. 104).

In West Germany, this family policy reticence towards an extensive system of primary education was no doubt due to the history of National Socialism and the state intervention in families and childhood; it was also related to competition with East Germany, which was well-known for its nationwide system of full-time child care. Even 17 years after the fall of the Berlin Wall, those in the Federal Republic who advocate expanding preschool education are accused of following the 'GDR ideology of state care by strangers', to quote the Catholic Bishop Mixa of Augsburg, for example (*Frankfurter Allgemeine Zeitung*, 23 February 2007, p. 1).

Following the end of communism in 1989, there was nonetheless a slow change of attitudes towards family policy. The expansion of kindergartens began in 1991 when a legal claim to a half-day place in a kindergarten was introduced. A change of attitude is also apparent in the current debates on ending the separation between child and youth welfare on the one hand and the education system on the other hand, and in the growing discussion of kindergarten's educational mission, the issue of charging fees for kindergarten and the discussion of increasing day care for children under age three.

And kindergarten is gradually starting to be viewed in Germany as an important institution for integrating immigrant children, as it was in the United States already in the nineteenth century, as described above. In connection with the discussions of deficits in preschool education primarily affecting children of immigrant backgrounds from families with low levels of education, the Federal Government Commissioner for Integration, Maria Böhmer, said in April 2006 that the integration of children with an immigrant background must start with kindergarten (*Süddeutsche Zeitung*, 1–2 April 2006, p. 1). Noting that children of immigrant backgrounds often lack German language skills when starting school, Böhmer favours a mandatory kindergarten year (*Frankfurter Allgemeine Zeitung*, 23 February 2007, p. 4).

5   Conclusion

On a number of issues related to the kindergarten movement, the German and American perspectives are diametrically opposed, as US historian Ann Taylor Allen noted in her comparison of the movements: the view of democracy, public education, gender and religion (Allen, 1989). Analysing the 'histories of education' also reveals fundamental differences in how the family is viewed, which are in turn linked to religion: according to Luther, the family constitutes the foundation for relations between the sexes and for the state order. If families, in particular mothers, in needy circumstances are unable to look after their young children, then in Germany this is the responsibility of the church as institution. Not that American society is less influenced by religion, but churches had less direct institutional influence on the educational system and the plurality of religions was more accepted. In Germany, the fact that kindergartens were not part of the educational system also has to do with the difficult compromise negotiated to end church involvement in education during the Weimar Republic: the state was to be in charge of the schools, while the preschool area largely remained in the hands of the churches. This continuing 'clericalisation' of preschool education was one reason for the West German *Kinderladen* movement around 1968 to found alternative institutions (Von Werder, 1977, p. 14). Against this background, the attitude in prewar Germany and the postwar Federal Republic can be summed up as follows: early childhood belongs to the institution of the family and to mothers and – if these are unavailable – to the institution of the church, in any case not the state or a public education system. This attitude is bolstered by specific and closely related attitudes towards the family, mothers, the mother–child bond and childhood.[9] One indication of the longevity of the German *Sonderweg* concerning issues of public care for young children is that one of the sharpest critics of expanding day care for children under three is a Catholic bishop, Bishop Mixa of Augsburg, supported by Catholic cardinals. He calls the initiative 'hostile to children' and sees it as an attack on the natural maternal role. When Cardinal Meisner describes this as a problem for 'the salvation of our people', he is taking much the same line as the nineteenth-century 'histories of education' cited here. Cardinal Lehmann even quotes the Bible to argue against excessive state involvement in child care (*Frankfurter Allgemeine Zeitung*, 26 February 2007, p. 1). One wonders whether this idea would ever occur to his French counterparts.

Notes

1. Some parts of this chapter have already appeared in Casale, Tröhler and Oelkers (2006), where they are analysed with regard to the national contexts of educational history and their historiographical problems. The present

chapter focuses on the different views of the relationship between family and public education for young children, discussed here also with regard to the longevity of attitudes and mentalities and in the context of the current debate over better daycare for young children in Germany.

2. For the precise history of the ban and the corresponding records, see Baader (1998; 1999).
3. Nohl (1930) p. 16. Here, the previously dominant image is reversed: Fröbel is seen as being closer to Fichte than Pestalozzi and idealised as a man of action, whereas the earlier histories pointed out that Fichte referred to Pestalozzi in his *Reden*.
4. Nohl does not mention Fröbel's connection to the revolution.
5. In *The Renewal of Life* (1836), Fröbel 'pointed to the United States as the country best fitted ... to receive his educational message and to profit thereby' (Fröbel, 1888, p. xx).
6. This first kindergarten was attended by German-speaking children (Allen, 1995, p. 87).
7. Halsey, 1968, pp. 495–496; Vandewalker, 1918, p. 604; Cubberly, 1920, p. 766. Schurz served as US senator from Missouri from 1869 to 1877 and Secretary of the Interior from 1877 to 1881 under President Hayes.
8. On the relationship between school, the modern self and the making of citizens in Dewey, see Popkewitz (2005).
9. On the history of the German mother, see Vinken (2001).

Bibliography

A. Allen, 'Kommt, laßt uns unsern Kindern leben. Kindergartenbewegung in Deutschland und in den Vereinigten Staaten, 1840–1914', *Zeitschrift für Pädagogik*, 35 (1989) 65–84

A. Allen, *Feminism and Motherhood in Germany, 1800–1941* (New Brunswick: Rutgers University Press, 1991)

A. Allen, 'American and German women in the kindergarten movement, 1850–1914', in H. Geitz, J. Heideking and J. Herbst (eds), *German Influences on education in the United States to 1917* (Cambridge: Cambridge University Press, 1995), 85–102

A. Allen, *Feminismus und Mütterlichkeit in Deutschland 1800–1914* (Weinheim: Beltz Verlag, 2000a)

A. Allen, 'Kindergarten', in J. Chastain (ed.), *Encyclopedia of revolutions of 1848* (2000b), available on the Internet at http://www.ohiou.edu/~Chastain/ip/kinderga.htm

M. Baader, ' "Alle wahren Demokraten tun es." Die Fröbelschen Kindergärten und der Zusammenhang von Erziehung, Revolution und Religion', in C. Jansen and T. Mergel (eds), *Die Revolutionen von 1848/49* (Göttingen: Vandenhoeck, 1998), 206–225

R. Casale, D. Tröhler and J. Oelkers (eds), *Methoden und Kontexte. Historiographische Probleme der Bildungsforschung* (Göttingen: Wallstein, 2006)

P. Cole, 'Fröbel', in P. Monroe (ed.), *A Cyclopedia of Education*, Vol. II (New York: Macmillan, 1918), 718–723

E. Cubberly, *Syllabus of Lectures on the History of Education*, 2nd edition (New York: Macmillan, 1904)

E. Cubberly, *The History of Education* (Boston: Houghton Mifflin, 1920)

T. Davidson, *A History of Education* (New York: Charles Scribners's Sons, 1901)

J. Dewey, *The School and Society* (Chicago: University of Chicago Press, 1899)

F. Fröbel, *Die Menschenerziehung* (Leipzig: A. Wienbrack, 1826)

F. Fröbel, *The Education of Man.* Translated and annotated by W. N. Hailmann (New York: D. Appleton and Company, 1888)

F. Fröbel, *Erneuerung des Lebens fordert das Jahr 1836* (Leipzig: Quelle und Meyer, 1933)

F. Fröbel, 'Die Menschenerziehung', in F. Fröbel (ed.), *Ausgewählte Schriften*, Vol. II (Stuttgart: Cotta, 1982)

F. Fröbel, 'Entwurf eines Planes zur Begründung und Ausführung eines Kindergartens', in F. Fröbel (ed.), *Ausgewählte Schriften*, Vol. I (Stuttgart: Cotta, 1982), 114–125

H. Göschel and C. Sachße, 'Theorie und Praxis in der Sozialarbeit. Ein Rückblick auf die Anfänge sozialer Berufsausbildung', in C. Sachße and F. Tennstedt (eds), *Jahrbuch der Sozialarbeit* 4 (Reinbek: Rowohlt, 1981), 422–443

G. Hall, 'The Pedagogy of the Kindergarten', in G. Hall (ed.), *Educational Problems*, vol. I (New York: Appleton, 1911), 1–41

G. Hall and J. Mansfield (eds), *Bibliography of Education* (Boston: D.C. Heath & Co., 1893)

W. Halsey (ed.), *Collier's encyclopedia* (New York: Macmillan, 1968)

H. Heiland, *Fröbel* (Reinbek: Rowohlt, 1982)

R. Hughes, *The making of citizens. A study in comparative education* (London: Walter Schott, 1902)

L. Kohlberg, 'Moralische Entwicklung und demokratische Erziehung', in G. Lind and J. Raschert (eds), *Moralische Entwicklung und demokratische Erziehung* (Weinheim: Beltz, 1987), 25–43

C. Mayer, 'Zur Kategorie "Beruf" in der Bildungsgeschichte von Frauen im 18. und 19. Jahrhundert', in E. Kleinau (ed.), *Frauen in pädagogischen Berufen* (Bad Heilbrunn: Klinkhardt, 1996), 14–38

P. Monroe (ed.), *A Brief Course in the History of Education* (London: Macmillan & Co., 1908)

P. Monroe (ed.), *A Textbook in the History of Education* (New York: MacMillan, 1915)

P. Monroe (ed.), *A Cyclopedia of Education* (New York: MacMillan, 1918)

H. Nohl and L. Pallat (eds), *Handbuch der Pädagogik* (Langensalza: Beltz, 1933)

F. Painter, *A History of Education* (New York: D. Appleton, 1896)

T. Popkewitz (ed.), *Inventing the Modern Self and John Dewey. Modernities and the Traveling of Pragmatism in Education* (New York: Palgrave Macmillan, 2005)

F. Regener, *Skizzen zur Geschichte der Pädagogik* (Langensalza: Beyer & Söhne, 1912)

K. Schmid, *Geschichte der Erziehung vom Anfang an bis auf unsere Zeit* (Stuttgart: Cotta, 1901)

L. Seely, *History of Education* (New York: American Book Company, 1899)

K. Scheiwe, 'Entwicklungstendenzen von Kindertagesstätten und Vorschulbetreuung', *Magazin der Universität Hildesheim*, 11 (2006) 51–52

N. Vandewalker, 'Kindergarten', in P. Monroe (ed.), *A Cyclopedia of Education*, Vol. III (New York: Macmillan, 1918), 598–606

B. Vinken, *Die deutsche Mutter. Der lange Schatten eines Mythos* (Munich/Zurich: Piper, 2001)

K. von Raumer, *Geschichte der Pädagogik vom Wiederaufblühen klassischer Studien bis auf unsere Zeit*, 3rd edition (Stuttgart: Samuel Liesching, 1857)

L. von Werder, 'Bedeutung und Entwicklung der Kinderladenbewegung in der Bundesrepublik', in L. von Werder (ed.), *Was kommt nach den Kinderläden?* (Berlin: Klaus Wagenbach, 1977), 7–58

H. White, 'Literaturtheorie und Geschichtsschreibung', in H. Nagl-Docekal (ed.), *Der Sinn des Historischen. Geschichtsphilosophische Debatten* (Frankfurt-am-Main: Fischer, 1996), 67–106

K. Wiggin and N. Smith, *The republic of childhood* (Boston: Houghton, Mifflin & Co., 1896)

H. Zeiher, 'Über den Umgang mit der Zeit bei Kindern', in M. Fölling-Albers (ed.), *Veränderte Kindheit – veränderte Grundschule* (Frankfurt-am-Main: Arbeitkreis Grundschule, 1989), 103–113

12
Maternalism and Truncated Professionalism – Historical Perspectives on Kindergarten Teachers

Ursula Rabe-Kleberg

Women's care for children is associated with several related but distinct concepts. Mother and motherhood refer to the objective fact of having a child of one's own. Maternalism and motherliness, by contrast, are subjective, culturally constructed concepts referring to the qualities associated with a mother's care for her child. Maternalism can be understood as a social and cultural strategy of dealing with motherhood. The concept of maternalism stems primarily from traditional relationships between genders and generations in specific societies and cultures. However, maternalism can also be seen more generally as a particular kind of cultural understanding of motherhood and as a specific way of dealing with mothers and their form of work and competence that is characteristic in Germany (Randall, 2000). Motherliness means having the personal qualities required to be a (good) mother. More generally, this is considered to be a gendered habitus – a gender-specific (female) trait that enables one to feel, think and act in a motherly way. These terms are distinct, but the boundaries around them are not hard and fast, so they overlap each other in a way that has a significant impact on the professionalisation of responsibilities traditionally associated with women, such as child care.

This essay will highlight the interdependency of professionalism and maternalism in an attempt to unravel the complexities of the two social phenomena. The focus of the discussion is on Germany, and I draw on concepts and practices in other countries to highlight the specificity of the German experience. I will first review the historical, social and cultural framework of the problem. Culturally, the image of a 'good mother' is determined by the effects of motherhood on the responsibilities, behaviour and competence of the mother. Next, I will assess the relationship between motherliness and the profession of early childhood education/child care in an attempt to elucidate the question of whether and how motherliness (and female qualities in general) can contribute to the formation of a profession. Alternatively, does the socially and culturally ascribed, specifically female aptitude for this work tend to hinder the development of child care as a profession? This double question has been an issue for over 150 years and it continues to emerge in constantly changing guises. Thirdly, based on a comparison of the maternal and professional relationship, I will discuss whether motherliness – defined as a general human aptitude and reflective ability – should be considered an essential feature of professional behaviour, that is, of the professional as such, independent of gender.

1 Maternalism and profession in Germany

A brief look at the historical background will shed more light on the specific developments in Germany and elucidate the still valid and effective workings of gender and generation relationships that we call maternalism.

During the eighteenth and nineteenth centuries in all modern societies, the middle-class family model developed with strong boundaries between inside and outside, private and public. It entailed a clear division of functions and labour and a hierarchical order of men and women, and of fathers and mothers (Horkheimer, 1936). When comparing nations, societies and cultures, it is essential to know in which of the strata, milieus or social groups the model first became established and which traditions it encountered there.

In Germany or, more precisely, in Prussia, decisive sociocultural changes occurred at the beginning of the nineteenth century. First of all, the idea of conjugal love and marital partnership combined with a romantic idealisation of everything feminine developed in literary and academic circles. A concept of profession that inseparably combined education and work developed in the historical and social milieu of Germany's emerging, educated middle class (*Bildungsbürgertum*). This is presumably the forerunner of the German's modern concept of profession, which, as a part of the public sphere, was 'naturally' reserved for men (Hausen, 1976; Kocka, 1991; Rabe-Kleberg, 1993).

As an alternative, women were offered the 'profession' or, rather, the 'calling' of motherhood (Campe, 1796; Niethammer, 1808/1968; Mayer, 1996; Rabe-Kleberg, 2003). But this concept differed fundamentally from the concept of male profession with its dominating, idealistic understanding of educational ideas associated with grammar schools and academics. It 'did without' any recognised certificates and thus forfeited the acknowledgement of social position and participation as opportunities for women. Then, the profession of mother and the development of motherliness as a 'professional' skill implied exclusion from the public sphere and inclusion in the private, family sphere.

A decisive factor is that this German concept of maternal duties developed in a section of the middle class in which small, two-generation family units had become established and accepted. The members of these families were rich in education but poor in terms of wealth. The housewife had neither servants nor governesses to whom she could delegate some of her work as a mother. Consequently, the image of a mother as a woman who is *solely* responsible for all child-raising duties was legitimated and increasingly promoted by (male) scholars in all disciplines (Hausen, 1976, Schütze, 1991; Wunder and Vanja, 1991).

The German understanding of the generation relationship is thus based on a type of motherhood determined by a strongly emotional element of ethical responsibility. Here the mother's main function is based on motherly love, which emotionally compensates for the coldness and rationality of society. In Horkheimer's (1936) reflections on the relationship between authority and family, he stressed the dialectic relationship between motherly love and fatherly authority. He believed that the mother's ability to compensate through love actively enables the recurring production of authoritarian coldness within society (by fathers). In more general terms, this means that the one-sided attribution of motherliness, i.e., the ability and readiness to provide emotional closeness and bonding and to exercise patience and reserve, to women determines not only hierarchical gender structures but also the limited development of the corresponding capabilities in males.

Together with the specific nature of the family model, this image of the mother was clearly attractive to all levels and classes in Germany and it gradually became established in all levels of society, including the lower middle and working classes. A glance across national borders shows that the developments in Germany were significantly different from those in France (Badinter, 1999), where the image of the mother is much more clearly based on the model of the aristocracy and upper middle class, or from those in Scandinavia (Haas, 1993), where a relatively balanced, agrarian division of labour in gender relationships persisted until far into the twentieth century, or from those in the United States, where a clear assignment of gender-specific characters only developed distinct contours around the turn of the twentieth century (Coltrane and Galt, 2000). Such historically determined cultural differences exert their effects to this day, and the strength of their 'sustainability' should not be underrated. In contrast to many other societies in Europe and America, it still serves as the basis of Germany's state welfare benefits structures (Kaufmann, 1982) and it shapes how society understands and treats maternalism and the professionalisation of traditionally female occupations.

The power of tradition in shaping the concept of maternalism to this day is particularly interesting to study in Germany in light of the division into two completely different political, economic, and cultural systems after World War II. Despite more than four decades of separation, the understanding of maternalism remained essentially the same in the two countries. I reject the theory that the role of women was completely different in the former East Germany (GDR). Although there was a fairly high level of social equality in the GDR, the function of women as mothers was supported and safeguarded against external influences through the appropriate infrastructures engineered by state policies, which were ironically dubbed 'Mummy policies' (Rabe-Kleberg, 1999). It is striking that, in both Eastern and Western Germany, the question of mothers and motherhood is still almost always discussed without due consideration of fathers or fatherhood. The lively debates seen especially in the United States and Scandinavia about the tasks of men in the generation relationship have only just started in Germany. The theory is that, because of this continuing focus on motherhood and maternalism, women and society are placing little or no pressure on men to examine and fulfil their responsibilities of fatherhood and fatherliness.

Two recent OECD reports addressed the relationship between maternalism and profession, and found that German society, especially in Western Germany, is traditionally characterised by a pronounced 'maternalism' that is used as an argument against children starting school early and against all-day child care and schools (OECD, 2004; 2005). Given this background, it is not surprising that so much criticism can be heard in Germany about the current introduction of academic courses for preschool teachers and child-care workers. These comments come from all areas of the sociopolitical spectrum and contain two repeated warnings. One is that girls who do not complete their secondary schooling will be excluded from the traditional female professions in which they have done so well for decades. This warning also takes a backhanded form: it is less problematic for girls than for boys to drop out of school, because, although the young women may not be able to read or write as well, not to mention their skills in maths, they are 'good with children' and 'motherly' and that, after all, is what counts most. The second warning expresses the fear that 'educated' young women must forfeit their motherliness and alienate themselves from children if they wish to enter the upper echelons of management. These arguments regard education and motherliness as two mutually exclusive principles. Apparently, some people expect or hope that motherliness will prevent or obstruct a woman from pursuing professional development and a career.

The concept of maternalism interferes with the professionalisation of child care in numerous ways. My research on the relation between parents and professionals and on experiences in cooperation with preschool teachers revealed other interesting findings.[1] Many of the teachers we interviewed reported that they only feel equal to and more self-assured with the mothers of the children in their kindergarten groups if they have children of their own. In other words, they implicitly see motherhood as a qualification for their work. The 'qualification' of being a mother to work in child care emerged in interviews with the directors of kindergartens as well. When we asked them about problems associated with their work, they tended to express uneasiness and reservations about child-care workers who pursue further education goals and are well-informed about the relevant current debates, but live as singles and have no children of their own. Based on numerous personal and professional biographical interviews carried out with child-care workers in recent years, we gained insight into the manner and intensity of influence of the teachers' experiences with their own mothers and children on their professional sphere. These experiences permeate the image of professional actors in an unconscious and uncontrolled way and are largely unrecognised and neglected by the profession itself. In this respect, motherhood is a 'dark', unexplored zone of professionalism.

2 Motherliness and child-raising as a profession

Are motherliness and professional competence compatible or incompatible or, more generally, how do they relate to each other? These questions are among the key issues of nearly all major discussions in the academic and policy-making communities about educational institutions and teaching professions, especially early childhood education. They focus on the necessary skills and training and the institutional scope of educational activities. The social and political value attached to the institutions dedicated to early childhood education and the people involved in them continues to be hotly debated.

Here, we differentiate between two levels in our search for answers. First, there is the level of the structure and development of the profession of child care and early education where motherliness is used as an argument as well as a counter-argument. Secondly, there is the level of preconditions and contents of professional behaviour, where motherliness is treated as a resource and used as a cover for 'hidden agendas'.

In the professional development of traditionally female occupations, it was argued that motherliness was a more or less natural competence of one specific gender: females. It was used as a counter-argument when deciding who was responsible and suitable for caring for and educating children outside the family, in kindergartens and primary schools. The choices were men, women or both. The question was, which abilities were these individuals required to have and how and where had they acquired their knowledge and relevant skills?

Historically, the merely symbolic or rhetorical professionalisation of motherly work in Germany made it difficult to establish women's professions modelled on those of men. In the area of childhood education, Fröbel failed in his attempts to create a profession for women which united education and work, as was the case for male professions (Fröbel, 1841). The idea of highly qualified (i.e., college-educated) kindergarten teachers failed in Germany after the 1848 revolution, but thrived in the United Kingdom and the United States. British and American women also fought for positions in teaching, social education, politics and society – but with more success than their German counterparts. Some decades later Helene Lange and her female comrades-in-arms in Germany tried to legitimise the claim to professionalism in child care with the concept of 'spiritual motherhood'. The idea was to make motherliness a more or less gender-specific form of professional competence. However, this type of 'motherly feminism' (Allen, 2000) brought women only into very 'modest' professions (Schütze, 1996).

This position on motherliness and maternalism was particularly easy to instrumentalise in counter-arguments against female professions and positions. Bureaucracies, male-dominated teachers' associations and educational theoreticians had no qualms about using maternalistic arguments against women. For example, around 1900 Prussian authorities refused to introduce state examinations for kindergarten teachers because, they claimed, one's qualification for being a kindergarten teacher, that is, motherliness, could not be determined by an exam

(Rabe-Kleberg, 1990). In contrast to France and Italy, only a few women in Prussia taught at primary schools at the turn of the last century. Men had become firmly established as teachers since the mid-nineteenth century, and they knew very well how to defend their positions politically. They staked a claim to knowledge and positioned it as a more valuable qualification than motherliness (Rabe-Kleberg, 2004). The now highly acclaimed book by the Swedish feminist Ellen Key was received in Germany with great controversy during the first decades of the twentieth century. Educators such as Nohl and Paulsen argued against the 'motherly principle' in education and maintained that boys needed strict male teachers (Key, 1900/1992; Nohl, 1933/1988; Paulsen, 1912).

'Spiritual motherhood' and the 'motherly principle' became arguments and counter-arguments in a power struggle for jobs, power and material rewards in professional development. These struggles can be seen as a 'professional battle', as an internal professional power struggle for exclusion and inclusion, for claims and influence (Abbott, 1988). In Germany, this struggle took place as a pronounced conflict between genders (Rabe-Kleberg, 1993).

How, then, was it possible for the education and care of children in kindergartens to be carried out for such a long time by women deprived of the necessary level of education and knowledge without causing an educational catastrophe or massive harm to the children? The answer may be that, probably up until the 1960s, the majority of kindergarten teachers in Germany were recruited from educated middle-class families who had two kinds of 'capital' as defined by Bourdieu (1987). In other words, they had a relatively good general education that greatly exceeded what was learned in school and they had a model of motherhood as a calling and motherliness as a natural female quality gained and consolidated through experience and socialisation in their families. Then, it obviously sufficed to use this initial capital and build it up with a relatively short course specifically designed for child-care specialists, an occupation usually only pursued until marriage. This 'capital' would not be completely wasted because the women's work as kindergarten teachers was thought to be a good preparation for motherhood and training in motherliness.

In the 1960s a shift in career orientation took place among young women. They started pushing back the boundaries. The daughters from educated middle-class families in West Germany started to make use of expanded education opportunities and moved into academic professions. In turn, the daughters of working-class families with lower school qualifications and aspirations began to enter the professional child-care sector that their better-heeled sisters were leaving behind. In subsequent years, a series of generally inadequate education and child-care reforms were introduced. Training programmes were lengthened and enhanced, but the question of competences and gender-specific qualifications remained unsolved. The state of affairs was repeatedly lamented in numerous specialist articles and discussions.

The 1960s also saw a shift in career orientation in East Germany. There, too, it was no longer possible to recruit female kindergarten teachers from the traditional social middle class after the 1960s, but for different reasons. The members of this social class did not conform to the interests of the regime, and kindergarten education had become an occupation for social climbers, that is, for working-class women in the GDR. In East Germany, the education of kindergarten teachers was ranked as equivalent to that of engineers (which served as a social mobility ladder for working-class boys). The authoritarian state did not leave anything to chance. Education, career development and the daily practice of professional child care were governed by an obligatory body of standardised knowledge and controlled by norms and rules (Rabe-Kleberg, 2003).[2]

The 'natural' motherliness of kindergarten teachers, although not explicitly required by the system, may well have served as a source of reward and recognition in conditions where intervention and control dominated childhood development. Why, then, were only women allowed to work in kindergartens in the GDR? Maybe the system more or less consciously drew on the resource that women offered for providing 'caring child care'.

It seems clear that both German systems rely on motherhood and motherliness as an acquired resource, but they do not recognise the professional skills they engender. Distinctions are made between education and specific professional knowledge. In some cases, they are thought to be contradictory to maternal qualities – the nurturing abilities that developed in a historical socialisation process embracing women of nearly all generations and classes. The transfer and acquisition of maternal qualities are left to chance, and the application and relevance of maternal aptitude in the professional context remains unrecognised and misunderstood.

3   Conclusion and outlook: Motherliness – professional behaviour 'in progress'?

As we have seen, the concept of maternalism developed within the historical evolution of gender relations in German society. It became an educated middle-class 'profession' or 'calling' requiring the specific knowledge and skills associated with 'motherliness'. These competences were thought to be not only essential to all women, but also an inherent part of the 'feminine nature'. All responsibility for raising the next generation was placed solely in the hands of women, creating a monopoly on the time of mothers. Although some change has occurred over the past few decades, the underlying concepts of maternalism and motherliness that are attributed to women continue to limit the professionalisation of child care.

Breaking out of the confines of traditional conceptions requires looking at things in a new way, and this is often helped by drawing comparisons with different areas. For example, it is instructive to consider the relationship of a mother with her child as having many similarities with the relationship between a professional and his or her client, although of course there are also many differences. Professional conduct intervenes in a person's material and social, physical and psychological existence. Ideally, the relationship is legitimised by voluntary engagement by the client, and by an alliance or bond based on mutual trust between the professional and the client. Respect and a high degree of responsibility are also needed for a successful outcome (Oevermann, 1996; Rabe-Kleberg, 1996; Schütze, 1996). Many of these elements are characteristic of the mother–child relationship, but they are defined in different terms: existential dependency of the child, mutual relationship and attachment, trust and respect, responsibility and care. All of these characteristics appear in normative concepts as well as in empirical descriptions of motherly relationships (Badinter, 1999; Schütze, 1991).

Maternal and professional relationships differ less in terms of required skills than in terms of social context and institutional structures where these skills are applied. The different contexts tend to be private vs. public, personal vs. professional, exclusive vs. universal, and emotionally expressive vs. emotionally controlled. They also differ in relation to the systematic professional knowledge required for these personally acquired skills. This specific knowledge is necessary in order to constantly reflect on one's own behaviour and that of the client, to substantiate it and to criticise it – in other words to monitor it. The paradox of proximity and distance and knowledge and uncertainty that occurs in child care cannot be overcome by motherly kindness on its own. It needs to be professionally managed, balanced and shaped.

Crossing borders is dangerous if it is not well-considered. Motherliness can be detrimental when applied to professional relationships in an unreflected and uncontrolled manner. A motherly attitude and the individual acquisition of the appropriate skills can be either helpful or harmful to the development of professional habitus and behaviour. It is not just women who need to cross borders consciously; men should also push back the boundaries limiting their roles and identities in society. Both women and men should systematically learn child-care skills as general human relationship and professional skills, instead of seeing motherliness as a gender-specific trait, cultural heritage and personal 'baggage'. Such a change in attitude must be accompanied by professionalisation in terms of both personal and professional development. This shift must be given top priority in the educational process and in the life-long process of critical self-reflection.

Notes

1. Most recently in the research project 'Elternhaus und Kindergarten' ('Child care at home and in kindergarten') as part of a programme funded by the Deutsche Forschungsgemeinschaft (DFG German Research Association).
2. In professional biographical narratives of the women involved the permanent and inescapable presence of this top-down pattern is confirmed by both critics and proponents (Musiol, 1998).

Bibliography

A. Abbott, *The System of Professions. An Essay on the Division of Expert Labor* (Chicago: Chicago University Press, 1988)

A. Allen, *Feminismus und Mütterlichkeit in Deutschland 1800–1914* (Weinheim: Deutscher Studien Verlag, 2000)

E. Badinter, *Die Mutterliebe: Geschichte eines Gefühls vom 17. Jahrhundert bis heute* (München: Piper, 1999)

P. Bourdieu, *Die feinen Unterschiede. Kritik der gesellschaftlichen Urteilskraft* (Frankfurt-am-Main: Suhrkamp, 1987)

J. Campe, *Väterlicher Rath für meine Tochter. Ein Gegenstück zum Theophron* (Paderborn: Hüttemann, 1988; originally 1796)

S. Coltrane and J. Galt, 'The History of Men's Caring. Evaluating Precedents for Father's Family Involvement', in M. Harrington Meyer (ed.), *Care Work: Gender, Labor and the Welfare State* (New York, London: Routledge, 2000), 15–36

F. Fröbel, 'Die Bildung von Kinderpflegerinnen: Kindermädchen und Kinderwärterinnen – überhaupt die Bildung zur ersten Kindererziehung und die Führung von Bewahranstalten – besonders den deutschen Kindergarten betreffend', in E. Hofmann (ed.), *Friedrich Fröbel. Ausgewählte Schriften, Bd. 4: Die Spielgaben* (Stuttgart: Klett-Cotta, 1982; originally 1841), 179–202

F. Fröbel, 'Die Kindergärten als um- und erfassende Pflege- und Erziehungsanstalten der Kindheit, der Kinder bis zum schulfähigen Alter und der deutschen Kindergarten als eine Musteranstalt dafür insbesondere', in E. Hofmann (ed.), *Friedrich Fröbel. Ausgewählte Schriften und Briefe von 1809–1851* (Godesberg: Küpper, 1951), 149–178

L. Haas, 'Nurturing Fathers and Working Mothers. Changing Gender Roles in Sweden', in J. Hood (ed.), *Men, Work and Family* (Newbury Park: Sage, 1993), 238–261

K. Hausen, 'Die Polarisierung der Geschlechtscharaktere. Eine Spiegelung der Dissoziation von Erwerbs- und Familienleben', in W. Conze (ed.), *Sozialgeschichte der Familie in der Neuzeit Europas* (Stuttgart: Klett, 1976), 363–393

M. Horkheimer (ed.), *Studien über Autorität und Familie* (Paris: Alcan, 1936)

F. Kaufmann, *Staatliche Sozialpolitik und Familie* (München: Oldenbourg, 1982)

E. Key, *Das Jahrhundert des Kindes* (Weinheim: Beltz, 1992; originally 1900)

J. Kocka, 'Bürgertum and professions in the nineteenth century: two alternative approaches', in M. Burrage and R. Torstendahl (eds), *Professions in Theory and History. Rethinking the Study of Professions* (London: Sage, 1991), 62–74

C. Mayer, 'Zur Kategorie "Beruf" in der Bildungsgeschichte von Frauen im 18. und 19. Jahrhundert', in E. Glumpler and E. Kleinau (eds), *Frauen in pädagogischen Berufen*, I (Bad Heilbrunn: Klinkhardt, 1996), 14–38

M. Musiol, '*Gewohntes*' und '*Verändertes*' im pädagogischen Handeln von Erzieherinnen in den neuen Bundesländern und die Transformation in Kindertageseinrichtungen (unpublished PhD, Halle-Wittenberg, 1998)

F. I. Niethammer, 'Der Streit des Philanthropismus und des Humanismus in der Theorie des Erziehungs-Unterrichts unserer Zeit', in F. I. Niethammer, *Philanthropismus – Humanismus. Texte zur Schulreform* (Weinheim: Beltz, 1968; originally 1808), 79–359

H. Nohl, *Pädagogik aus dreißig Jahren* (Frankfurt-am-Main: Suhrkamp, 1988; originally 1933)

OECD, OECD Early Childhood Policy Review 2002–2004 Background Report Germany (Munich: DJI, 2004)

OECD, *Starting Strong* (Paris: OECD, 2005)

U. Oevermann, 'Theoretische Skizze einer revidierten Theorie professionellen Handelns', in A. Combe and W. Helsper (eds), *Pädagogische Professionalität* (Frankfurt-am-Main: Suhrkamp, 1996), 70–182

F. Paulsen, 'Väter und Söhne', in F. Paulsen (ed.), *Gesammelte pädagogische Abhandlungen* (Stuttgart: Cotta, 1912), 497–561

U. Rabe-Kleberg, *Besser gebildet und doch nicht gleich! Frauen und Bildung in der Arbeitsgesellschaft* (Bielefeld: Kleine, 1990)

U. Rabe-Kleberg, *Verantwortlichkeit und Macht - Ein Beitrag zum Verhältnis von Geschlecht und Beruf angesichts der Krise traditioneller Frauenberufe* (Bielefeld: Kleine, 1993)

U. Rabe-Kleberg, 'Professionalität und Geschlechterverhältnis. Oder: Was ist "semi" an traditionellen Frauenberufen?', in A. Combe and W. Helsper (eds), *Pädagogische Professionalität* (Frankfurt-am-Main: Suhrkamp, 1996), 276–302

U. Rabe-Kleberg, 'Wie aus Berufen für Frauen Frauenberufe werden. – Ein Beitrag zur Transformation des Geschlechterverhältnisses', in H. M. Nickel, S. Völkel and H. Hüning (eds), *Transformation, Unternehmerreorganisation, Geschlechterforschung* (Opladen: Leske und Budrich, 1999), 93–107

U. Rabe-Kleberg, *Gendermainstreaming und Kindergarten. Eine Expertise im Auftrag des Bundesministeriums für Familie, Senioren, Frauen und Jugend* (Weinheim: Beltz, 2003)

U. Rabe-Kleberg, 'Feminisierung der Erziehung. Chancen oder Gefahren für die Bildungsprozesse von Mädchen und Jungen?', in Sachverständigenkommission 12. Kinder- und Jugendbericht (ed.), *Materialien zum 12. Kinder- und Jugendbericht, II, Steuerung frühkindlicher Bildung, Betreuung und Erziehung* (München: Deutsches Jugendinstitut, 2004), 135–172

V. Randall, *The Politics of Child Daycare in Britain* (Oxford: Oxford University Press, 2000)

F. Schütze, 'Organisationszwänge und hoheitsstaatliche Rahmenbedingungen im Sozialwesen: Ihre Auswirkungen auf die Paradoxien des professionellen Handelns', in A. Combe and W. Helsper (eds), *Pädagogische Professionalität* (Frankfurt-am-Main: Suhrkamp, 1996), 183–275

Y. Schütze, *Die gute Mutter: zur Geschichte des normativen Musters 'Mutterliebe'* (Bielefeld: Kleine, 1991)

H. Wunder and C. Vanja, *Wandel der Geschlechterbeziehungen zu Beginn der Neuzeit* (Frankfurt-am-Main: Suhrkamp, 1991)

13

Money Matters – Experiments in Financing Public Child Care

Margarete Schuler-Harms

1 Introduction

Money matters. Adequate and long-term financing is an essential condition for public child care and preschools. But financial resources are limited. Financing has therefore to follow the principles of effectiveness and efficiency. Financing also helps to regulate the quality of services, as does the framework of legal requirements and proper staff training. Money not only ensures adequate capacities, it also regulates the supply of child care and preschools to meet families' needs in terms of both quantity and quality. Even demand itself can be influenced by the type of financing, because the freedom of families in choosing a (public or private) care or education institution depends on the families' means.

Common ways of financing preschools are for the state either to organise the preschools itself or to give direct subsidies to intermediaries (e.g., the churches) running the preschools. In this article, I will focus on two ways of financing public child care which are less common: vouchers and the (originally) French *caisse familiale*. My purpose is to explore ways of financing which have the potential to improve the quality and efficiency of care and education of preschool children. I will try to point out which targets can be pursued through which modes of financing and which dysfunctional impacts are to be expected.

2 Voucher experiments

2.1 The term 'voucher'

A voucher is a document which states that its holder or another person indicated in the document is entitled to certain goods or services to be provided by the issuer of the voucher (Friedman, 1955). Thus the voucher enables the recipient to acquire services from the provider at a more or less specified value. Accordingly a voucher includes the promise to render cash benefits out of public funds for a certain purpose specified in the voucher. The voucher also includes a declaration of value which restricts its extent. If the issuer is not identical to the provider of the product or service, the voucher creates a multipolar contractual relationship between the issuer, the provider and the recipient of the service. In this multipolar relationship the recipient establishes his or her claim to the product or service as well as showing his or her ability to render consideration in return by presenting the voucher.

In the case of vouchers for child care or education, the issuer of the voucher is different from the provider of the service. The voucher is issued by a government agency. Voucher schemes primarily work when the state does not provide the public services itself but uses third parties to perform its duties (in the context of child care and education the third parties are private or charitable services/organisations). Voucher schemes are even suitable for financing a service if the state only works as an intermediary between the provider and the recipient of a service. The result is a trilateral relationship between the government issuer, the provider of the product or service and the recipient, who is legitimated by the voucher.

In the relationship between the issuer and the recipient, the voucher represents a unilateral and binding government promise to render a service. In this way vouchers also put citizens in a position to purchase products or services. In order to do that, vouchers belong to the mode of what is called subject sponsorship, in contrast to object sponsorship in which the service provider is funded directly. The voucher itself is received by the families or the parents, who can cash the voucher at the child-care or educational institution of their choice. So the voucher constitutes both the entitled person and the intended use. Furthermore, the voucher may also include additional conditions for the eligibility of the holder to cash the voucher.

When the holder of the voucher has chosen a provider, he enters into a private law contract. By presenting and handing over the voucher the holder proves his eligibility to receive the offered service under conditions determined by the state. Afterwards the provider cashes the vouchers at regular intervals at the issuing agency. The conditions for rendering the service can be specified by the voucher or by agreements between the service provider and the government agency.

In legal terms, the most interesting contractual relationship is that between the issuing government agency and the service provider. This relationship decides both who is entitled to offer the service specified in the voucher and who is entitled to receive it. However, too strict a limitation on one certain service provider (e.g., by committing oneself to one educational institution due to local criteria) would contradict the intended purpose of voucher schemes to create freedom of choice and competition between providers. Nonetheless, in relation to the provider, the state determines the extent to which it will leave the choice of services up to the entitled person. In this relationship the state decides to what extent it will enable options for the beneficiaries and to what extent it will limit the choice, for example by imposing legal restrictions concerning the quality of services offered. So within the scope of voucher schemes the state is flexible in terms of regulation and deregulation of specific services offered.

2.2 Functions of voucher schemes

Freedom of choice seems to be the first priority of voucher schemes (Levin, 2000, p. 104; Levin and Schwartz, 2007, p. 6). Vouchers allow recipients of a service to choose the care or educational institution on their own. This function indeed also aims to protect the recipients' personal liberty. But its primary goal is to create competition with the purpose of establishing adequate choice that is suitable to all requirements. However, this suitability can be provided only through freedom of choice and the resulting competition under two preconditions.

First of all, for there to be freedom of choice, there must be a range of products or services on offer. Voucher schemes aim to develop or deregulate markets. They prove to be an exceedingly flexible way to control markets: subject sponsorship permits services to be provided in a purpose- and requirement-oriented way at the transition from governmental provision to a pluralistic market of providers. It is irrelevant whether private providers compete only with each other or with charitable or governmental providers. So a nursery voucher scheme does not need to distinguish whether an institution is run by a private company, a charitable organisation, a local authority or parental initiative. At the same time, different forms of care, such as daycare centres or childminders, can be guaranteed consistently.

Secondly, both freedom of choice and competition require that recipients be able to make reasonable, quality-oriented choices. Only then does a voucher scheme generate the positive effects of fulfilling requirements and ensuring quality within the competition between providers. Families must therefore be aware of the specific services on offer. They also have to be able to choose in a manner that meets their own needs as well as ensuring optimal quality and efficiency in objective terms. Voucher schemes thus require not only simple conditions for those entitled to purchase a voucher, but also a minimum of information and transparency about type and extent of the concrete service. In particular, voucher use makes sense only if all essential information about what is on offer can be provided. This is most notably possible in all cases where the offer can be standardised under certain criteria (Münder, 1999, p. 49; Stutzer and Dürsteler, 2005, p. 3 f.). If offer and demand are profoundly standardised, a real choice can be made by all recipients. In principle such standardisation is possible within child care and preschool.

Voucher schemes furthermore allow a flexible use of governmental regulation and control to guarantee high-quality and efficient services which meet requirements. Vouchers themselves guarantee a flexible classification of personal freedom in choice and governmental regulation of offerings. By launching voucher schemes, the state no longer has to perform these duties itself, without becoming subject to the law of the market in general. The voucher scheme, rather, permits the government to move from acting to activating behaviour.

Lastly, voucher schemes provide both direct transfer payments and distributive justice between recipients of the services. In this respect, vouchers especially allow flexible arrangements: their value may either be the same for all families or vary by family income; it is also possible to reserve vouchers for families with lower incomes (selective vs. universal vouchers, Chen and West, 2000, p. 1520 ff.). Vouchers can be used as the sole means of payment in legal relations between service provider and recipient. Or they can be supplemented with private family funds (open-ended vouchers). It is even possible for schools to be reimbursed by the state directly rather than through vouchers (quasi-voucher scheme). A good example is the Georgia Pre-K approach (evaluated by Levin and Schwartz, 2007).

Voucher schemes are thus profoundly flexible instruments[1] to guarantee adequate, high-quality and efficient services. However, to function properly, they require enormous and special governmental diligence. Further, the use of voucher schemes is basically limited to services that can be standardised, and such schemes only develop their potential in the context of service recipients who have or can develop the required competence to realise and use their choices. For both reasons, voucher schemes are self-evident in the field of child care and education. Nevertheless – and against all theoretical advantages – voucher schemes are rarely used in European care and educational systems.

2.3   Voucher experiments in the context of public daycare and preschool services in Europe

United Kingdom: Nursery education voucher scheme

In 1996 a nursery education voucher scheme was established experimentally on a regional level in five districts of the United Kingdom and was extended to the national level in the spring of 1997 (for England and Wales). Only two months after its nationwide launch, however, the newly elected Labour Party ended the voucher scheme experiment.

The voucher was designed to be 'open-ended', that is parents were allowed to combine the voucher with private family funds if they sent their children to private institutions or those run by charitable organisations. Public institutions were not permitted to accept private funds. Parents entitled to benefits were identified by the register of child benefit recipients and were sent the application form afterwards by post. Families who wanted care vouchers returned the completed application forms to the administration agency in charge. After careful consideration of the entitlement the agency automatically sent the requested care vouchers to the families at the beginning of each term. Only those institutions with the appropriate licence were entitled to cash vouchers. The licence was granted to institutions prepared not only to fulfil certain standards for output and input, but also to be surveyed by the competent authority. Input standards such as requirements for carer:child ratios or for staff training already existed before the voucher scheme was started. By contrast, an extensive catalogue of output standards for learning and socialisation outcomes was established when the voucher scheme was launched.

Admittedly, the test and operating stage was too short to permit final judgement of the voucher scheme. Overall, the main criticism was that the voucher scheme did not increase efficiency but only raised costs. The output standards proved impossible to measure or control. The value of the voucher was too low to provide an adequate supply of services suitable for all requirements. And finally, beneficiaries with low levels of education, especially immigrant families, did not use the care voucher very often.

The Kita-Card programme in Hamburg

In the summer of 2003 a project with child-care vouchers was launched in Hamburg. However, the Hamburg Act on Aid for Children in Child Care and Day-Care Institutions (*Hamburger Gesetz zur Förderung von Kindern in Tageseinrichtungen und in der Tagespflege*) did not contain the term 'voucher', referring instead to a 'decision on an application for grant-in-aid' (explanation and evaluation by Näther, 2000; Falck, 2004). The entitlement to reimbursement depends on whether a child has a legal claim to or was at least granted a place in a child-care institution. The aid depends on income level: the price of child-care services was negotiated between the City of Hamburg and the individual providers, and families are reimbursed on a sliding scale depending on family income. Both quality of care and compensation are guaranteed by agreements between the City of Hamburg and the Alliance for Funding Bodies of Youth Welfare Services, as well as the Hamburg Federation of Day-Care Centres and the Federation of Miscellaneous Service Providers. This agreement governs all modalities for payments to service providers. The Hamburg voucher scheme was long criticised for being ponderous and inefficient, but the initial difficulties with drawing and cashing the voucher seem to have been resolved recently. The number of children in care has increased, according to the Hamburg Senator for Social Affairs. In addition, the institutions and the funding bodies are demonstrating great creative potential as they flexibly broaden their choice oriented to the demand. The demand-oriented scheme has led to major growth, appetite for innovation and quality competition.

In the meantime some political parties have proposed nursery voucher schemes in other federal states. For example, the free-market FDP party has proposed child-care vouchers or cash benefits which can be redeemed for child care provided by associations, companies, parent initiatives or childminders; the party also says the voucher scheme should be accompanied by quality assurance, for which a certification system is recommended.[2]

2.4 Summary

The limited experience shows that the working conditions of voucher schemes have to be carefully regulated and evaluated. A voucher scheme requires particular administrative effort which must be related to the object of quality assurance and must be organised so that families with less informational and educational competence are capable of making their choice. Aside from that, a voucher scheme requires quality management, which should not be limited to generating family demand and competition between the providers. National standards, either set unilaterally or negotiated with providers, remain necessary. These standards have to be reachable and available for documentation without causing enormous financial and personnel expenses. They also need to be comprehensible for families and have to allow a comparison concerning the quality of the institutions. And, ultimately, the value has to be high enough to generate high-quality services and to allow lower-income families to participate.

3 The *caisse familiale* model

3.1 Principle of the *caisse familiale*

A *caisse familiale* is an institution which enjoys state sponsorship while maintaining a certain distance from direct management by the state. Its purpose is to fulfil certain tasks, generally of a financial nature, in the area of family policy. The French *Caisses allocations familiales*, which have existed for about 100 years, are the classic example, but family assurance associations have been formed in other European countries as well. In Germany, the idea of creating a *Familienkasse* on the *caisse familiale* model has recently been under discussion.

There is a wide range of possibilities for structuring such an association. The major variables are, firstly, the way the financial resources are acquired, secondly the degree of budgetary independence under the law, and thirdly the degree of organisational autonomy.

3.2 The European forms of a family assurance association

The caisses allocations familiales model

The French *caisses allocations familiales* are responsible for all key services of family policy, including, for example, child benefits (*Allocation pour Jeunes Enfants*, APJE), the benefits for single parents with young children (*Allocation de Parent Isolé*, API), special benefits for disabled children, assistance with accommodation and removals, and school supplements (*Allocation Parentale d'Education*) as well as benefits at the beginning of the school year (*Allocation de Rentrée Scolaire*). Also included are assistance for the employment of child-care workers and basic assistance (*Minima sociaux*), which is not restricted to claimants with families. The financial authorities, on the other hand, are responsible for the *quotient familial*, a special form of tax allowance which is an important component of family policy. To show the scale: in 1999, the *caisses allocations familiales* in France employed 31,007 people.

The financial capital was accumulated over decades from the contributions of French employers. Since the early 1990s, the contributions have been supplemented by an increasing proportion of state funds.[3] In 1999 nearly 60 percent of the income of the associations came from social insurance contributions by employers and about 40 percent from state funds, including 4.5 percent from contributions taken over by the state, about 14 percent from tax and approximately. 20 percent from the *Contribution Sociale Généralisée* (CSG), a kind of family tax levied as a social contribution.[4]

The *Caisse Familiale* is made up of a national association, the *Caisse Nationale d'Allocation familiale* (CNAF), which acts as an umbrella organisation, and 125 *Caisses Allocations Familiales* with limited spheres of responsibility. For the majority of the associations this responsibility is a regional one, but there are still a few that serve particular employment groups (Deter, 2003, p. 96; Spieß and Thomasius, 2004, p. 55). To a large extent, the *Caisse familiale* is independently organised. The CNAF is organised as a public institution; the CAFs are run as private entities, in common with other organisations in the sphere of social security in France.

The CNAF and the CAFs are run by a management board and a director. The CNAF's management board consists of 35 persons, and the boards of the regional CAFs each include 24 people. The board members represent the associations of employers, employees, professional associations and chambers of commerce according to fixed proportions. There are also expert civil servants appointed by the state (Deter, 2003, p. 97). The directors are responsible for setting up and executing the decisions of the management board.[5] The director of the CNAF is appointed by the board of management in accordance with the recommendation of the French government. In turn, he appoints the directors and chief accountants of the CAFs after a formal selection process. The CNAF is responsible for monitoring the CAFs' compliance with legal and technical requirements as well as the service provided. CNAF itself stands under the supervision of the Ministry for Employment and Solidarity, which is responsible for social security (Deter, 2003, p. 81; Spieß and Thomasius, 2004, p. 57 f.).

Family assurance in Germany

The model of the child benefit associations   In Germany the tax-financed child benefit has been managed and paid by child-benefit associations (*Kindergeldkassen*). These have been organised as public institutions. The Federal Employment Agency (Bundesagentur für Arbeit, BA) is responsible for implementing this. The BA's administrative structure made it possible to divide these responsibilities into three levels: local employment agencies, regional employment offices, and the BA as the central organisation.

At the end of the 1990s, nearly all aspects of child benefit were integrated into the income tax system (§§ 31, 62 ff. EStG, BKGG[6];

Gitter and Schmid, 2001, § 39 marginal numbers 1, 13 ff.). The Federal Finance Office now has responsibility for effecting the payment of child benefit. However, the BA – through its *Familienkassen*, formerly known as *Kindergeldkassen* –is still responsible for financing child benefits. At the beginning of 2006, the *Familienkassen* were given greater organisational independence within the BA; furthermore, they are now no longer organised on three administrative levels, like the employment offices, but on two levels.

There have been repeated attempts in Germany to organise a greater number of family benefits within a family assurance association. A variety of financial and organisational models have been considered.

The idea of a parafiscal levy in the form of social insurance
In 2001, the *Wissenschaftliche Beirat für Familienfragen* (scientific advisory board for family matters) drew up a transfer model for real transfers and finance streams between children, workers and pensioners, showing these within an 'intergenerational benefits adjustment' (Wiss. Beirat, 2001, p. 206, 208, fig. 7.3–2). The transfer relationships between these generations are interpreted as credit relationships in which the earlier contributions of the employed generation to children correspond to the – temporally delayed – capital provision for pensioners. According to this model, the prefinancing of children's needs should not come from tax revenues, but – like old-age pensions – from contributions made by the population during their economically active period. The money is to be managed through an endowment fund.

The Advisory Board did not give any further details as to how this fund should be administered. A research fellow in public economy, Spieß, suggests establishing a 'family parafiscus'. By this she means an organisation characterised by group-oriented self-management and its own budget. This 'parafiscus' would be organised as a special fund. It would finance all benefits within family policy, including children's homes, which fall within the remit of the regions (*Länder*) and communes. Two ways of carrying this out have been suggested. The first alternative would be to use the associations that already exist within the BA (*Familienkassen*) as executive agencies having a greater range of responsibilities. As the parafiscus's tasks would include supporting providers of daycare for children, Spieß suggests the second alternative of setting up 'executive agencies' at local level. The organisation of the federal parafiscus should be carried out on the model of existing social insurance institutions (Spieß and Thomasius, 2004, p. 98 ff.).

Drawing on these suggestions, in 2005 the Commission for the 7th Report on the Family recommended setting up a family assurance association, to be financed from contributions and with organisational independence, like a social insurance institution. The German Federal Government has largely ignored the Commission's recommendation.

The idea of a tax-financed family fund Another view is that family benefits should be increasingly financed from taxes. It has, for instance, been suggested that allowances for the expense of bringing up children within individual social security systems should be replaced by a universal tax financing system, concentrating all monetary transfers in favour of families within a central institution. According to this concept, no new, expensive administrative agency would be required. This idea is clearly based on the model of the Family Settlement Fund in Austria, which is administered by the Ministry for Social Security, Generations and Consumer Protection (Bauer, 2002, p. 17; Spieß and Thomasius, 2004, p. 63).

3.3 Evaluation

The German discussion, in particular, shows that the idea of a *caisse familiale* is linked to a wide variety of expectations. First of all, there is an expectation of greater transparency in benefits for families (whether financial benefits, services or benefits in kind), and consequently greater effectiveness and efficiency of family policy. Secondly, the suggestion of setting up a family assurance association aims at creating an organisation that would be more independent of national politics with its four-year electoral cycle. Finally, these suggestions aim to create greater acceptance of family policies involving larger expenditure by making the contributions of the population and the benefits to families better reflect the relationship across three generations between old-age insurance and family provision.

In my own view it is doubtful whether and under which preconditions a *caisse familiale* model could fulfil such expectations in Germany. To create transparency and effectiveness, family policy first needs to be more closely oriented to the needs of families. Unlike in France or Belgium, family policy in Germany has been seen for decades as just an aspect of social policy, whilst it remained taboo to orient family policy on the basis of demographic changes. The first thing that is needed in Germany is to abandon this reliance on existing models.

I also doubt that greater independence of national politics can be achieved without other measures. The special political influence of the French *caisse familiale* derives from their importance as significant players in the domain of family policy. But their competence and the influence need to be seen and understood in the context of other institutional conditions. In France, family policy is based on a broad social consensus supported (both alongside the family assurance associations and within them) by social partners and by powerful family organisations. On the government side, family policy is tied to the Ministry for Family and Children, and is closely linked to the Work and Social Ministry. Interministerial delegations subordinate to the Family Ministry guarantee the effectiveness of family policy as an interdepartmental responsibility. The centralised structure of the French state further simplifies the organisation and the influence of a family assurance association. The success of the *caisse familiale* model depends on these preconditions. Careful efforts would be needed to apply this model in another country, especially one with a federal structure. As long as institutional care for children and funding for this care in Germany remain the responsibility of the regions, setting up a *caisse familiale* on the French model cannot solve this problem.

4   Conclusion

Depending on their design, vouchers can be flexible tools to regulate and finance public child care and preschools. A voucher gives families freedom of choice, makes efficient use of public funds and also provides the necessary degree of regulation in the competition among providers. Vouchers can also be a tool to fight poverty of children and families.

By contrast, the arguments for and against the *caisse familiale* model must be carefully balanced. The alleged advantages of the French model are not only based on the independence of the *caisse* but also the result of a centralised state system (in contrast to the German), the traditional orientation of French politics on demographic targets and the continuous consulting between the departments about tasks and tools for compliance. Thus, there are many different basic conditions which determine whether or not a *caisse familiale* model promotes public child care and preschools.

Notes

1. Differences between voucher plans are understood in the dimensions of finance, regulation and information: Levin (2000), p. 97 ff.

2. FDP Baden-Württemberg, in April 2005, FDP Hessen, in February 2006; Alliance 90/The Greens (Bündnis 90/Die Grünen), Vertices-paper 11.4.06.
3. Deter (2003), p. 94, speaks about a change to a 'fundamental structural principle'.
4. A contribution of 1.1 percent on all income from employment, capital, savings and transfers; the money raised is paid to the family associations (Deter, 2003, p. 94).
5. Spieß/Thomasius (2004), p. 57, also mention a 'management official', whose role presumably corresponds to the 'accounting director' in Deter (2003), p. 98, although this function is not listed as a 'management function'.
6. The Bundeskindergeldgesetz (Federal Child Benefit Law) covers children who get the child benefit in their own right (orphans) or in that of their brothers or sisters.

Bibliography

H. Bauer, *Ausgabeneinsparungen im föderalen Staat* (Wien: KDZ, 2002) (http://www.iv-mitgliederservice.at/iv-all/dokumente/doc_2064.pdf)

Z. Chen and G. West, 'Selective Versus Universal Vouchers: Modeling Median Voter Preferences in Education', *American Economic Review*, 90 (2000) 1520–1534

G. Deter, 'Französische Familienpolitik, Funktion und Arbeitsweise der Caisse Familiale in Frankreich', *Konrad-Adenauer-Stiftung, Aktuelle Informationen* (2003) 76–126

O. Falck, 'Das Hamburger 'Kita-Gutscheinsystem' – besser als sein Ruf?', *Sozialer Fortschritt*, 53 (2004) 68–74

M. Friedman, 'The Role of Government in Education', in R. Solo (ed.), *Economics and the Public Interest* (Piscataway, NJ: Rutgers University Press, 1955), 123–144

W. Gitter and J. Schmid, *Sozialrecht* (Munich: Beck, 2001)

H. Levin, 'Recent Developments in the Economics of Education: Educational Vouchers', in M. Weis and H. Weißhaupt (eds), *Bildungsökonomie und Neue Steuerung* (Frankfurt-am-Main: Lang, 2000), 97–114

H. Levin and H. Schwartz, 'Educational Vouchers for Universal Preschools', *Economics of Education Review*, 26 (2007) 3–16

J. Münder, *Finanzierungssystem der Kindertagesbetreuung in Hamburg* (Hamburg: Behörde für Schule, Jugend und Berufsbildung, 1999)

J. Näther, 'Die Kita-Card. Ein neues Modell zur Planung und Finanzierung der Kindertagesbetreuung in Hamburg', *Zentralblatt für Jugendrecht*, 87 (2000) 143–146

K. Spieß and S. Thomasius, *Parafiskalische Modelle zur Finanzierung familienpolitischer Leistungen* (Berlin: DIW, 2004)

A. Stutzer and R. Dürsteler, *Versagen in der staatlichen Krippenförderung – Betreuungsgutscheine als Alternative* (Basle: Centre for Research in Economics, Management and the Arts, 2005)

Wissenschaftlicher Beirat für Familienfragen, *Gerechtigkeit für Familien – Zur Begründung und Weiterentwicklung des Familienlasten- und -leistungsausgleichs* (Stuttgart: Bundesministerium für Familie, Senioren, Frauen und Jugend, 2001)

14
Basic Legal Principles of Public Responsibility for Children

Ingo Richter

The responsibility for schools has always been quite clear, because there are public schools run by the state and/or by local communities, and there are private schools, organised by private initiative. As for child care before school age, the division between the public and the private sphere is not so clear, because the churches and the welfare organisations play an important role in early child care. It has always been difficult to apply the traditional legal principles to the child-care organisations: the universality principle, the individual rights approach, the subsidiarity principle and the basic distinction between public and private law. In our times the application of these principles gets even more difficult because of new theoretical approaches to the organisation of state and society, only to mention the two key notions: New Governance and New Federalism. Although these principles apply in many Western societies, examples are mostly taken from German law and politics.

1 The Universality Principle

The constitutions of liberal states do not mention the responsibility of the state, whereas the constitutions of the communist states did. The historical mission of political liberalism was and still is to restrict the power of the state. This means that the functions of the state are not enumerated in the constitution.[1] This is the reason why we do not know whether child care is a state function.[2]

Under what is known as the universality principle the state can fulfil all tasks as long as it does not intervene in the private liberties of its citizens. For federal states there is a fundamental rule for the distribution of power between the federation and the states: all competences which are not enumerated in the federal constitution as competences of the federation are competences of the states (Art. 30 of the German Constitution). As far as child care is concerned, we therefore have to look into the federal constitution to see whether a given matter is mentioned there as a federal concern. In Art. 74 No 7, the German Constitution mentions 'öffentliche Fürsorge' (public social assistance or public care) as a federal concern. From this it has been inferred that the federation has the legislative competence in child-care matters,[3] leaving implementation and administration to the states (Art. 84 of the German Constitution). This is the constitutional basis for the Children and Youth Act of 1990. And what is true for Germany also holds for the other European constitutions. Since the texts do not mention early child care, the state is free to organise any kind of preschool child-care system as long as it does not infringe the individual rights of citizens.

2 Individual rights

The rights of the child and the rights of parents are individual rights. Both are guaranteed in the international declarations of human rights and in the constitutions of many nations.

The 1966 International Convention on Economic, Social and Cultural Rights mentions the right to education and the freedom of parents to choose private schools (Art. 13). Early child care at that time probably was not regarded as part of the educational system and was therefore not mentioned. Since the 1966 Convention on Civil and Political Rights protects the family (Art. 23), early child care under the Conventions of 1966 has to be regarded as part of family life and protected against state intervention. But this does not prevent the signatory states or local communities from creating public institutions for early child care, as long as children are not obliged to attend them.

The 1989 Convention on the Rights of the Child also guarantees the right to education as a right to schooling (Art. 28). Early child care as a right of the child is mentioned only with regard to the case of working parents and the case of disability (Art. 18 III and Art. 23 II) as a right of access to existing facilities. In the case of state intervention in the family in the best interest of the child, the Convention speaks of protection and help, but not of a right to early child care in public institutions (Art. 20). The 1989 Convention on the Rights of the Child thus ultimately does not go any further than the conventions of 1966. It does not guarantee a human right to early child care, but it does guarantee the right of parents to care for their children, and this right has always to be pursued in the best interest of the child. But it is still the parents who have the right to decide whether family child care or public child care is in the best interest of the child.

Many national constitutions guarantee the right of the parents to care for, educate and instruct their children (e.g., Art. 6 (2) of the German Constitution). If constitutions do not address this expressly – as is the case in the American or the French constitutions, for example – this right is part of the general liberty enshrined in the texts of the constitutions. There is no doubt about this, and in all such countries courts have acknowledged this right of parents. These national constitutions do not provide for a right of the child, at least not in the texts. The International Convention on the Rights of the Child is a treaty between the member states of the United Nations that have signed and ratified the Convention.[4] Therefore it only binds the contracting parties, the states, and it does not directly give rights to the citizens of the states. This is a matter left to the transposition of the convention into national law by national parliaments. As long as this not has been achieved, children cannot rely on the rights set out in the Convention on the Rights of the Child.[5] The right of the child therefore has to be interpreted as part of the general liberty clause of the constitutions.

To sum up, there is a right of the child and there is a right of parents under international and under national law, but we cannot say that the conventions and constitutions regulate public responsibility for child care or provide for public institutions of early child care. So if states create systems of early child care, we have to examine carefully the problem of an infringement of the rights of the child and the rights of parents. There are two questions here:

- If public child care were mandatory – like schooling – we would have to ask whether this infringes the rights of the child and the rights of parents. Can the state force parents to send their preschool-age children to public child-care institutions? And prevent parents from caring for their own children 24 hours a day? I admit that this is a rather theoretical question, because no state does this. A much more interesting constitutional issue would be the question of school age (six or five or even younger?) and afternoon school attendance (which is currently an issue in Germany). But that is a question of schooling, not of preschool child care. Therefore I will leave it at that.
- If public child care is voluntary – as it is everywhere – and if there are parents who do not make use of this opportunity and prefer to care for their children themselves – as there are everywhere – one could ask whether it is contrary to the equality clause of the constitution

that the children in public child care profit from child care while others do not, and whether the state is allowed to spend money for public child care, instead of giving the same amount of money to parents for their own private child care. The answer is easy: we make use of our constitutional rights at our own cost. The state is not obliged to pay. If there is a subsidised public railroad system, we cannot ask the state to pay for our gasoline if we prefer to use our own private car. The same is true for private schools. Parents have to pay fees, even though public schools are free of cost, and the same would also be true for early child care.

3   Public and private responsibility

In law the distinction between public and private law dates back to the Roman Empire: public law regulates matters of public interest and private law covers matters of private interest. But this does not help us that much. For our purpose here, which is child care, I will look at the actors, not the users.

- If the state or the local community is the actor, then there is public responsibility. It is true that the state or the local community can make use of private law regulation, for example, contract law. But if they act in the public interest, there is public responsibility and they are bound by public law principles, and in particular by the fundamental constitutional rights. It is also true that private actors can fulfil public functions. They can be called upon or even obliged by the state to do so. In this case public law applies, welfare organisations in early child care being an example.
- If welfare organisations in the broadest sense are the actors, there is also public responsibility, because these actors fulfil public functions, are largely financed by tax money and basically regulated by public law. Even if they are corporations under private law, the Children and Youth Act applies to them and they are bound by the fundamental constitutional rights.
- Commercial child-care institutions and self-help groups as well as neighbourhood groups are private actors, even if they are subsidised by tax money, and even if they are open to all users. This means that private law applies to them. If the state or local communities want to impose early child-care duties on them, they must do this through private law contracts. Using contracts, the state or local communities

can provide money under certain conditions, for example, they can demand that the regulations on public early child care be applied.

We therefore find that there is private responsibility in the cases of the family and business but public responsibility in the cases of welfare, local communities, and the state.

4   The Subsidiarity principle

This principle – derived from early twentieth-century Catholic philosophy of the state[6] – is a very simple rule for the distribution of power between the private and the public domain on the one hand, and within the public domain between the different actors or institutions involved on the other. It states that the 'lower-level' actor or institution should be given preference over the 'higher-level' actor or institution, on the condition that they are able to fulfil their task. To put it bluntly: family before state, welfare organisations (particularly church-related welfare) before state, local community before state, member state before federal state. In this traditional form the principle is of no great value for the organisation of society, because everything depends on the definition of 'lower' and 'higher' and 'ability'. Also, a kind of modernisation of the principle – known as the new subsidiarity principle – which relies more on modern forms of social organisation like self-help groups and NGOs does not get us any further, because the approach is just too simple and too ideological. We should therefore not infer from the subsidiarity principle that child care should be primarily with the family and, if there is no family, then child care should be organised by welfare organisations – before the local communities or the state would be allowed to step in. The subsidiarity principle – the old as well as the new – is a principle of social policy without any constitutional value. There is no constitution in the world that has integrated this principle into its catalogue of basic constitutional principles. The German Constitutional Court – asked by local communities in the 1970s to decide on public responsibility for early child-care and youth policy – in fact ruled that the subsidiarity principle is not a general principle of German constitutional law.[7] But the court left it to the states to choose the subsidiarity principle as guidance for the organisation of social policy, for example for early child care. And that is what the German Bundestag did in 1990. In organising early child care in Germany, in the Children and Youth Act, it opted for central elements of the subsidiarity principle.

Even if constitutions do not integrate the subsidiarity principle as such into the text, some choose certain elements of it. In theory, federalism is certainly close to the subsidiarity principle. As a general rule it can be said that power is invested in the states if the constitution does not expressly give it to the federation. The European Union has also adopted the subsidiarity principle for the separation of powers between the union and the member states (Art. 5 of the Amsterdam Treaty), and the new treaty or constitution – or whatever it may be called – will certainly make use of the subsidiarity principle as well in order to safeguard the cohesion of the Union.[8]

5   New governance

This is one of the buzzwords of the day.[9] It claims to do justice to the complexity of modern societies and to be open to the future. It goes beyond the traditional distinction between state and civil society that characterised the nineteenth century in continental Europe. It leaves behind the contradiction between public and private. It also encompasses business organisations like big corporations and business associations, NGOs and welfare organisations, trade unions and the media. But new governance means a new encompassing look, not only at organisational features but also at procedures and control. New governance goes beyond the classic triad of the liberal state: legislation – administration – jurisprudence, and talks about new forms of administration like programming, planning by objectives, new management, contracting, public–private partnership, benchmarking, controlling, etc., to mention only a few key words of the debate (Buchs, 2007). For our purpose here I will restrict myself to just a few notions that may be of relevance for the public responsibility for child care.

5.1   A mixed child-care system

Just as we speak of a mixed economy, and sometimes a mixed educational system (Richter, 1996, p. 107), we could envision a mixed child-care system. This would mean that all the players (the family and family-related organisations, welfare and business, local communities and the state) are regarded as parts of one system, that they work together and are interdependent.

This would imply:

- that all 'players' are free to offer early child care;
- that they compete for parents and children and for public funding;

- that the state can regulate competition, but that the state is restricted to this form of regulation;
- that local communities are responsible for planning and counselling;
- that the providers of early child care cooperate on the basis of contracts in order to meet demand.[10]

5.2   Public–private partnership (PPP)

Until now we have been thinking of exclusive organisations. An organisation is either communal or welfare, state or family, commerce or welfare. According to traditional European constitutional theory of the state, there cannot be partnership between the state on the one hand and private social organisations on the other. The state, according to this theory, can never be on the same footing with the family or the firm. And the same is true for the other side. The theory of the family has no room for state intervention in family life, with rare exceptions in the best interest of the child, and the economic theory of the firm forbids state intervention in private business, with rare exceptions in the interest of the public good. But that is wrong under new governance. We have to think of how to organise the cooperation between the partners for the best interest of the child and the family. When an enterprise organises child care for its workers' children together with a church-run welfare organisation, when a local community outsources the management of its local daycare centre, when autonomous parents' groups are allowed to use the former local fire station without paying for it – and we could add many other examples – then we speak of successful public–private partnership. But we have always to keep in mind that the state has to act in the best interest of the child. PPP does not mean that the state and local communities seek to rid themselves of their public responsibility by leaving early child care exclusively to welfare organisations and business. And PPP does not mean that churches can monopolise early child care in their own interest and that businesses can offer early child care to their workers only in the interest of the firm. The duty to serve the best interest of the child and fair relationships between the private and the public sphere are necessary conditions for the public–private partnership under new governance.

5.3   NGOs

Child care is in the public interest, but the public interest nowadays is not only represented by the state and local communities. Be it a local initiative, for example, to channel heavy traffic away from the local daycare centre, or an international organisation like UNICEF, what we have is citizens uniting in order to do something for the public good, for example, for child care. Therefore new governance integrates NGOs. Protest movements are listened to. Parents' initiatives are given opportunities to try out their ideas. The local planning of child care provides for NGO participation. NGOs are very popular nowadays and the public expects wonders from their work for the public good. But what are NGOs, speaking in legal or administrative terms? What is their function within new governance? Sometimes the Catholic Church and the labour unions claim to be the world's biggest NGOs. Greenpeace, Amnesty International, and Human Rights Watch, which surely can make the claim, were founded by private initiatives. But they are now very rich and very influential international organisations, bigger and richer than many states in the world, and certainly much more influential. But what is the basis of their influence? They lack democratic legitimacy, at least in the usual sense of the word (Richter, 2006, p. 9). And this question must be asked even in early child care. Parent self-help groups have the right to organise child care for their own children and they are entitled to public funding. But when they claim a say in local child-care policy? Why and on what grounds? New governance does not care for the traditional legitimisation process. Working in the public interest and doing good seem to be enough.

5.4 Contracts

Compared with schooling, early child care is not that structured and regulated by statute law, although the pluralistic structure of the field would call for some regulation. But welfare organisations rely on their constitutional rights in any case, and local communities invoke their constitutional right to self-government. And, in fact, child care cannot really be regulated by the legislative branch. To the extent that child care is in fact regulated by legislation, the laws of course have to be followed, but the main problems of child care cannot be solved by legislation. Caring is a personal relationship that resists regulation by law. State and local statutes can regulate the relations between the state and providers of child care, including the financial, personnel, and organisational conditions of early child care. The substance will always remain unregulated. Since statute law is less relevant for early child care, the most important instrument of regulation is the contract. Contract law differs in some important aspects from statute law. Under contract law the partners are on the same level, they are deemed to be equal, even if in reality they are not. Contracts permit flexibility. Goals can better be set by contract than by statute. Contracts may be less transparent, but they do make it easier to monitor target achievement. Early child care in this way is becoming a field for experiments in contract law. There might be some unrealistic hope, but contract management seems to serve new governance.

5.5   The new role of the state

New governance is not, as it may seem, governance without the state. Under new governance the state assumes a new role. Instead of regulating everything by law and instead of running the institutions of child care itself, the state's function under the new governance scheme is to guarantee the functioning of the system. Public responsibility under the new governance system means that the state guarantees the quality of the child-care system. All parents have a right to child care. All children ought to find a place. The institutions will be run by professionals, but parent participation is not excluded. There is choice, but also a core curriculum. Public responsibility means that the state guarantees the quality of child care and that the organisation of child care will be a mixed system.

6   New federalism

Federalism is an old principle of state organisation, used in order to establish a vertical division of power or to integrate states or regions, to bring them into a closer relationship in a nation-state. I will not go into the details of the theory of federal states here.

Federal states may be organised in two different ways:

- All state functions, that is, legislation, administration, and jurisdiction, can be divided completely between the federation and the states ('layer-cake' theory) – this is particularly true for the United States, as for the legislation, for example, Art. 1 Sec. 8 ('The Congress shall have the power ... to make all laws which shall be necessary and proper for carrying into execution the foregoing powers, and other powers vested by this constitution in the government of the United States, or in any department or officer thereof').
- State functions are divided between the federation and the states, but not completely ('marble-cake' theory). In the central European federal states, for example, in Austria, Germany and Switzerland, the federation and the states share the legislative function as well as

jurisdiction, as far as the federal level is concerned, whereas administration has traditionally been separate (in Germany, for example, Art. 78 of the Federal Constitution regulates the shared legislation of the federal and the state level).

But what seems clear in theory may be quite different in practice. Early child care is a good example. In the United States there is no federal legislative power in early childhood education. So the legislative power is with the states. Nevertheless, in the 1970s, because of the federal government's spending power (Tribe, 1988, p. 256), the US government provided millions of dollars to fund early childhood education, in particular for the famous Head Start programme. This money was given directly to local projects, and no state legislation was needed, because under American constitutional law direct contracting with the receivers of the funds is possible. Not so in Germany. Under German constitutional law the federal level has legislative power at least for early child care. The federation is entitled to spend money for models, experiments, research, etc., not for personnel and maintenance in general. But this federal money must be given to the states, because the federal government cannot contract directly with the recipients (Art. 104 a (1) Federal Constitution). This is the reason why implementing federal programmes for child care in the United States can be a federal task, whereas in Germany it must be left to the states.

All this is traditional federalism, and a lot of problems emerge when we go into the details. But in the 1970s a new theory of federalism was developed, known as new federalism or cooperative federalism. The federation and the states are expected not to divide but to share power. There was talk of shared legislation, which in a way exists already in Central Europe, of shared planning, of shared administration, and even of shared taxes and spending power. Following numerous discussions, parts of this programme were implemented, for example, in child care in Germany.

I will therefore give a short overview of the implementation of cooperative federalism in child care in Germany.

- As I mentioned, there is a federal legislative power that was used to promulgate federal laws, including the law on child care.
- Federal laws in Germany have to be passed by the Bundestag and by the Bundesrat, the upper house.
- The German Children and Youth Act of 26 June 1990 guarantees a right to preschool care and education for all children aged three to

six and calls on local communities also to provide public child care for children up to age three on demand. But it is local communities that have to provide the places and the personnel, and to pay the bill.

- The law also provides for a certain organisation of local children and youth administrations as well as some procedures for planning and administration.
- The federation itself has only restricted powers in child-care matters. The law only allows the federation 'to give incentives' (*Anregungsfunktion*) in this field. This makes possible federal reporting (*Kinder- und Jugendberichterstattung*), model projects, organised and financed by federal programmes, and a federal children and youth plan with considerable federal money.

These main features of the German federal system in child care persist, although in 2007, after protracted conflicts between the federal and the state governments, the Bundestag came up with a reform of the German federal system. This reform sought to abolish cooperative federalism, stating that it had failed. But public responsibility for child care in the German federal system was not affected by this reform.

A concluding remark: In its edition of 21 July 2001, the *Frankfurter Allgemeine Zeitung*, a leading German newspaper, argued that the state had no business in child care, because children need love, intimacy, and time, and the state, a cold impersonal bureaucratic machine, is unable to educate and give a human example; only the family, only parents, can care for their children, the newspaper said. Although there is a basic conflict of interest between the state and the family, child care calls for a mixed system of different actors, one being the family and one the state. In federal systems there is no clear and logical division of power between the federation and the member states, and in federal systems public responsibility for child care changes over time.

Notes

1. In federal states the federal constitution enumerates the powers of the federation, for example, in foreign affairs or in defence, telecommunications or air traffic, but the aim of this is only to separate the powers of the federation and the member states, not to legitimise the functions of government as such.
2. In France the preamble of the Constitution of 1946, which was integrated into the present constitution of the Fifth Republic of 1958, says: 'L'organisation de l'enseignement publique gratuit et laïque a tous les degrés est un devoir de l'Etat' (The organisation of public instruction, which is free of charge and secular at all levels, is a duty of the state). The reason for

this rather exceptional article was the implementation of the separation of state and church in France, which was a very difficult and painful process, and only a public educational system seemed to guarantee the separation of church and state. Child care in *crèches* before the *ecole maternelle* is not part of 'enseignement'.

3. *Entscheidungen des Bundesverfassungsgerichts*, 11, 105 and 22, 180. At the time these decisions were taken, early child care was in fact part of the social assistance system, because early child care in public institutions at that time was only for needy families. Now this condition has completely changed, because early child care has become a constitutional right for everyone.

4. All member states except Somalia and the United States have signed and ratified the Convention.

5. Many states that signed and ratified the Convention made formal reservations, e.g., the Muslim states with the famous Sharia reservation. But Germany did as well, and there has always been a debate on abandoning the reservations and integrating the rights of the child into the text of the constitution (while ratifying the Convention the German government on 5 April 1992 made three reservations: 1. Under German law there is no right of the child to common custody of the parents in case of birth out of wedlock; 2. in criminal law the right to counsel and the right to appeal are not guaranteed in the case of minor offences; 3. illegal immigrants under German law are not treated as legals, and different treatment of nationals and non-nationals is permitted).

6. Its best known formulation stems from the Papal Encyclica 'Quadragesimo anno' of 1931.

7. *Entscheidungen des Bundesverfassungsgerichts*, 22, 180.

8. See No. 3 of the fundamental principles in Art. I-11 of the Draft for a Constitution for Europe as of 18 June 2004, as published by the Council of the European Union ('Under the principle of subsidiarity, in areas which do not fall within its exclusive competence, the Union shall only act if and insofar as the objectives of the proposed action cannot be sufficiently achieved by Member States, either at central level or at regional and local level, but can rather, by reason of scale or effects of the proposed action, be better achieved at Union level').

9. European Union White Paper 'European Governance' COM (2001) 428 of 25 July 2001 and many other papers since.

10. This model was proposed by the Commission of the 11th German Children and Youth Report in 2002, called *fachlich regulierter Qualitätswettbewerb* (*Elfter Kinder- und Jugendbericht* 2002, p. 256).

Bibliography

M. Buchs, *New Governance in European Social Policy: The Open Method of Coordination* (London: Palgrave, 2007)

Elfter Kinder- und Jugendbericht – Bericht über die Lebenssituation junger Menschen und die Leistungen der Kinder- und Jugendhilfe (Berlin: BFSFJ, 2002)

I. Richter, 'Die öffentliche Schule im Umbau des Sozialstaates', *Zeitschrift für Pädagogik*, 34 (1996) 107–118

I. Richter, 'Das Gehirn und die Bildungspolitik – ein Kommentar', *Recht der Jugend und des Bildungswesens* (2006) 421–424

I. Richter, S. Berking and R. Muller-Schmid (eds), *Building a Transnational Civil Society – Global Issues and Global Actors* (New York: Palgrave, 2006)

L. H. Tribe, *American Constitutional Law,* 2nd edition (Mineola: The Foundation Press, 1988)

Index

America, *see* United States
Austria, 26, 32, 33f, 53, 181, 231, 242

Baltic states, 33, 34
Belgium, 3ff, 11, 21, 25ff, 31ff, **43ff**, 65, 76, 181f, 205, 231

CAF/CNAF, *see* Caisse Familiale
Caisse Familiale, 19f, 61, 161f, 168, 175, 177f, 222, 228ff
centralisation/decentralisation, 3, 8, 10, 12, 14f, 18, 29, 54, 61, 76, 139, 154, **157ff**, **172ff**
child, right of a child, 191
child protection, 44f, 51, 161
children under three, 3, 12, 61, 66, 159, 168f, 174, 190f, 206
church, 2, 6, 11ff, 24, **27ff**, 32, **44ff**, **53ff**, 72ff, **78ff**, 88ff, 100, 136, 183f, 187, 198f, 206, 222, 234, 238, 240f
church, Catholic, 11f, 46, 55, 72, 75, **78ff**, 84, 88, **90ff**, 100, 241
church, Protestant, 6, 14, 29f, 34, 92
citizenship, 17, 68f, 85, 105, 148, 153, 182, 204
class, 4, 6, 7ff, **12ff**, 16, **26ff**, 66, 74, 77ff, 83ff, 93, 99, **102ff**, 116f, 120f, 130ff, 138, 143ff, 167, 171, 183, 198, 211f, 216ff, 225, 228, 239
class, middle, 8, 30, 106ff, 111, 116, 183, 198, 211f, 216ff
class, upper, 83ff, 105, 116, 130
class, working, 8, 28, 30, 108, 111, 115ff, 130ff, 198, 212, 216f
compatibility of employment and family life, 4, 6f, 9f, 13, 18, 20, **32f**, 55, 60
competences, 2, 8, 10, 13, 15, 19, 24, 54, 182, 189ff, 217f, 234f
competences, administrative, 15

competences, financing, 10, 182, 190, 222ff
competences, legislative, 182, 189, 191
constitution, 16, 46, 47, 79, 94, **181ff**, 234ff
constraints, 8, 13, 15, 85, 160, 169, 175, 181, 188
courts, 44, 186, 236
crèches, 27, 39, 61, 63, 111f, 129, 139, 144, 160ff, 168, 171, **173ff**, 188, 194, 245
curricula, 15, 20, 49, 78, 80, 95, 109, 131, 139, 187

decentralisation, *see* centralisation/ decentralisation
Denmark, 3, 8, 13f, 18, 25f, 32f, 36, 38f, 44, **126ff**, 142, 153f, 192

education, 1ff, 28ff, 36f, 40, 43ff, 52f, 55, 58, 62, 65ff, **72ff**, **89ff**, 101f, **105ff**, 125, 130f, 136f, 142ff, **157ff**, **162ff**, **181ff**, 196ff, 211f, 214ff, 219, 222ff, 235, 239, 243, 245
employers, 16, 20, 48, 136, 145, 161, 228f
employment, 3, 7f, 10f, 13ff, 20, 27f, 31, 34, 37, 51, 57, 60ff, 67ff, 77, 83, 88, 121, 123, 126f, 132, 134, 136ff, 140, 142, 144ff, 151f, 154, 158, 177, 190f, 228ff
employment, mothers', 51, 138
England, 17, 19, 105, 107, 120, 198, 204, 226
equality/inequality, 13, 23, 24, 27, 30f, 60, 75ff, 81f, 119f, 126, 132, 136f, 140, 142ff, 150, 152ff, 163, 174, 213, 236
ethnicity, 143
EU, *see* European Union

European Union, 3, 16, 19, 24, 45, 60, 68, 72, 76, 78, 83f, 122, 126f, 140, 154, 180, 190, 239, 245

family policy, 8, 10f, 13, 19, 23f, 27, 31ff, 37, 40, 54f, 57ff, 65, 88, 154, 161, 205, 228, 230ff
fascism, 12
federalism, 15, 181f, 189, 192ff, 234, 239, 242ff
fees, 9, 17, 100, 103, 128, 130, 158, 162, 164f, 168, 175, 177, 188, 205, 237
fertility, 59f, 66, 138, 154, *see* also pronatalism
finances, 20, 34, **222ff**
Finland, 26, 27, 32f, 142, 148, 153f
France, 3ff, 8f, 11f, 14, 21, 25ff, 31ff, 37ff, 43ff, 51, 54f, **57ff**, 76, 142, **157ff**, 164, **166ff**, 181f, 204, 212, 216, 228f, 231f, 244f
Fröbel, 8, 21, 45f, 50, 107, 130, 144, 181, **183f, 196ff**, 215

gender, 4, 8, 13f, 16, 18, 20, 23f, 27, 31, 45, 57, 60, 63, 68, 75f, 81f, 85, 119f, 126f, 132, 134, 136f, 140, 143ff, 147, 149ff, 206, **210ff**
Germany, 3, 6, 8, 10, 13ff, 19, 21, 24, 26ff, **32ff**, 40, 58, 130, 142, **180ff**, **196ff**, 203ff, **210ff**, 228ff, 235ff, 242ff
governance, 12, 14f, 18f, 157, 160, 164, 174ff, 234, **239ff**, 245
grandparents, 37ff, 55
group size, child-staff ratio, 9, 101, 158, 160, 163ff, 171f

historical institutionalism, *see* institutionalism

ideal type, 4
institutionalism, historical, 131, 139
Italy, 3f, 8f, 11f, 25f, 32, 76, **88ff**, 142, 181, 216

juncture, turning point, 2, 11ff, 31, 59f, 67, 89, 95, 98, 135, 139

law, 3, 11, 44f, 47, 51, 57f, 60f, 77, 80, 89ff, 96ff, 102, 133, 142f, 159ff, 167, 180, 182, 185ff, 193ff, 223, 225, 228, 233f, 236ff, 241ff
legislation, 45, 69, 90, 93, 98ff, 128f, 131, 133ff, 167, 181f, 185, 188ff, 239, 241ff
liberalism, 29, 46, 234
lone parent, 190f

market, 1, 7, 10f, 16, 18f, 24, 30ff, 43, 50ff, 62f, 67ff, 75, 83, 93, 98, 106, 119ff, 128, 136ff, 144ff, **150ff**, 188, 224f, 227
maternalism, 4, 18, 210ff
migration, 5, 95, 106, 182, 194
ministry, 10, 15, 77, 89ff, 112f, 123, 131, 133, 163f, 171, 173, 184, 198, 229, 231f
Montessori, 50, 92, 107f, 117, 130
mothers, 1, 6, 12, 17, 32, 39, 44f, 48, 50f, 59, 62, 67f, 73, 81, 83f, 88, 91, 93, 106, 111ff, 128, 132ff, 146, 150ff, 188, 199f, 206, 210ff, 218, 220
multicultural, 85, 119, 152
municipalities, 15, 19, 47ff, 61, 76, 89f, 97, 128, 133, 138, 140, 147, 150, **159ff**, 173, 175f, 182ff, 187ff

the Netherlands, **25f**, 29, 32f, 36, 53, 137, 142
Norway, 137, 142, 153f
nursery school, 16, 36, 108ff, 123, 144

parents, 6ff, 12, 15, 17, 19, 23f, 28, 37ff, 47, 51ff, 61ff, 69, 73, 78, 82f, 88, 101, 103, 107f, 115ff, 121, 128, 130, 134, 136ff, 142ff, 152, 154, 159, 161, 163ff, 169ff, 187ff, 198, 203, 214, 223, 226, 228, 235ff
parents, parental rights, 60, 182, 187
parties, political, 53, 55, 58, 74, 77, 81, 95, 126, **132ff**, 140, 161ff, 176, 184, 189, 194, 223, 227, 236
path dependency, 1ff
pedagogical ideas, **130ff**, 139, 183, 197
Pestalozzi, 144, 183, 197ff, **202f**, 207

pillarisation, 11, 29, 52f

pluralism, 13, **28ff**

poverty, 7, 10, 13, 58, 60, 68, 92, 121, 145, 147, 152, 188, 232

professionalisation, 9, 18, 61, 210, 213ff, 218f

pronatalism, 54, 59, 152

Protestantism, 6, 14, 29, 30, 34, 92

reconciliation, *see* compatibility of employment and family

religion, 28, 47, 51, 74, 79f, 106, 154, 199, **206**

republicanism, 5, 80

responsibility, public/private, 3, 30, 44, 47f, 55, 61, **89ff**, 94f, 100f, 112f, 116, 118ff, 132f, 144, 148, 150, 153, **159ff**, 165ff, 174, 176, 181, 184, 200, 206, 212, 218, 229ff, **234ff**

rights, 15f, 57, 59f, 68, 76, 94, 143, 150ff, 167, 176, 182, 185, 187f, 190, 192f, **234ff**, 241, 245

Scandinavia, 15, 23, 25ff, **29ff**, 39, **126ff**, **142ff**, **162ff**, 178, 181, 212f

school, 2ff, 9, 12, 15f, 24, 36, 44ff, 61, 66f, 75, **89ff**, **106ff**, 127ff, 138ff, 147, 157ff, 167, 171ff, 180ff, 196, 199ff, 212ff, 225, 228, **234ff**, 241

service economy, 13, 27, 32

socialism, socialists, 48, 53, 95f, 161, 198, 205

Spain, 3f, 8f, 11f, 26, 32, 37f, **72ff**, 181

staff, 8f, 16, 18, 20, 51, 77f, 84, 90ff, 97ff, 108, 112ff, 119, 122, 130, 135, 139, 147ff, 157ff, 171,ff, 176, 187f, 185, 222, 226

steiner, 128

subsidiarity, 94

Sweden, 3, 8, 10, 12, 14f, 18, 25f, 32f, 36, 38f, 137, 142, 146ff, 153f, **157ff**, **162ff**

targeting, 6, 9, 13

taxes, 17, 24, 63, 79f, 85, 121, 128, 134, 138, 143, 151, 164f, 228ff, 237, 243

teacher, 6, 9, 18, 47ff, 66, 77, 91, 95ff, 101ff, 107ff, 113ff, 121, 130, 147, 149, 159, 167, 171, 176, 178, 188, 198, 203, **213ff**

trade unions, 18, 48, 81, 163, 239

unemployment, 11, 13, 34, 57, 60ff, 134, 137

United Kingdom, 3, 6, 10ff, 24ff, 32ff, **105f**, 129, 137, 215, **226**

United States, 3, 5, 19, 21, 35, 94, 142, 178, **196f**, **200ff**, 212ff, 236, 242ff

universality, 28, 101, 234

vouchers, 19, 193, **222ff**